ml

The Canning of Fish and Meat

The Canning of Fish and Meat

Edited by

R.J. FOOTITT

and

A.S LEWIS

John West Foods Ltd.
Liverpool

BLACKIE ACADEMIC & PROFESSIONAL
An Imprint of Chapman & Hall

London · Glasgow · Weinheim · New York · Tokyo · Melbourne · Madras

Published by
Blackie Academic and Professional, an imprint of Chapman & Hall,
Wester Cleddens Road, Bishopbriggs, Glasgow G64 2NZ

Chapman & Hall, 2–6 Boundary Row, London SE1 8HN, UK

Blackie Academic & Professional, Wester Cleddens Road, Bishopbriggs, Glasgow G64 2NZ, UK

Chapman & Hall GmbH, Pappelallee 3, 69469 Weinheim, Germany

Chapman & Hall USA, One Penn Plaza, 41st Floor, New York NY 10119, USA

Chapman & Hall Japan, ITP-Japan, Kyowa Building, 3F, 2-2-1 Hirakawacho, Chiyoda-ku, Tokyo 102, Japan

DA Book (Aust.) Pty Ltd, 648 Whitehorse Road, Mitcham 3132, Victoria, Australia

Chapman & Hall India, R. Seshadri, 32 Second Main Road, CIT East, Madras 600 035, India

First edition 1995

© 1995 Chapman & Hall

Typeset in 10/12pt Times by Cambrian Typesetters, Frimley, Surrey

Printed in Great Britain by St Edmundsbury Press, Bury St Edmunds, Suffolk

ISBN 0 7514 0011 4

A catalogue record for this book is available from the British Library
Library of Congress Catalog Card Number: 94–78794

∞ Printed on permanent acid-free text paper, manufactured in accordance with ANSI/NISO Z39.48-1992 (Permanence of Paper).

Preface

Canning as a preservation process has proved its value in its contribution to the preservation, distribution, and storage of world food supplies, and is a traditional way of preserving fish and meat. With increasing concern for the environment, it has much to offer with its use of readily recyclable container materials and product stability at ambient conditions, as well as long life.

For some foods, such as fish and meat, the character of the canned product has become an accepted and sought after quality by the consumer but for other foods, other methods of preservation have delivered a 'fresher' character.

However, there is a growing realisation that these other methods of preservation of foods carry critical control requirements through the whole distribution chain, which, considered together with environmental implications of energy usage and packaging recycling potential, has led to a resurgence of interest in canning.

Increasingly, in the major markets, legislative control of fish canning is following (and extending) the style previously only applied to canned meat, with enormous implications for fish canneries worldwide.

Until now, no book has drawn together practical guidance in a single volume. This book sets out to fill the gap. Each stage of the canning process is dealt with sequentially, starting from the acquisition of raw material and its preparation, through can supply, filling, seaming, heat processing and storage, to distribution. The essential services of factory and equipment cleaning, and the requirements of support laboratory facilities are also detailed, and specific practical advice on the design and construction of canneries is given.

Authorship is drawn from the collective experience of industry including British Columbia Packers, CMB and Unilever; of the two major trade research associations in the United Kingdom, Campden Food and Drink RA and Leatherhead Food RA; and also the academic world, represented by the University of Humberside, bringing together in a single volume the combined experience of industry, research and academia.

The Canning of Fish and Meat is a book which will be of practical use to the canmaking and canning industries, to food brokers and retailers, and to students training for and graduating into the industry.

R.J.F.
A.S.L.

Contributors

K. Barber	British Columbia Packers Ltd., Box 5000, Vancouver, British Columbia, V6B 4A8, Canada
P. Bird	Lever Industrial Limited, PO Box 100, Runcorn, Cheshire WA7 3JZ, UK
L. Bratt	The Campden Food & Drink Research Association, Chipping Campden, Glos GL55 6LD, UK
R.J. Footitt	John West Foods Ltd., West House, Bixteth Street, Liverpool L3 9SR, UK
A. Garthwaite	University of Humberside, Humber Lodge, 61 Bargate, Grimsby DN34 5AA, UK
P. Harris	Unilever Research Laboratory, Colworth House, Sharnbrook, Bedford MK44 1LQ, UK
R.J. Hart	Leatherhead Food R.A., Randalls Road, Leatherhead, Surrey, UK
G. Hazle	Exel Logistics, The Merton Centre, 45 St. Peters St., Bedford MK40 2UB, UK
R. Heroux	British Columbia Packers Ltd., Box 5000, Vancouver, British Columbia, V6B 4A8, Canada
M. Hutchinson	British Columbia Packers Ltd., Box 5000, Vancouver, British Columbia, V6B 4A8, Canada
A.S. Lewis	John West Foods Ltd., West House, Bixteth Street, Liverpool L3 9SR, UK
P. Moran	CMB Packaging Technology, Denchworth Road, Wantage OX12 3B, UK
F. Nolte	British Columbia Packers Ltd., c/o Pacific Fishing Co. Ltd., PO Box 4, Levuka, Ovalau, Fiji
P. Robinson	Union International plc, 14 West Smithfield, London EC14 9JN, UK
M.A. Terry	Exel Logistics, The Merton Centre, 45 St. Peters St., Bedford MK40 2UB, UK

A.W. Timperley   The Campden Food & Drink Research Association, Chipping Campden, Glos GL55 6LD, UK

T.A. Turner   CMB Packaging Technology, Denchworth Road, Wantage OX12 3B, UK

Contents

1 Raw material sourcing   **1**
P. HARRIS

1.1	Introduction	1
1.2	Supply of fish	1
1.3	Finding fish	2
1.4	Catching fish	4
	1.4.1 Surrounding nets	5
	1.4.2 Towed nets	7
	1.4.3 Static nets	8
	1.4.4 Line and hook	9
1.5	By-catch	11
1.6	On-board handling of fish	11
	1.6.1 Size of fish	11
	1.6.2 Metabolic rate	12
	1.6.3 Catching practice	12
	1.6.4 Handling fish	12
1.7	Quality retention	13
	1.7.1 Cooling with ice	14
	1.7.2 Boxing in ice	14
	1.7.3 Ice-chilled sea water (CSW)	14
	1.7.4 Refrigerated sea water (RSW)	15
	1.7.5 Freezing	15
1.8	Fish farming	15
1.9	Conclusions	15
References		16

2 Fish raw material   **17**
A. GARTHWAITE

2.1	Introduction	17
2.2	Transportation	17
	2.2.1 Spoilage factors	17
	2.2.2 Protection in transportation	19
2.3	Reception and testing	21
2.4	Storage	25
2.5	Defrosting frozen fish	26
	2.5.1 Air thawing	27
	2.5.2 Air blast thawing	28
	2.5.3 Water thawing	29
	2.5.4 Vacuum thawing	30
	2.5.5 Other methods of thawing	31
2.6	Fish preparation	31
	2.6.1 Heading	32
	2.6.2 Filleting	33
	2.6.3 Skinning	34
	2.6.4 Smoking	35
	2.6.5 Pre-cooking	38

2.7 Storing prepared fish 40
2.8 Chemical indicators of quality 41
References and Bibliography 41
Appendix: Sources of machinery 42

3 Meat raw materials 44
R.J. HART

3.1 Introduction 44
3.2 Specifications and quality assurance 44
3.3 Sampling procedures 46
3.4 Identity of meat 47
    3.4.1 Species 47
    3.4.2 Age and sex 47
    3.4.3 Other factors 48
    3.4.4 Chemical composition 48
3.5 Manufacturing quality factors 49
    3.5.1 Functionality of meat proteins 49
    3.5.2 Curing of meat products with nitrite 50
    3.5.3 The importance of meat pH 51
    3.5.4 pH changes in meat after slaughter 52
    3.5.5 Chilling and freezing 54
    3.5.6 Transport and delivery 56
3.6 Physical condition of meat 57
3.7 Microbiology of meat raw materials 57
    3.7.1 Spoilage bacteria 57
    3.7.2 Food-poisoning bacteria 58
3.8 Summary 58
References 59

4 Canning factory standards 60
A.W. TIMPERLEY

4.1 Introduction 60
4.2 Factory environment 60
    4.2.1 Location and surroundings 60
    4.2.2 Vehicles and roadways 61
4.3 Factory structure 61
    4.3.1 External walls 61
    4.3.2 Access ways 61
    4.3.3 Pest-proofing 62
4.4 Production area 66
    4.4.1 Internal walls 66
    4.4.2 Floors 72
    4.4.3 Ceilings 74
    4.4.4 Lighting 74
    4.4.5 Ventilation 75
4.5 Factory layout 75
    4.5.1 Separation of processes 75
    4.5.2 Separation of personnel 76
4.6 Services 77
    4.6.1 General water supply 77
    4.6.2 Water for cooling purposes 78
    4.6.3 General steam supply 78
    4.6.4 Potable steam supply 78
    4.6.5 Other services 79
    4.6.6 Effluent 79

4.7	Personal hygiene		79
	4.7.1	Health control	81
	4.7.2	Protective clothing	81
	4.7.3	Sanitary accommodation	82
	4.7.4	Staff amenities	82
4.8	Equipment		82
	4.8.1	Hygienic design	82
	4.8.2	Installation	86
Further reading			87

5 Cans and lids

T.A. TURNER

			88
5.1	Introduction		88
5.2	Metals used in can manufacture		88
	5.2.1	Steel	88
	5.2.2	Tin-free steels (TFS) and blackplate	91
	5.2.3	Aluminium	92
	5.2.4	Mechanical properties	94
5.3	Methods of container manufacture		95
	5.3.1	Three-piece can manufacture	96
	5.3.2	Two-piece can manufacture	100
	5.3.3	Can ends	104
5.4	Selection of a can-making route		107
	5.4.1	Product(s) to be packed	108
	5.4.2	Size of the market and the manufacturing unit	108
5.5	Mechanical properties of containers and ends		109
	5.5.1	General	109
	5.5.2	Axial strength	110
	5.5.3	Panelling resistance	110
	5.5.4	Peaking resistance	111
	5.5.5	Measurement of mechanical properties	111
	5.5.6	Secondary processes	112
5.6	Coatings		113
	5.6.1	General classification	113
	5.6.2	Protective internal coatings	113
5.7	Functions of can lacquers/enamels		119
	5.7.1	Internal corrosion protection	119
	5.7.2	Protection of the product	120
	5.7.3	Facilitating manufacture	121
	5.7.4	Base for decoration	123
	5.7.5	External corrosion and abrasion resistance	123
5.8	Methods of lacquer application		123
	5.8.1	Roller coating in sheet form	123
	5.8.2	Coil coating	124
	5.8.3	Spraying	124
	5.8.4	Electrocoating	125
5.9	Container corrosion; theory and practice		125
	5.9.1	External corrosion	125
	5.9.2	Internal corrosion	126
	5.9.3	Theory	130
	5.9.10	Recycling	133
	5.10.1	Technical factors	134
	5.10.2	Economics	134
Bibliography			134

6   Filling operations   **136**
    A.S LEWIS, R. HEROUX, F. NOLTE and
    P. ROBINSON

    6.1   Introduction   136
    6.2   Hand filling   137
          6.2.1   Meat products   137
          6.2.2   Fish products   137
    6.3   Mechanical filling – general considerations   138
    6.4   Meat filling   140
    6.5   Fish filling   142
    6.6   Liquid fillers   147
    6.7   Fillers for fish and meat products in sauce   150
    6.8   Operational safety   150
    6.9   Control of the filling operation   152
    Acknowledgement   155
    Manufacturers of filling machines   156

7   Can seaming   **159**
    P. MORAN

    7.1   Introduction   159
    7.2   Can seaming   161
          7.2.1   Double seamers   161
          7.2.2   Irregular seamers   161
          7.2.3   Round can seamers   161
          7.2.4   Irregular can seaming   162
          7.2.5   Round can seaming   163
    7.3   Double seam acceptability   164
          7.3.1   Double seam appraisal   164
          7.3.2   Dimensional setting and control of double seamers   166
    7.4   Target setting   166
    7.5   Seamer maintenance procedures   171
    7.6   Double seaming technology developments   171
    Glossary of terms and definitions   172

8   Heat treatment   **178**
    L. BRATT

    8.1   Introduction   178
    8.2   Aims of the retorting process and commercial sterility   178
    8.3   The requirements for a retorting system   179
          8.3.1   Pressure vessel   179
          8.3.2   Can location   179
          8.3.3   Heat transfer medium   179
          8.3.4   Control system   180
          8.3.5   Venting and condensate removal   180
          8.3.6   Rotation   180
    8.4   The classification and selection of sterilising systems   180
          8.4.1   Manufacturing output   181
          8.4.2   Available factory space   181
          8.4.3   Requirement for rotation   181
          8.4.4   Overpressure   181
          8.4.5   Factory location   182

8.5   Batch retorts   182
      8.5.1   Steam retorts   182
      8.5.2   Steam–air retorts   184
      8.5.3   Full immersion water retorts   186
      8.5.4   Showered water retorts   188
8.6   Continuous sterilisers   188
      8.6.1   Fundamental considerations   188
      8.6.2   Hydrostatic cookers   191
      8.6.3   Reel and spiral cooker/coolers   191
8.7   Instrumentation and control of sterilising systems   191
      8.7.1   Temperature   193
      8.7.2   Time   193
      8.7.3   Pressure   193
      8.7.4   Rotation speed/batch retorts   194
      8.7.5   Continuous steriliser speeds   194
      8.7.6   Water level   194
      8.7.7   Water flow rate   194
      8.7.8   Instrumentation   194
      8.7.9   Temperature measurement – the master temperature indicator (MTI) 195
      8.7.10 Mercury-in-glass thermometers   196
      8.7.11 Platinum resistance thermometers (PRTs)   196
      8.7.12 Temperature – recorder controller   196
      8.7.13 Pressure measurement   198
      8.7.14 Control systems   198
8.8   Establishment of thermal process   199
      8.8.1   The scheduled process   202
      8.8.2   Special considerations for canned cured meats   203
      8.8.3   Thermal process verification   204
      8.8.4   Temperature distribution tests   204
      8.8.5   Thermal process evaluation   205
      8.8.6   Calculation methods   207
8.9   Procedures and records   208
8.10 Retort operation   208
8.11 Process audit reconciliation   209
Suggested further reading   210
Principal European suppliers of retorts and sterilisers   211

9   Warehousing and distribution   212
G. HAZLE and M.A. TERRY

9.1   Recent trends   212
9.2   The storage problem   214
9.3   Brightstacking   215
9.4   Block-stacking   215
9.5   Semi-automated warehouse systems   216
9.6   Despatch   218
9.7   Pallets versus hand stow versus slipsheets   218
9.8   Electronic data interchange   218
9.9   Stock control   219
9.10 Third-party contracts   219
9.11 Performance measurement   220
9.12 Imports   220
9.13 Distribution and shipping   221
      9.13.1 Road haulage   221
      9.13.2 Containers   222

10   Laboratory services   **223**
    M . HUTCHINSON

    10.1   Laboratory facilities   223
           10.1.1 Location of laboratories   223
           10.1.2 Laboratory design   223
           10.1.3 Technicians and procedures   224
           10.1.4 Sampling plans   224
    10.2   Analytical testing   225
    10.3   Microbiological testing   225
    10.4   Analyses recommended for cannery water and retort cooling water   226
    10.5   Swab testing   227
    10.6   Incubation tests   228
    10.7   Sterility testing   229
           10.7.1 Examination of containers   230
           10.7.2 Cleaning the container   230
           10.7.3 Opening the container   230
           10.7.4 Inoculation   231
           10.7.5 Interpretation of results   231
    10.8   Types of spoilage   235
    10.9   Consumer illness complaints   235
    10.10 Botulism   237
    10.11 Staphylococcal poisoning   238
    Bibliography   238
    Laboratory in-house quality assurance and accreditation   239
        Quality assurance   239
        Accreditation   240
        ISO 9000   241
    Acknowledgement   242
    Reference   242
    Introduction to Quality Indicators   242
        Ammonia   242
        Total volatile bases (TVB)   243
        K-value analysis   244
        Ethanol   245
        The Torry meter   246
        Total crude protein   246
        Estimation of moisture   248
        Total ash   248
        Crude fat: Goldfisch method   249
        Salt analysis   250
        Salt determination in solutions   251
        Total carbohydrates calculated as dextrose   251
        Qualitative determination for starch   253
        Histamine determination: Fluorometric method   253
        Quantitative determination of nitrite by the Griess–Ilosvay reaction   256
        Qualitative determination of nitrite   258
        Quantitative determination of hydroxyproline   259
        Phosphate determination   262
        Free fatty acids in oils   264
        Estimation of moisture and volatiles in oils   265
        Peroxide value   266
        Determination of Iodine number: Rosemund Kuhnenn method   266

11 Cleaning   **270**
    K. BARBER AND P. BIRD

    11.1   Introduction to cleaning in the fish canning industry   270
           11.1.1 Cleaners and sanitisers   271
           11.1.2 Methods and equipment   280
           11.1.3 Applying HACCP principles to cleaning   282
    11.2   Introduction to cleaning in the meat industry   286
           11.2.1 Slaughterhouse   289
           11.2.2 Raw meat department   291
           11.2.3 General factory cleaning   293
           11.2.4 Personal hygiene   293
    Bibliography   294
    Appendices 1–11   295

Index   **305**

1 Raw material sourcing
P. HARRIS

1.1 Introduction

There are more than 20 000 different species of fish in the world, but less than 200 of them are of commercial significance. Almost without exception, the fish which are used for canning come from the sea (as opposed to freshwater or farmed fish), this means that they are 'wild' and therefore have to be hunted. Because the fish are wild there is only limited control over the quality of these fish with regard to nutritional state etc., in contrast to farmed fish or animals, whose rearing, whether for fish or meat, is controlled as the first stage in the manufacture of fish or meat products.

The quality of fish will vary according to the season when the fish can either be well fed or spawning, when a significant proportion of the fish flesh is converted to reproductive tissue, thus making the fish of poorer quality. Most fish species are fragile and can be easily damaged leading to rapid spoilage and loss of original quality. Also, fishing is governed by the weather which means that the availability of fish to a cannery can be uncertain.

Sea fish are often classified according to the part of the sea in which they normally live, this in turn will influence the type of method used for catching them. Demersal fish live mainly on the sea bottom and typical examples are cod, haddock, whiting and the flat fish. Pelagic fish live in the middle and surface waters of the seas and examples of these are the herring, mackerel, sardine and tuna. The demersal fish are mainly the 'white' fish, whereas the pelagic fish are mainly the 'fatty' fish, although there are many exceptions. The majority of fish which are canned are pelagic.

This chapter will cover the main fishing methods which are used to catch fish for canning, and list some of the on-board handling procedures and their influence on the quality of the fish.

1.2 Supply of fish

Until the end of the last century, it was considered that the supply of fish from the seas was limitless. Therefore, fish in the sea were common property and did not belong to anybody; they only became property by the law of capture. With the advent of steam-powered fishing boats came the ability to catch vast quantities of fish and thus the capability of overfishing. This ability to overfish and deplete stocks of particular species to such an extent that fishing for that species was no longer viable, lead to countries claiming 'ownership' of the seas, first by the 3 mile then 200 mile limits. This was supplemented by stock surveys which were used to set total allowable catches (TAC) and quotas of that TAC to be divided amongst the various countries; management of this TAC/quota system is by international treaty. The formation of the EU has improved the management of TAC and quotas within the community, but there are still many obstacles to overcome with the rest of the world.

The question of the continued supply of fish for the foreseeable future is still unresolved. Of 146 species of fish currently recorded by the FAO of the UN

- 7 species are underutilised,
- 39 species have some room for further exploitation,
- 49 species are fished to their maximum, and
- 51 species are overfished.

It is considered that 90% of the North Atlantic fish stocks are overfished, some by as much as four times the sustainable yield.

Most of the overfished stocks are demersal and not pelagic, which is good news for the canners!

1.3 Finding fish

Before a fisherman can catch the fish, he must first find them. There are two problems related to finding fish: (i) establishing their location in the vast ocean; and (ii) having got to the right part of the ocean, finding *exactly* where the fish are. Historically, these problems had to be overcome by the experience of the fisherman, either learnt or passed down from generation to generation. Over the years, knowledge would be built up of the relationship between the presence of fish and factors like time of the year, water temperature, and thermoclines or upswellings. Today, the use of satellites and on-board sensors and computers allow the monitoring and processing of such data to generate maps predicting the likely location of the target fish.

The task of finding pelagic fish is easier than for demersals because pelagic fish have the tendency to form shoals where large numbers of the same species gather together making location possible. Also, these shoals often swim so close to the surface as to create a surface pattern which renders the shoal visible from above. If the fish come close to the shore, as is the case with sardines and herring, it is common to site a lookout at a high vantage point to observe this surface disturbance and alert the fishermen who immediately take to their boats. If the shoals are at a distance it will be necessary to use a helicopter as is the case in part of the American tuna fishing. Industry aerial observation can be either direct during the daytime, or at night by using specially adapted TV cameras which are sensitive to the bioluminescence created by shoals of fish such as herring, menhaden and anchovy.

These methods aid the fisherman to identify the approximate location of the target fish, but other methods are needed to establish the *exact* location of the fish before they can be captured. This need can be fulfilled by echo-sounders or sonar equipment which are installed on the fishing vessel. Both pieces of equipment work on the principle of transmitting an acoustic signal and processing the echo which is returned from the seabed or fish shoal to give a display in which distinctive features can be identified and located in relation to the ship. An echo-sounder is used to monitor the sea directly below the vessel and tends to be used primarily in demersal fishing. The sonar is mounted in a movable housing such that it can be moved (within limits) horizontally and vertically and thus can be 'pointed' at a distance of 0.5 km or more from the fishing vessel allowing location of pelagic shoals. Both echo-sounder and sonar are capable of indicating range, bearing and depth of the fish and the data can be output to a coloured video monitor to enable better discrimination and detail.

Another useful feature of the pelagic fish is their tendency to congregate around floating debris (whether it is idle curiosity or some profound biological reason has yet to be established). This characteristic is often exploited by the fishermen deliberately creating floating debris in the form of a recoverable raft (called a payao in the Philippines) which is left floating for a period before the fisherman returns to hopefully collect his reward. Thus, the fisherman is not so much finding the fish, but rather letting the fish find him. Other methods which are used for 'attracting' the fish are the use of lights at night. This is particularly popular in the Mediterranean where it is called 'lampara' (from the Italian lampo, meaning lamp). The final method of attracting fish is of course by the use of bait, either in the form of baited hooks, or by throwing bait into the water – known as chumming – in order to first encourage the formation of a shoal followed by a feeding frenzy thus enabling relatively easy capture of the fish.

One fishery which has minimum problems locating fish is that for salmon, both Atlantic and Pacific species. Here, the fish not only return to their native rivers to spawn, but do so at set times each year.

(a)

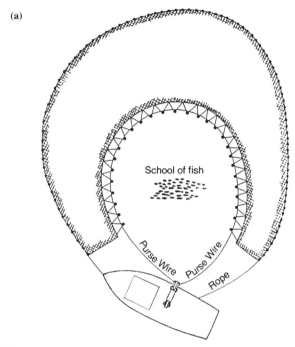

Figure 1.1 Purse seining. (a) A school of fish surrounded by a purse seine net. Hauling on the purse wire reduces the size of the net under the shoal of fish effectively trapping them. (b), (c) The side and plan view of the fishing vessel setting the net; the direction of travel is shown by a dotted line.

1.4 Catching fish

In the introduction, it was stated that sea fish are classified according to the area of the sea which they normally occupy, and this influenced the type of method employed for their capture. If, for example, the sea is 500 m deep, a demersal fisherman will be fishing at a maximum height of 12 m from the bottom; thus, he is only interested in 2.5% of the total depth of the sea. By contrast, the pelagic fisherman is interested in the remaining 97.5%. Since most of the fish used for canning are pelagic, the methods used for catching demersal fish will not be further discussed.

There is a wide variety of methods employed for catching fish (Von Brandt, 1984) but this chapter will only concentrate on the main methods which are extensively used for catching fish used for canning. These fishing methods can be broadly classified into four basic types:

- surrounding nets,
- towed nets,

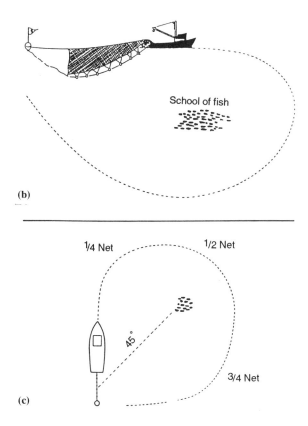

(b)

(c)

- static nets, and
- line and hook.

1.4.1 Surrounding nets

As described above, the pelagic fish have a tendency to form large shoals of the same species. This behaviour is exploited by the fisherman who can surround the shoal with a net to prevent the fish escaping. The most important type of surround net is the purse-seine which is used extensively for mackerel, herring, sardine and tuna (Figure 1.1).

The basic method of purse-seining is to form a wall of netting around the shoal of fish and when the shoal has been completely encircled, the bottom of the net is pulled together trapping the fish in a pool of water (Figure 1.1a). This pool is made smaller by hauling in the net until eventually the pool is small enough to allow the fish to be taken aboard. The nets are usually made of nylon with a mesh size appropriate to the species being hunted. They are made of large sections of netting joined together and mounted on a headline (at the top), a sole-rope (at the bottom) and gables (side ropes). These nets may be up to 800 m long and 200 m deep. It is critical that the net sinks quickly when it is set. To aid this, lead weights are fitted to the sole-rope, and floats are fitted to the headline to prevent the net sinking. The bottom edge of the net is pulled together by means of a line passed through rings, called purse rings, which are mounted at intervals below the sole-rope.

When a decision to fish a shoal has been made, careful attention must be made to the direction of the tide and wind, and the direction of movement of the shoal in order to avoid escape of the fish before the net is 'pursed'. The vessel moves to its starting position and lowers a buoy into the water to which is attached a line connected to the headline of the net, and one end of the pursing line (Figure 1.1b). Net is paid out as the vessel moves round the shoal, the circle being completed when the vessel has returned to the buoy which it first dropped (Figure 1.1c). The pursing line and the line attached to the headline are recovered from the buoy, and pursing of the net is completed without delay. When pursing is complete, the two ends of the net are hauled aboard using a power block in order to reduce the volume of water surrounded by the net. Fish can then be recovered from the net using a lifting net called a brailer, or fish and water are pumped out using a fish pump.

Two types of fish pump are commonly used. The submersible which pumps water and fish continuously but has the disadvantage that it is difficult to control the ratio of fish to water which can lead to the risk of bruising the fish with a consequent loss of quality. More recently, there has been an increased use of the pressure/vacuum (P/V) pump. The principle of this pump is that an accumulation tank of 500–1500 litres is alternately put under vacuum and pressure by a water-ring vacuum-pump. The fish, together with some water are sucked from the nets through a hose via a valve into the accumulation tank. When the tank is full it is pressurised by changing the vacuum and pressure side connections from the tank to the pump. The fish–water mixture flows out of the tank and the fish are removed from the water by a strainer. It is claimed that the P/V pump treats the fish more gently than any other type of fish pump, but the disadvantage is that it has a lower capacity than submersible pumps due to its alternating action.

The method of purse-seine fishing outlined above involves the use of one vessel but some fisheries use two. In this case, each vessel carries about half of the net, and the vessels start setting it simultaneously starting with the middle of the net with each vessel moving in the opposite direction to its partner until they meet at the opposite side of the circle.

Other surround netting methods which are worth noting are ring netting, and lampara nets.

The principle of ring netting is very similar to the purse-seine, except the net is not pursed (i.e. there are no purse rings or purse line). Instead, when the fish have been surrounded, the bottom of the net is hauled in faster than the top causing a portion of the net to go underneath the shoal of fish and thus preventing their escape. Care must be taken to ensure that the top of the net does not sink due the weight of catch or hauling the bottom of the net too fast, since this would allow fish to escape.

The lampara net is shaped like a horseshoe so that the centre of the net forms a bag. Fish are attracted to the area by means of the light, and the net is set in a similar way to that used in purse-seining. However, the lampara net does not have the means to purse, but hauling on both ends of the net causes the fish to be captured in the bag-like centre portion of the net.

1.4.2 Towed nets

Trawling is the name given to the fishing method which involves the towing of a net to catch fish. This method is also used for catching demersal fish, but whereas the demersal trawl is towed along the bottom of the sea for many hours in order to capture widely dispersed fish, the mid-water pelagic trawl is only towed for minutes in order to pass through and capture a shoal of fish. Much of the pelagic fishery vessel's time is spent locating a shoal of fish, and this is where the sophisticated electronic equipment is required, not only to find the shoal of fish, but also to control the movements of the vessel and depth of the net to ensure that the shoal is captured.

The mid-water trawl net is shaped like a cone with the mouth of the net being somewhat oval or square depending on the design. Wing-shaped extensions of netting at each side of the net mouth are attached to the ropes used for towing. Very wide mesh netting is often used for these wings of netting in order to reduce the drag on the net while it is being towed. Boards – called otter-boards – are fitted to the towing ropes in order to help keep the mouth of the net open whilst it is being towed. This is further aided by floats which are fitted to the top rope, and weights fitted to the bottom rope of the net mouth (Figure 1.2). The principle of trawling is to

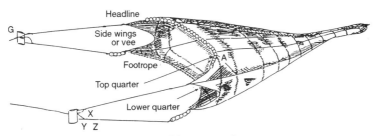

Figure 1.2 Mid-water trawl net.

tow the net through a shoal of fish so that the fish enter the mouth of the net, undersized fish will pass through the mesh of the net, but the marketable fish will be captured in the end of the net called the codend.

The mesh size of the net will depend on the species being hunted, although it is quite common for the first part of the net – after the mouth – to have large mesh (again to reduce the drag), the main body of the net to have a mesh of an intermediate size, and the codend (where the fish are captured) to have the smallest and strongest mesh.

A critical part of mid-water trawling is to know when to haul in the net. If the net is hauled too early, then too few fish are caught; however, if the net is hauled too late, then an excessive catch may be achieved which could burst the net or make the net too heavy to handle on board. Also, too many fish in the net can lead to damage of the fish causing a reduction in quality. Modern electronics have a part to play here since, by the use of sensors fitted to the net, the skipper can monitor not only the position of the net but also its contents.

Mid-water trawling can be carried out by a single vessel or a pair of vessels.

1.4.3 Static nets

The most important method of static net fishing is that of drift netting, which is probably one of the oldest forms of net fishing (Figure 1.3). It is used to catch all types of pelagic fish including mackerel, herring, pilchard and tuna, it is also used to catch salmon. The drift net consists of a curtain of net which has a series of floats attached to the top, and weights on the bottom to create a vertical wall of net; the fixing of the floats will govern how far below the surface of the sea that the net hangs (Figure 1.3a). The mesh size is chosen to allow the heads of the desired fish to just pass through and thus become enmeshed in the net by their gills (this is why this method of fishing is also called gill netting). Drift nets can be up to 100 m deep, and a number of nets can be joined together to make a net of up to 2.5 km in length (the maximum length recommended by the UN Washington Convention). The material from which the mesh of the net is made needs to be practically invisible in water because an approaching fish must not realise that it is confronted with an impenetrable barrier otherwise it will try to swim round the net.

As in the other methods of fishing described above, the drift net fisherman still needs to locate a shoal of fish if he is to be successful. Having located a shoal, the nets are set ahead of the direction in which the shoal is moving (this requires either a lot of experience about how fish move or the use of modern electronics) (Figure 1.3b). The drifting operation can last for a number of hours depending on conditions and the size of the shoal. At the end of the drifting operation the net is hauled

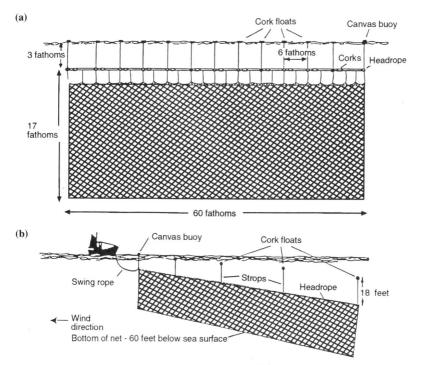

Figure 1.3 Drift net. (a) Detail of the drift net. (b) How the drift net is set.

aboard and the fish shaken out of the net. Sometimes, if the catch is very heavy, the net has to be stored with the fish still attached until the vessel has returned to shore before the fish can be removed.

The advantages of drift netting are that this form of fishing does not require a powerful vessel because the nets are relatively light, and the catch is brought aboard in stages – unlike trawling. Perhaps the most important advantage is the fact that drift netting can be a very selective form of fishing. The mesh size and the setting of the net can accurately select the size of fish to be caught, and this may become of increasing importance with the present emphasis on conservation fishery management. This of course can only come about providing the correct mesh size and length of net are used, and that they are used properly. Abuse of this fishing method in the past by using drift nets up to 50 km in length on the high seas has lead to drift netting being referred to as a 'wall of death'.

1.4.4 Line and hook

The line and hook methods of fishing are probably the most simple. There are a number of variations on the method, but all are based on the principle of a line (or lines) attached to the vessel at one end and a hook to catch the fish on the other end; the hook can be baited or consist of an artificial lure. The use of weights and floats on the line can control the desired fishing depth. The line can be static using an anchor and buoy, a method commonly used to catch tuna and mackerel. The line can also be allowed to drift which enables a greater part of the sea to be covered. A variation on the drift line is to actually tow the line and this is called trolling (Figure 1.4). Trolling is particularly applicable when the target fish have a high individual value and high quality is necessary, typical examples are salmon and tuna. A number of lures or baited hooks are towed behind a slow moving vessel, the fish being hooked after snapping at the lure, and held by the mouth until they can be brought aboard as the line is pulled in.

The line can be attached to a pole or rod, and again, this method of fishing is usually only applied to pelagic species such as tuna which have a high individual value. The fishing gear consists of a bamboo pole 3–4 m in length to which is attached a line having a feather or other lure fixed to a barbless hook. When a shoal is located, the fishermen take their positions and begin 'chumming' with bait to bring the fish to a feeding frenzy. Each man casts his line as the vessel passes slowly through the school, as the fish snap at the lure, the fisherman heaves on his pole to fling the fish behind him onto the deck of the boat. As the hook is barbless, the fish becomes disengaged from the hook when it hits the deck and slides away from the fisherman.

Although the landings of fish caught by line and hook are often low, they generally fetch a high price because the fish are usually undamaged and of a better appearance than fish caught by other methods.

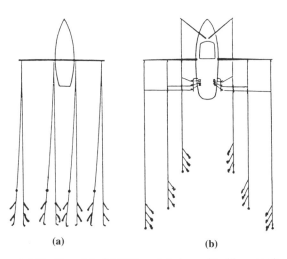

Figure 1.4 Trolling. (a), (b) Different designs of trolling vessels.

1.5 By-catch

The fishing methods described above seek to catch a particular species – the target species – of fish. However, none of these methods is precise and other species of fish are often caught at the same time, and these are referred to as the by-catch. Because of the enforcement of TAC, this by-catch is often discarded. The main problem of discards is that there is a very high mortality rate associated with most fishing methods, consequently these discards are usually dead. Therefore, accidentally catching juvenile and non-target species fish can have serious consequences on fish stocks.

Another possible form of by-catch is the accidental capture of marine mammals and birds in the nets, and some fishing methods are more prone to this problem than others. Apart from the damage that a large marine mammal such as a whale can do to the fisherman's nets, there is increasing pressure from the consumer to ensure that catching a particular species of fish does not cause harm to marine mammals. It can be difficult at times for the fisherman to avoid catching these mammals when they are trying to catch the same fish as the fisherman. However, fishermen are now taking steps to ensure that even if they accidentally catch a marine mammal, the animal is released from the net without harm. This can take the form of divers being sent into the pool created by the purse-seine net and aiding the trapped animal to escape. Also, by more careful monitoring of drift nets the mammal which has become enmeshed in the net can be released before it comes to harm.

1.6 On-board handling of fish

Fish for canning must be of the highest quality. In comparison with most animal products, fish spoil much more rapidly, and pelagic fish tend to be more susceptible than other species (Whittle *et al.*, 1990). Thus, the storage life of herring on ice is about 5 days whereas that of cod is 12–15 days. There are a number of reasons for this, including the following:

- size of fish,
- metabolic rate,
- catching practice, and
- handling of fish.

1.6.1 Size of fish

Many of the pelagic species are small, so their surface area to volume ratio is greater than in larger fish. As the major spoilage processes occur on the surface of the fish due to microbial action (Shewan, 1971), small fish will tend to spoil more rapidly than large fish.

1.6.2 Metabolic rate

Pelagic fish tend to be very active in their life-style and have very active enzymes in their tissues. Many of these enzymes remain active long after the fish has died causing breakdown of proteins and fat which leads to deterioration of the texture and flavour of the fish (Sikorski *et al.*, 1990).

1.6.3 Catching practice

Modern fishing vessels can catch pelagic fish in very large numbers and unless extreme care is taken, physical damage will occur from the sheer weight and compression of fish in the net. This damage can be extreme at certain times of the year when the fish are soft because of feeding or spawning. Damage can also be caused by the pumps used to transfer fish as described earlier. This physical damage is not only undesirable from the viewpoint of acceptability, and machine processing, but it can disrupt the viscera and cause damage to the skin releasing bacteria and enzymes to accelerate deterioration. Further physical damage may ensue from bulk storage of the fish on board ship.

1.6.4 Handling fish

1.6.4.1 Rigor mortis. When death occurs, the fish go through rigor mortis, the outward sign of which is a stiffening of the fish's body. All fish go through rigor, it cannot be stopped but it can be delayed or suspended by adjusting the temperature (Iwamoto *et al.*, 1987). After a period of time, rigor will be resolved and the fish flesh will return to being soft and pliable. The time taken for a fish to enter rigor and for rigor to be resolved depends on a number factors including temperature, the nutritional state and the size of the fish. Usually, small pelagic fish go into rigor within 2–4 h after death, the larger pelagics take longer – up to 1 day – and stay in rigor for a longer period.

If fish in rigor are treated roughly, the resultant fish flesh will be of poor quality – the fillet will gape and the water-holding capacity of the flesh will be reduced leading to high drip loss and cook-out, and a tough dry texture on eating (Burt and Hardy, 1992).

1.6.4.2 Evisceration. Pelagic fish, particularly the smaller species, are rarely eviscerated (or gutted) immediately after capture. If a fish is not eviscerated, then the digestive enzymes continue to function but without the normal control mechanisms which are active when the fish is alive. This means that these digestive enzymes will digest the internal organs and eventually the fish flesh including the belly wall leading to a condition known as belly burst. To illustrate the problems that this can cause during subsequent processing, when the quantity of sardines beheaded by a nobbing machine decreased from 160 kg per person per hour to 60 kg per person per hour the proportion of belly burst increased from zero towards 100% (Jensen, 1983).

An additional advantage of immediate evisceration is that this step also leads to bleeding of the fish which, in turn, leads to a whiter flesh of the cooked fish.

Thus, it can be seen that the quality deterioration of the fish is caused by microbiological spoilage, and the continued action of the digestive enzymes, and both of these processes are accelerated by physical damage. Since it is well known that fish for canning need to be of the highest possible quality, steps must be taken to ensure that the initial quality of the fish is retained.

1.7 Quality retention

The one factor which has the most important role to play in helping to retain the initial quality of the fish is their temperature. In order to land the best quality fresh fish it is essential to cool fish as quickly as possible to a temperature just above freezing point (Huss, 1983). Only a few hours delay at 15–20°C will reduce the storage life of fish by several days (Hansen and Jensen, 1982).

Traditionally, offshore fishing with big vessels has been for fish-meal or oil production while the coastal fisheries have supplied the fresh fish market and the fish canning industry. When the distance from the fishing ground to the canning plant is short, the fishing vessels may deliver their catches at short intervals (often within hours of catching) without the need for chilling the fish. However, some kind of chilling method is essential if good quality is to be maintained when fishing in more distant waters, or when the catching period is long. If fish of the scombroid family (e.g. tuna, bonito and mackerel) are not stored chilled, microbial conversion of histidine to histamine will occur. High levels of histamine (>5 mg/100 g) have been implicated in scombrotoxin poisoning; although there is no conclusive evidence that histamine itself is the cause (Clifford et al., 1989).

There are a number of methods available to achieve on-board chilling of the fish which include the following:
- cooling with ice,
- boxing in ice,
- ice-chilled sea water (CSW),

- refrigerated sea water (RSW), and
- freezing.

These are summarised below, but more details of transportation systems are given in chapter 2.

1.7.1 Cooling with ice

Cooling the catch by the addition of ice is used extensively, particularly on smaller fishing boats. On larger fishing vessels, where the volume of catch can be large, it can be particularly difficult to ensure an adequate mixing of the ice with fish especially when it is quite normal to transfer fish from the nets at a rate of 300 tonnes/h. If 10–15% ice is needed to cool the fish, then 30–45 tonnes/h ice must be added and efficiently mixed with the fish; to ensure this requires effective mechanical equipment and monitoring. The iced fish are then normally stored in a fish hold which can lead to their physical damage due the compressive forces exerted by the weight of the fish.

1.7.2 Boxing in ice

Ideally, alternate layers of fish and ice are formed in a box. The boxes are usually made of plastic for strength and so that they can be easily cleaned. The boxes should be designed so that they can be stacked on top of one another in such a way that the bottom of a box rests on the top of the box below and not on the fish. The main advantages of boxing are that the fish are not subjected to the static pressure that they would otherwise suffer if they were stored in bulk, and they are easier to unload. Also, the boxed fish will be untouched until they are processed. All of these factors will contribute to retaining the quality of the fish.

The disadvantages are that it takes time and effort to mix the fish with the ice, and the empty boxes and the ice are kept separate until they are filled, and this takes up space. This means that unless there is investment in mechanisation, boxing is restricted to the smaller vessels.

1.7.3 Ice-chilled sea water (CSW)

The CSW system was developed to minimise the physical damage caused by storing iced fish in bulk. The CSW system consists of an insulated tank (instead of a hold) which contains a mixture of ice and sea water, the fish are then transferred directly to the CSW tank. The heat transfer from fish to water is effective, and more rapid cooling can be achieved than with ice alone. In order to avoid anaerobic conditions in the tank, and to avoid localised hot spots, it is common to pump air into the bottom of the tank via perforated pipes – the CSW-champagne method (Jensen and Hansen, 1983).

1.7.4 Refrigerated sea water (RSW)

A variation on the CSW system is to use a refrigeration plant to cool the sea water which is then continuously pumped through the insulated tank containing the fish. The advantage of this variation is that the vessel does not need to be equipped with ice bins.

The disadvantage of both the CSW and RSW is that there can be some undesirable uptake of salt by the fish from the sea water which is used.

1.7.5 Freezing

When the fish required for canning can only be caught at a considerable distance from the canning factories, then icing of these fish will not be sufficient to prevent unacceptable quality deterioration; the fish must be frozen. Freezing is a common practice in some tuna fisheries, e.g. skipjack tuna (*Euthynnus pelamis* or *Katsuwonus pelamis*) which is usually caught by purse-seine fishing mainly in the western Pacific and Indian oceans. They are frozen on-board ship as whole fish using a concentrated (23%) brine, to a temperature of -10 to $-12°C$ and may be held on-board ship either in the brine or more usually in dry frozen storage for up to 3 months. Sometimes the fish are held in refrigerated sea water ($-2°C$) for a day before freezing. This method of freezing is slow and takes about 36 h to reach a backbone temperature of $-5°C$ for 1.5–2.5 kg fish, and 84 h for these same fish to reach a backbone temperature of $-12°C$ (Lampilla and Brown, 1986). After landing, the fish are held in frozen storage at -18 to $-20°C$ for up to 4 months before the fish are used for canning.

The big advantage of freezing fish is that the cannery does not have to be located close to the fishery, it can be on the other side of the world!

1.8 Fish farming

To date, fish farming does not contribute significantly to the supply of fish for canning. For example, Chile produced 37 000 tonnes of farmed salmon in 1992, consisting of a mixture of Atlantic salmon and Coho. Of these, around 200 tonnes were used for canning. There is some work in Canada and Russia where fish farming is used to hatch Pacific salmon eggs for release in the wild to boost the native stock, and the importance of this type of activity will increase in the future.

1.9 Conclusions

This chapter has outlined the steps which are necessary in order for a cannery to receive fish which are of the best quality. Because the fish are wild, they have to be found and then caught. Capturing the fish is not the end of the challenge, it is really the beginning. Unless the fish are handled properly, they will deteriorate to such an extent as to render them inedible and thus virtually worthless. Since fishing is classed as one of the most dangerous occupations, it is important that the fisherman does everything possible to retain the quality of his precious catch.

Fish will start deteriorating from the moment that they are caught. The two most important factors in retaining quality are time and temperature. The quicker that fish can be chilled to around freezing point, and the sooner that the fish are processed, then the better the quality of the fish. Even if these steps are taken, all of this sound practice can be totally undermined if the fish are physically damaged.

Therefore, quickly cooled fish which have been handled carefully and delivered from the fishery with the minimum delay, will make the perfect starting raw material for any cannery.

References

Burt, J.R. and Hardy, R. (1992) Composition and deterioration of pelagic fish. In *Pelagic Fish: The Resource and its Exploitation* (ed. Burt, J.R., Hardy, R. and Whittle, K.J.). Fishing News Books, Oxford, UK, pp. 115–141.

Clifford, M.N., Walker, R., Wright, J., Hardy, R. and Murray, C.K. (1989) Studies with volunteers on the role of histamine in suspected scombrotoxicosis. *J. Sci. Food Agric.*, **47**, 365–375.

Hansen, P. and Jensen, J. (1982) Bulk handling and chilling of large catches of small fish. Part 1: Quality and storage life. *Infofish Marketing Dig.*, **November**, 26–28.

Huss, H.H. (1983) *Fersk Fisk. Kvalitet og Holdbarhed* [Fresh fish. Quality and quality changes]. Ministry of Fisheries, Technological Laboratory, Lyngby.

Iwamoto, M., Yamanaka, H., Watabe, S. and Hashimoto, K. (1987) Effect of storage temperature on rigor mortis and ATP degradation in plaice *Paralichthys olivaceus* muscle. *J. Food Sci.*, **52**, 1514–1517.

Jensen, J. (1983) Bulk handling and chilling of large catches of small fish. Part IV: Handling on shore. *Infofish Marketing Dig.*, **3**, 38–41.

Jensen, J. and Hansen, P. (1983) Bulk handling and chilling of large catches of small fish. Part II: Purse seine catches. *Infofish Marketing Dig.*, **1**, 34–38.

Lampilla, L.A. and Brown, W.D. (1986) Changes in the microstructure of skipjack tuna during storage and heat treatment. *Food Microstruct.*, **5**, 25–31.

Shewan, J.M. (1971) The microbiology of fish and fishery products—a progress report. *J. Appl. Bacteriol.*, **34**, 299–315.

Sikorski, Z.E., Kolakowska, A. and Burt, J.R. (1990) Post harvest biochemical and microbial changes. In *Marine Food: Resources, Nutritional Composition and Preservation*. CRC Press Inc., Boca Raton, FL, USA, pp. 53–75.

Von Brandt, A. (1984) *Fish Catching Methods of the World* (3rd edn), Fishing News Books, Oxford, UK.

Whittle, K.J., Hardy, R. and Hobbs, G. (1990) Chilled fish and fisheries products. In *Chilled Foods – The State of the Art* (ed. Gormley, T.R.). Elsevier Applied Science, London, UK, pp. 87–116.

2 Fish raw material
A. GARTHWAITE

2.1 Introduction

Preserved fish is presented to the consumer in many forms, but no matter which form the consumer purchases, the quality of the end-product will reflect the quality of the raw material used in its preparation. Like any other food product it is impossible to produce a premium-quality canned fish product using second-rate raw materials. The handling and storage of the fish as a raw material, together with preliminary processing operations prior to packing, are major factors influencing the final product quality.

This chapter attempts to outline some of the problems and procedures together with quality assurance methods which are used in canneries to control the quality of the raw material being packed.

2.2 Transportation

The term 'canned fish' includes both fish and shellfish. By far the greater percentage of fish which is canned is caught by fishing vessels which hunt for their catch in waters where the desired species are known to congregate in large numbers at certain times of the year. Many such catches are seasonal, and consequently when species are caught in excess of the capacity of the canneries they must be preserved by other methods for use at a later date. The handling of the fish from the point of capture to reception at the cannery, when carried out correctly, will result in the cannery producing a product of excellent quality. However, poor handling of the catch may result in rejection of the fish at the cannery door.

2.2.1 Spoilage factors

Fresh fish and shellfish are very susceptible to spoilage and as a consequence may be expected to undergo some degree of deterioration between catching and delivery to the cannery reception area. The deterioration is caused mainly by enzymic reactions in the fish tissues due to autolysis which begins as soon as the fish dies, and also due to increases in the number of bacteria present in or on the surface of the fish if they are allowed to multiply. Physical damage due to mishandling the catch, both during netting operations and also after depositing on the deck or on dry land, may also affect quality due to bruising and/or temperature abuse. In the case of fatty fish, the availability of oxygen over prolonged periods will result in the development of rancidity to a point where the fish becomes unacceptable for further processing.

Fatty fish contain high levels of unsaturated fatty acids which are susceptible to attack by atmospheric oxygen leading to rancidity. Hence, fatty fish, such as sardines, always have a shorter storage life than lean fish.

Rancid flavours can range from that of a mild cod liver oil to an acrid burning taste which is objectionable. Rancidity development in frozen fatty fish is difficult to control. The rate of lipid oxidation is influenced by several factors which have been described in detail by Hardy *et al.* (1979) and Labuza (1970).

Higher rates of oxidation occur with increased

- concentration of unsaturated fatty acids present,
- access of oxygen to the fish flesh,
- temperature of storage, and
- exposure to light.

The reactions leading to rancidity development are also catalysed by the presence of haematin compounds and transition metals.

In addition, the water activity of the fish flesh influences rancidity development. The salt and moisture content of the fish flesh can also have an effect. For example, according to Borgstrom (1965), it is generally recognised that the practice of freezing in common salt brine contributes to rancid flavours on frozen storage of fatty fish. Atkin *et al.* (1982) also state that the salt absorbed during brine freezing can accelerate deterioration in cold storage. Where fatty fish are to be frozen this should take place as soon after catching as possible. Research on Indian sardines frozen quickly and stored at −23°C found that they remained in an acceptable condition for 20 weeks. However, similar fish held in ice for 3 days prior to freezing were found to be unacceptable after only 2 weeks frozen storage (Shenoy and Pillai, 1974).

The relationship between temperature and spoilage rate due to enzymes and microorganisms is well known and much work has been done relating the spoilage of fish caught in cold waters to the storage temperature and time. Work on tropical species is less available but in both cases it is known that by reducing the temperature of the stored fish the spoilage rates may be greatly reduced.

The process of rigor mortis is also enzymic in origin, and results from the enzymes involved in maintaining the muscle in a state of relaxation ceasing to work. The muscle contracts and the fish becomes stiff. If the fish is whole the skeleton will prevent any shortening which will occur if the fillet has been removed from the bone. The time taken for rigor to commence depends upon a number of factors:

- poor condition, exhaustion, and high temperatures cause rapid onset of rigor;
- well fed, quick catching and low temperatures delay the onset of rigor.

It is best to keep the fish cool because at higher temperatures the muscle contraction during rigor may be so strong that the flesh tears resulting in ragged fillets when finally processed. It is better to freeze whole fish before they go into rigor when freezing at sea. It is also important that the fish is kept as cool as possible whilst waiting to be processed into the frozen state.

2.2.2 Protection in transportation

In practice it is normal to reduce the temperature of storage of fresh fish to temperatures approaching 0°C. This may be achieved by using ice or a combination of ice and water or refrigerated sea water. The ice acts as a heat sink, absorbing heat from the fish and its surroundings and bringing the temperature of the fish down to that of the melting ice (0°C). The fish must be correctly packed with the ice. It is important that the ice be placed below and above the fish in order to achieve reasonable rates of heat transfer which result in rapid cooling of the catch. Where shoaling fish are caught in large quantities, the time taken to ice the catch adequately may be excessive and in such cases it is usual for the fish to be intimately mixed with refrigerated or chilled sea water at a temperature between −1 and 0°C. This has the effect of rapidly cooling the fish immediately after catching. The fish is held in tanks on board the fishing vessel from which they may be pumped ashore.

Many shoaling fish destined for use by canneries are frozen at sea. Here they may be packed into vertical plate freezers (Figure 2.1) and may be frozen in a polythene bag to which clean sea water has been added. This both improves the rate of freezing and also acts as a protection during subsequent storage reducing the risks of freezer-burn.

Ice is cheap, harmless and portable, having a very large cooling effect for a given weight, and allows rapid cooling through intimate contact between the fish and ice. This ensures the fish are kept moist, preventing them from drying on the surface. In tropical climates the quantity of ice required to cool the fish and keep it cool until landing is considerably greater than the requirements in cooler climates. With the use of ice there is always a danger that the fishermen put too much fish and ice in a box. Stacking such boxes, one box on top of another, results in boxes resting on the ice at the top of the box below, rather than resting on the walls of the box. This

Figure 2.1 A vertical plate freezer. A robust, heavy-duty unit with a range of freezing capacities. Ideal for applications on land or at sea.

may produce bruising of the fish due to pressure which may be considerable when the boxes are stacked six or ten high in the hold of the fishing vessel.

Studies in tropical climates have shown that for such conditions the general rule of 50% fish to 50% ice is sometimes inadequate and the use of higher proportions results in higher costs for ice. The use of dry ice as an aid to transportation of fish in ice is now being studied practically. Dry ice is the solid form of carbon dioxide which reverts to the gaseous form at a temperature of $-79°C$. Although it has no harmful effects on the fish, when it is placed too close or in direct contact with the fish it will cause the fish to freeze, which may result in a loss of quality. Studies in the use of dry ice in fish handling (Putro *et al.*, 1989) concluded that the incorporation of dry ice could significantly reduce the amount of ice used to 1:4:0.2 (ice:fish:dry ice), and the cooling efficiency of ice, as well as the amount of fish transported in a given volume, were improved. The study showed that the temperatures at the thermal centres were significantly lower using dry ice in conjunction with ice than by using ice alone. The use of dry ice for the chilling/transportation of shrimp was found to be more effective than for fish such as milk fish (250 g) and skipjack (3.5–5.0 kg), though in all cases there was a significant improvement in the quality of the raw material when compared with samples using ice only as the chilling medium. Though the economics of such a system require further studies, the commercial possibilities for this technology are very interesting.

Where fish or shellfish are to be moved from the point of capture to the cannery for processing they should be transported as quickly as possible and under conditions which are as cool as possible. Obviously, where the raw material is in a frozen state it should be transported in refrigerated holds which should have a maximum temperature of −20°C, or in refrigerated transport where the same maximum temperature applies. The maximum recommended storage temperature for frozen fish is −30°C. This is often not achieved in cold stores in the tropics and is due to lack of insulation in the store coupled with insufficient capacity of the refrigeration plant. Where refrigerated transport used in tropical countries has been imported second-hand from cooler climates, the insulation of the box and the capacity of the refrigeration compressor are often not capable of coping with the ambient temperatures in the tropics which may be 20°C greater than those for which the refrigeration system was designed. With such vehicles there is a danger that the temperature of the frozen product will rise during transportation, and subsequent cooling would result in recrystallisation of the ice causing textural problems and drip loss during further processing.

2.3 Reception and testing

When batches of fish are received at the factory their physical and chemical attributes should be checked against those laid down in the buying specifications. Before off-loading from the transport the temperature of the fish at various positions in the load should be checked to ensure it is below the maximum stipulated in the specification. Typical temperatures of 0°C for fresh fish and −18°C for frozen fish are ideal for acceptance in the plant. However, in the case of freshly caught fish and shellfish the maximum temperature may be set somewhat higher dependent upon the circumstances prevailing with that particular species.

Once the temperature of the load has been checked and is within acceptable limits, the priority is to off-load the fish into chilled or cold storage as rapidly as possible. At this point it is best to separate species where such an operation has not already been carried out. With fresh fish and shellfish, a visual check for quality should be made during the off-loading procedure in order to check consistency throughout the load.

The separate species should be held in separate containers, labelled with information identifying species, size, origin and date of intake. This also allows a visual check for quality to be made. Tables 2.1 and 2.2 are typical examples of grading systems used for salmon and tuna.

Table 2.1 Quality grades for Pacific salmon (grades are based on the number and seriousness of defects in external appearance)

Characteristics	Premium grade No. 1	Standard grade No. 2	Utility grade No. 3
Skin			
Colour	Typical for sea-run fish; good sheen, good contrast between dark dorsal and light ventral surfaces, no watermarks, no belly burn	Some dulling of colour and sheen; line between dark dorsal and light ventral surfaces less distinct; moderate cherry belly permitted	May be very dull; may be little distinction between dark dorsal and light ventricle surfaces; cherry belly and watermarks may be extreme
Slime	Clear	Dull and cloudy	Thick, dull and copious
Net marks	No indentation, no skin perforation	May have slight to moderate indentation	May have moderate to heavy indentation; skin may be perforated
Scars	None except small, well-healed scars	Well-healed scars permitted	Scars permitted
Cuts or punctures	No cuts or punctures	Small cuts and punctures permitted	Cuts and punctures permitted
Scales	Nil to slight scale loss; not more than 25% lost	Can have moderate to heavy scale loss; can have 25–75% lost	Can have total loss of scales
Fins	Must not lose not more than 75% of caudal fin	Fin loss or mutilation permitted	Fin loss or mutilation permitted
Eyes	Bright and clear; should protrude	Dull	Milky or cloudy, sunken
Gills	Normal appearance; bright red to pink, free of slime	Pink to grey	Grey to greenish; slimy
Belly cavity (if dressed)			
Colour	Fresh colour typical for species	Slight fading of natural colour; may have slight dark discoloration from viscera	Noticeable loss of natural colour; dark discoloration from viscera may be moderate to extreme
Bruising	No bruises	No more than one small bruise	Bruises permitted
Belly burn	No belly burn; no protruding ribs	May have slight to moderate belly burn; less than 10% of ribs protruding	Belly burn can be moderate to serious; protruding ribs permitted
Cuts or tears	Not more than 2.5 cm total length of cuts or tears	Not more than 5 cm total length of cuts and tears	Cuts and tears permitted
Cleaning	Thorough; no oesophagus, gills, viscera, kidney, or blood remain	Thorough; no oesophagus, gills, viscera, kidney remain; traces of blood permitted	Traces of blood and kidney permitted
Odour	Fresh odour; no abnormal odour	Loss of fresh odour; no sour or abnormal odour	May have slight off-odour, but no trace of decomposition

Table 2.2 Grade standards: Whole or butchered tuna intended for processing

Grade factors	Grade A	Grade B	Grade C	Reject
Odour: Belly cavity and cut through flesh at nape	Fresh characteristic odours	No odour	Slightly stale odour or uncharacteristic odours *not* associated with taint or decomposition	Any detectable odour associated with taint or decomposition such as ammonia, bilge, sour.
Belly cavity: Internal organs and belly wall	Smooth, bright, no evidence of burn; organs bright, firm, characteristic colour	Slight burn, slightly rough peritoneum; organs slightly soft with loss of lustre, red discoloration evident	Breakdown of belly wall, no holes to skin, excessively rough peritoneum; organs bleached and soft; 10% of belly wall affected by protruding bones; cracks if bent 90°	Burns through to skin, greater than 10% of belly wall has protruding bones; organs show liquefaction, and/or grey or green colours evident
Physical damage: Edible portion of fish	No evidence of mutilation or damage	Slight mutilation or deformation; no evidence of splitting	Slight splitting; less than 10% of fish slightly smashed or broken to expose muscle	Greater than 10% of the fish is split, smashed or mutilated to expose muscle
Texture	Firm and elastic	Slightly soft	Soft	Excessively soft and mushy
Eyes	Clear, bright, protruding	Sunken, cloudy-white or reddish	Sunken, dull white or red. Centre of eye liquefied	Not assigned
Gills	Characteristic odour and blood red appearance	No odour, pale red to brown red colour	Uncharacteristic odours not associated with taint or decomposition, dark brown to yellow brown colour	Grade D Detectable odours associated with taint and decomposition; white-yellow colour and slimy appearance

Grades are assigned to each sample unit examined using the combination of factors given above. The assigned grade cannot be higher than the lowest grade for any of the grading factors.

The importance of such visual checks cannot be overemphasised and should be supervised by an experienced quality assurance officer or operative. With frozen fish this is not normally possible. However, checks on correct packaging and lack of damage to packaging may be made at this time. When the raw material is in cold storage further checks can be undertaken.

The sexual maturity of salmon must be assessed as the change in preparation for breeding affects the eating quality. Konagaya (1983) suggests an increased protease activity in the muscle of chum salmon during spawning migration causes softening of the muscle tissue. However, Yamashita and Konagaya (1991) state that it is probable that it is the participation of phagocytes rich in cathepsins which cause the extensive muscle softening of the mature salmon. Farmed salmon are fed diets rich in carotenoids to produce the red colour favoured by the consumer. Diets may also contain antibiotics, considered necessary in intensive farming, though carry-over of residues should be avoided in fish destined for use in canning.

Where possible, it is best to keep the fish in the same boxes or containers without re-icing as the less the fish is handled, the longer the quality will be maintained. It may be necessary, however, during the off-loading procedure to re-ice the fish. With some species the fish may be off-loaded, separated from ice, washed and re-iced prior to placing in chilled storage to await further processing.

The raw material specification is broken down into a number of attributes. First, the species will need identifying; secondly, the size will be stated.

Fish which have been mechanically graded should fall within a specified weight range. However, where fish are of mixed sizes, a better indication will be given by 'percent usable fish' which is the percentage by weight of fish in the required weight range. A minimum acceptable percentage should be stated for this specification.

The general condition of the fish may be specified in different ways depending upon whether the fish is fresh or frozen. An example of this for *Sprattus sprattus* will be as follows:

- Fresh fish:
    - shining, iridescent with bright colour,
    - slightly protruding eyes;
    - little or no blood staining at the gills;
    - fresh odour;
    - fresh seaweedy or slight oily odour;
    - containing no feed;
    - free from disease and with no obvious infestation with parasites;
    - minimum of damage; and
    - no burst bellies.

- Frozen fish:
  - general appearance good;
  - fairly firm flesh;
  - eyes flat or only slightly sunken;
  - odour slightly oily or neutral with no off-odours particularly at the gills;
  - containing no feed;
  - no burst bellies;
  - very little skinning or damage;
  - no evidence of disease or parasitic infestation;
  - blocks well glazed to minimise the development of rancidity.

For some species, the fat content of the fish will normally be specified. In the case of fresh fish of known origin samples may be taken on a daily basis to check the variation of fat content throughout the season in order to correlate variations in texture or eating qualities in the final product with variations in the fat content of the fish. In the case of frozen raw material the fat content must be checked to ensure that it falls within the acceptable range laid down in the product raw material specifications prior to the fish being defrosted in the cannery. The fat content of fresh fish should be monitored throughout the year, to provide evidence of seasonal variations (day-to-day variations should be insignificant).

An example of this is Atlantic mackerel which may have an oil content as high as 34% at the beginning of the season and fall to 13% by the end of the season. The very high oil content causes problems in handling during cooking, giving a very soft product. Also, when used in cans which have sauces added, the high percentage cook-out of oil dramatically affects the sauce texture and appearance after processing in the can.

Frozen blocks should be checked for weight of fish after thawing as this will affect the yield and consequent overall profitability of the operation. In the case of fresh fish, weight checks should be made on a random basis on receipt at the factory.

2.4 Storage

Where fresh fish is being used by the cannery the delay between catching and landing should be as short as possible, ideally less than 12 h. Where this period is likely to be exceeded there must be some form of refrigeration to hold the product at 0°C, such as boxing and icing, or use of refrigerated sea water, to minimise quality deterioration. Once the fish has been accepted in the factory the maintenance of a fish temperature of 0°C is essential if accelerated spoilage is to be avoided. Ideally, storage should be in clean plastic boxes where the fish is mixed with ice and the boxes held in an insulated chilled room operating at between 1 and 2°C; this allows the ice to melt thereby cooling the fish with cold melt water and the relatively low temperature of the surrounding air ensures that ice is not wasted by absorbing heat from the air. The result is a reduced usage of ice and the quality of fish is maintained.

An alternative method of storing fresh fish is to use refrigerated fresh water. The water may be cooled to 0–2°C by adding ice or by using a mechanical refrigeration method. There are some advantages to be had in using this method; the bulk of fish in water can be handled mechanically in the factory and, where the fish have already been stored in refrigerated sea water on-board the fishing vessel, this may be an advantage when using pumping for off-loading ship to shore. The fish are less likely to be bruised using such techniques and, where cooling is required, the cooling will be fairly uniform throughout the total mass of fish.

Where frozen fish is to be stored the temperature of the cold store should ideally be at −30°C. At this temperature fatty fish may be kept for up to 6 months with little deterioration in quality. The main problem in extending cold storage of fatty fish is rancidity; the degree of rancidity is accentuated by higher temperatures, inadequate glazing of the block and extended period of storage. Lipid oxidation proceeds rapidly at temperatures as low as −18°C. Below this temperature, the rate of oxidation decreases quickly. Fat oxidation rate is reduced by a factor of 2 or 3 for every 10°C reduction in temperature. As storage progresses, denaturation of protein causes toughening of the flesh of the fish.

In order to maintain quality, it is essential that good practices be followed in chilled store and cold store management. Strict rotation of stock must be observed. For traceability purposes all pallets should bear a sequentially numbered ticket which states the product, its production date and the source of raw material. Other items which may appear on the ticket could be quality grade, count per kilogram, date into store, etc. Where wooden pallets are used, frozen blocks should not be placed directly on to them but a suitable plastic liner placed between the block and the wooden pallet. Ideally, blocks should be individually glazed and bagged, this will help reduce the rate of oxidation of the fish oil.

2.5 Defrosting frozen fish

Large quantities of fish are frozen as a means of preservation and storage prior to use in the canning process. The defrosting of this fish is of considerable interest to the processor. Careful thawing is essential if product quality is to be retained. Generally, rapid thawing is more advantageous as it limits the exposure of the product to high temperatures which cause deterioration in quality.

When frozen fish is thawed in air or water, the surface ice melts to form a layer of water. Because water has a lower thermal conductivity as well as a lower thermal diffusivity than ice, the rate at which heat is conducted to the frozen part of the fish is reduced as the thickness of the water layer increases. Effectively, as the fish defrosts so the thawed outer surface acts as an insulator to heat transfer. During the freezing process, as the layer of ice builds up, so the heat transfer rate increases, consequently it takes longer to defrost material by simple heat transfer than it does to freeze the same material over the same temperature range, using similar parameters.

There are two main groups of thawing methods used today. The first group includes those methods whereby heat is conducted into the fish from the surface whilst the second group is concerned with methods where heat is generated uniformly throughout the fish.

Whichever method is used the system should avoid:

- localised overheating of the fish,
- excessive drip loss,
- dehydration, and
- bacterial growth.

There are a number of systems used for application of heat to the surface of the fish. These include exposure to still or moving warm air, spraying with water, immersion in water; or condensation of water vapour on the surface. In all these methods the outside of the fish thaws first and, as mentioned earlier, reduces the ability to conduct heat, thus increasing the thawing time. These methods are also limited by the need to avoid overheating the fish. In the UK it is recommended that the temperatures should not exceed 20°C (Jason, 1981) but in tropical countries this is often impossible to achieve without the use of chilled storage facilities. The use of higher temperatures for the heating medium increases the rate of heat transfer, but may result in localised overheating which could lead to the cooking of the fish, and a consequent break up of the flesh.

2.5.1 Air thawing

Thawing in still air may be considered the simplest of the thawing methods for frozen blocks of whole fish and, whilst for small quantities it is an inexpensive method, it is not without its drawbacks. The temperature of the air should be between 15° and 20°C. Lower temperatures result in extremely slow thawing rates resulting in softening of the flesh and reduced yield in further processing. Higher temperatures also result in product deterioration and at temperatures greater than 30°C some fish from colder waters may cook resulting in break up of the flesh.

Thawing in still air is feasible for small quantities. It has the disadvantages of requiring a considerable amount of space, handling and the time taken to defrost is often very long (normally 10–24 h depending on the size of the fish block). It does, however, have the advantage that little equipment is required.

2.5.2 Air blast thawing

Frozen fish can be thawed much more rapidly under controlled conditions using air blast thawing, typically saving 70% of the thawing time (Figure 2.2).

Thawing in still air requires long periods of time because the rate of heat transfer between air and fish is very low. This rate of heat transfer may be increased by using high velocity air passing across the frozen fish. Velocities of 8–10 m/s are used in industrial units; above this speed, little increase in heat transfer rate is achieved (Burgess *et al.*, 1967).

Thawing using moving air may be continuous or batch operated. Continuous thawing systems utilise a conveyor-belt on which the frozen blocks of fish are placed and carried through a blast thawer where air at temperatures between 15° and 20°C is blown across the conveyor-belt. In batch thawers, frozen blocks are loaded onto special racks or trolleys. The trays are designed for maximum air flow, resulting in a minimum processing time (Figure 2.3).

Because of the moving air over the surface of the product, the avoidance of dehydration is essential to achieve high yields with no deterioration in quality of the product. This is achieved by using air which is as nearly saturated as possible. Heat exchangers and banks of water sprays in the

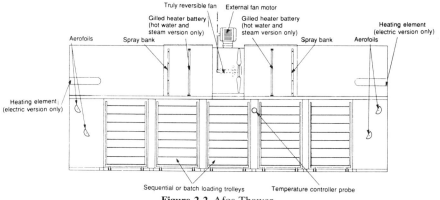

Figure 2.2 Afos Thawer.

Figure 2.3 Continuous thawer. Product is placed on infeed conveyor and heated air circulation is controlled by a number of fan units. The use of separate defrosting zones allows for temperature sensing and humidity control. (Courtesy of Cabinplant.)

plenum chambers of air blast thawers are used to achieve the desired objective. Frequent cleaning of air blast thawers is vital for both hygienic and operational considerations.

2.5.3 Water thawing

Where an ample supply of clean water is available, thawing in warm water may be a cheap and simple method of thawing frozen fish. The fish may be immersed in the water or the water sprayed over the fish or even a combination of the two.

Whilst thawing in water is simple and inexpensive it may cause the fish to lose quality in terms of flavour and appearance, and if water is absorbed during the thawing process this may cause problems in subsequent operations during the canning process.

Thawing of frozen blocks using water is more rapid than air thawing due to higher rates of heat transfer between the product and water. As with air blast thawing, the velocity of water passing over the product greatly influences the rate of thawing, and velocities of 0.5–2 cm/s are used commercially. Where the higher velocity of water is used at temperatures of 18°C, blocks 100 mm thick may be defrosted in periods of 4.5 h (Jason).

Typical immersion thawers consist of a tank in which vertical baffles are placed causing the water to flow backwards and forwards across the tank as it moves from the inlet end to the outlet at the opposite end. The fish blocks are placed between the baffles and the flow of water should be such that the fish blocks at the downstream end of the tank do not thaw too slowly. In practice it is normal for a usage rate of 4 tonnes of water per tonne of fish to be thawed. Continuous thawers may use sprays and immersion as shown in Figure 2.4. Alternatively, blocks of frozen fish may be conveyed through a tank of moving water which defrosts the block and thus gives a continuous feed to a production line. Such thawers may have problems due to scales and pieces of fish becoming trapped in the circulation systems of the thawer. Filtration systems and thorough cleaning on a daily basis are essential for this type of equipment.

2.5.4 Vacuum thawing

Vacuum thawers consist of air-tight chambers into which the fish is loaded using trolleys. A vacuum is drawn and water in a tray over the base of the chamber is heated filling the chamber with water vapour. The temperature of the water vapour is typically between 18° and 20°C and the vapour condenses on the cold surface of the fish where the latent heat of vaporisation is absorbed by the fish. Heat transfer to the product is much more rapid than the previous method of thawing.

Figure 2.4 Continuous immersion thawer. Product is submerged into a water bath and defrosted by means of recirculated water. A water flume and elevator are used for discharge from the defroster. (Courtesy of Cabinplant.)

Equivalent thawing times may be reduced from 20 h in air to less than 1 h in a vacuum thawing unit and the water usage of such units is low. However, care must be taken that gases released from the fish as thawing proceeds do not cause rupturing of flesh (e.g. belly burst in herring and mackerel).

The advantages of this method of defrosting are that with the exception of a vacuum pump there are no moving parts, hence the possibility of mechanical breakdown is reduced compared to the previous method. Also, as the vapour is distilled from water in the tank it condenses onto the fish in a pure state, so there is no risk of contamination from bacteria which may accumulate within the system. Cleaning for this method is by means of a CIP system within the chamber.

2.5.5 Other methods of thawing

Di-electric heating consists of placing the fish between two parallel metal plates across which a high-frequency alternating voltage is applied. The electrical frequency causes dipoles in the water to oscillate as the electrical field direction changes. The frictional energy produced heats the fish resulting in defrosting of the block. Rapid thawing of the product is possible but localised overheating may cause problems. This can be avoided by applying the di-electric effect for short periods interspersed with a tempering period in order to dissipate the heat produced.

Defrosting using microwave heating is also possible. Again, localised heating is a problem with this method.

Though the use of electrical methods of thawing results in a much more rapid defrosting of products, it is very costly in terms of capital expenditure. However, if correctly applied it can result in good quality thawed fish with reduced drip loss from the product.

The choice of thawing method will depend on a number of factors including the throughput required and whether batch or continuous operations are to be considered. The capital cost of the equipment, the floor area required for its installation and subsequent labour requirements, the maintenance and other running costs and availability of steam and hot water will also influence the decision.

2.6 Fish preparation

During the production operation, visual inspection is of paramount importance for determining the quality of the raw material entering the can. Where there is a delay prior to further processing in the cannery this enables further quality checks to be made prior to the packing operation.

2.6.1 Heading

'Heading' involves removing the head of the fish from the body and is achieved by two different methods. The simplest method is by means of a straight cut perpendicular to the backbone of the fish made just behind the head. This method is simple and fast but results in a reduced yield. The second method is termed a V-cut where the cut is made from behind the gills but slanting diagonally forward to the point of the backbone. This achieves an increase in yield from meat which is located near the back bone at the dorsal side of the fish. Such a cut may be used where heading is carried out by hand or where the value of the fish flesh saved is sufficient to pay for the increased cost of machinery or labour required to carry out such an operation. Where machines are used, the heads may be removed using a circular saw for both types of cut whereas the straight cut may utilise a bandsaw or guillotine. Heading machines are normally adjusted to accept fish of a certain length and shape.

Using a straight-cut machine, fish are normally headed by loading onto a slatted conveyor-belt, the nose of each fish being pressed against an end plate. The conveyor moves the fish towards the saw blade or guillotine which removes the head. This in turn is guided down a chute to a waste collection point, whilst the body of the fish moves onto the next part of the process. Some straight head cutting machines are modified to remove the head and pull out the viscera at the same time. Such an operation is known as 'nobbing' (Figure 2.5).

To achieve the V-cut, a machine with two rotating blades is used and the position of the blades is adjusted to yield as much meat as possible whilst still removing the collar-bone and pectoral fins with the head.

For smaller fish such as sardine and sild and even mackerel, machinery is a viable alternative where the cost of manual labour is high. However, for larger fish the manual removal of the head will result in greater economies of yield.

Where shrimps and prawns are used for canning, they must also undergo a deheading operation. In many parts of the tropics, especially in the countries of South East Asia, this operation is carried out by hand. The operation is achieved by squeezing the shrimp just in front of the tail section between thumb and fingers, then, with a slight twist, removing the head from the tail. Mechanical removal of the head is achieved by using either a guillotine or rotating knife which cuts off the head after the shrimp is correctly positioned on a slatted conveyor-belt similar to that described for the deheading of fish. This operation is often carried out at the same time as peeling of shrimps and prawns.

Figure 2.5 Orientation of sardines for nobbing. (Courtesy of International Fish Canners.)

2.6.2 *Filleting*

The process of removing the complete musculature from each side of a fish is known as filleting. This may be achieved manually or by using machines. For the canning industry, because of the large quantities of fish processed daily, it is usual for the smaller species to be filleted using a machine. Filleting machines are available commercially for many species of fish but the canning industry is mainly concerned with herring, mackerel and pilchards (Figure 2.6).

With mechanised filleting the species such as herring, pilchards and small mackerel may all be filleted using the same machine. This is because they have similar bone structures. The fish are conveyed into the machine oriented relative to the filleting blades. Automatic orientation of the fish is now the norm although some machines still utilise manual orientation. Headed and gutted fish are conveyed into the machine held in a guide which presents the fish to the circular filleting blades. The blades are at fixed angles and the distance from the guides is determined by the thickness of the fish and the distance from the body cavity to the exterior

Figure 2.6 Herring filleting machine. (Courtesy of Baader (UK) Ltd.)

surface of the fish. The angles of the blades relative to the guide will be determined by the skeletal structure and the contours of the external surface of the fish species. Adjustments to the position of the blades are made in order that as much meat as possible is removed with the fillet thus increasing the yield using the machine. Such machines are designed to accept an optimum length of fish. Where fish that are larger or smaller than this optimum size are filleted on the machine, the yield will be reduced.

These machines, whilst not removing as much flesh as a skilled filleter, do process greater quantities of fish in a given time. The capacity of such machines may be up to 300 fish a minute where machines are fed by up to four operators. This greatly reduces the labour cost of the filleting operation. Against this increased efficiency, water consumption must be considered, which may be up to 40 litres/min. The water must be of potable quality and an adequate supply is essential for the operation of such automatic machines.

2.6.3 Skinning

The decision to remove the skin or not will depend upon the product to be produced. Some fish have hard scales which need to be removed before the fish is further processed and placed in the can. Herring is such a fish and the scales are removed from the skin by rubbing against a rough surface in such a manner to remove the scales. Generally, automatic scalers consist of a horizontal cylinder fabricated from horizontal metal bars or having a rough internal surface. Fish are fed into one end of the cylinder, where the slope of the axis and the rotational speed will determine how long the fish are in the scaler before being discharged at the other end. The fish tumble inside the rotating cylinder and as the fish move across the rough internal surface the scales are removed. As with filleting machines large quantities of water are required in this case in order to wash the fish to assist in the removal of the scales and carry them away.

For fish with soft skins, such as mackerel, caustic peeling is preferable. This entails feeding the fish on a continuous basis through a tank containing caustic soda solution at a pH of between 11 and 13. The recommended strength is to achieve a pH of 11. However, when operating to this pH excessive subsequent trimming of fins and skin is sometimes required and pH values of up to 13 are used in order to avoid extra labour later in the process. On leaving the caustic tank the fish are immersed in a neutralising tank using hydrochloric acid operating at a pH of 3. The fish are subsequently washed using water jet sprays and loose skin is removed during the washing process. At the end of the process the fish should be at a pH of 7. The total time period from entering the caustic bath to leaving the acid bath will be in the region of 20 min.

2.6.4 Smoking

Traditionally, the objective of smoking fish was to increase the shelf-life of the raw material. With modern smoking, procedures are designed to impart the desired sensory characteristics to the fish uniformly and with consistency from one batch to another. Where the fish are to be smoked prior to canning, the extension of shelf-life of the product is not in consideration as the subsequent sterilisation process will achieve a much longer shelf-life than is possible with the smoking process alone. The smoking of fish may be divided into two types, cold smoking at temperatures below 30°C and hot smoking where temperatures greater than 80°C are achieved. Cold smoked fish are usually non-fatty fish such as haddock and cod. Here, the process imparts a smoke flavour which satisfies the demands of the consumer.

The hot smoking process is used mainly for fatty fish such as herring and mackerel and with shellfish it is generally limited to oysters and mussels.

Poly-aromatic hydrocarbons (PAH) are some of the hundreds of constituents of wood smoke. They are of particular interest because they are carcinogenic, the most important one being 3,4-benzpyrene. Concentrations of PAH are influenced by the method of smoke generation, temperature of combustion, the available air supply, type of wood, length of time of smoking and smoke temperature. High temperature smoking is best to limit the PAH concentration in the smoke and ultimately in the product (Maga, 1987).

All smoked fish are salted prior to the smoking process. The prepared fillet or shellfish meat is submerged in a brine solution long enough to absorb salt to a desired concentration. The concentration achieved can be varied depending upon the product and the customers' requirements.

Generally, fully automatic brining machines are employed by the industry (Figure 2.7). The machine consists of a tank containing brine solution and mechanised conveyor-belt and paddle system normally with variable speed control. This is used to pass the fish through the brine tank at a pre-set rate, thus ensuring that the fish are immersed in the brine for the ideal length of time. This will ensure a consistent quality of product and a constant salt content in the finished product. The fish enters the system via an elevated conveyor hopper which is fed from the filleting machines or is hand loaded at a rate determined by the requirements of the processing line subsequent to the briner. The salted fish leaving the brining tank will be placed on trays, which when fully loaded are positioned onto smoking trolleys for transportation into the smoking kilns.

The concentration of brine solution used may vary between 50 and 100% saturation. High concentrations of salt will permit shorter dwell times in the brine in order to achieve the desired salt concentration in the end-product.

Figure 2.7 Sardines entering a continuous brining machine. (Courtesy of International Fish Canners.)

As an indication, for mackerel fillets passed through a continuous brining system utilising brine which is over 90% saturation the residence time will be between 1 and 2 min in order to achieve the final salt concentration of around 3%. The final figure will depend upon three factors. Firstly, the brine concentration; secondly, the length of time the fillet is left in the brine; and thirdly, the percentage fat content of the fish. The greater the fat content of the fish the slower the salt uptake.

In the case of shellfish such as mussels, these are immersed in brine for 4–5 min using a brine concentration of 50%. The meats are then drained and dipped in vegetable oil before being laid on mesh trays to drain. Oysters are prepared in a similar manner and in both cases the shellfish may be placed immediately in the kiln.

Where fish, whole or in fillet form, have been brined prior to smoking, they are laid on mesh trays constructed from stainless steel or plastic-coated steel and left to drain for a period of 0.5–1 h.

Smoking kilns are of two main types: traditional, where the fish is placed directly over source of smoke, typically a chimney structure; or a modern mechanical kiln consisting of a main cabinet with an air circulating fan, exhaust fan, heat exchangers and controls and a separate smoke generation chamber connected to the main cabinet (Figure 2.8). Smoke generated from sawdust is used in preference to smoke from burning wood, this produces a cooler fire and more smoke as the sawdust smoulders rather than burns and gives a smoke with more flavouring properties.

Modern smoke generators feed sawdust slowly onto a hot surface producing full smoke output in a matter of minutes, and requiring little attention other than to keep the hopper filled with sawdust. A sawdust feed hopper is fitted with variable speed output drive which provides

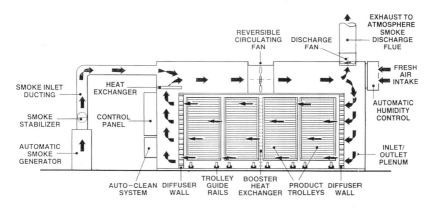

Figure 2.8 Modern mechanical fish-smoking kiln. (Courtesy of Afos Ltd, Manor Estate, Anlaby, Hull, UK.)

controlled quantities of sawdust to an electrically heated combustion plate. The volume of combustion air is also varied providing maximum control of smoke density with economy of sawdust usage.

The smoking cabinet is a self-contained unit which includes an air circulating fan, an exhaust fan, heat exchangers and humidifiers. Depending upon the design, the smoke/air flow may be vertical or horizontal. Some kilns allow for reversal of the direction of air flow thus ensuring greater uniformity of smoke uptake by the product on the trolleys. Modern mechanical kilns incorporating the latest production technology and microprocessor controls allow programming which will ensure a consistent smoked product and also guarantee yields at the end of the process. This is a distinct advantage to the smoked fish canner where reduction in the amount of drying which takes place during the smoking process may give both higher yields and a better quality finished product in the can.

Operation of the smoking kiln is such that air is circulated around the smoke house and conditioned to the correct temperature (using thermostats) and humidity (using water sprays) in the heat exchangers located in a plenum. The humidity is monitored by humidity detectors positioned in the air stream. Smoke is drawn into the kiln from the smoke generator through a connecting duct and mixed with recirculating air and fresh air before passing through the heat exchanger to ensure the correct temperature is maintained. Fans circulate the mixture of smoke and air at a controlled velocity aimed at maximum deposition of smoke flavour in the fish. The smoke generator is normally positioned outside the production area and the smoke is drawn into the kiln via an extended duct leading from the generator to the kiln.

The choice of wood used for smoking depends upon the types of wood available and the desired flavour in the final product. Almost any hard wood may be used but resinous soft wood should not be used as it results in high PAH levels in the smoked fish. Because of this, hard wood chips or sawdust are generally preferred. Where available, oak is normally the preferred type of wood for hot smoking of fish. However, other woods such as hickory, cedar and eucalyptus may also be used to produce smoke and in some parts of the world coconut husks, spent sugar cane, or rice husks may be used.

2.6.5 Pre-cooking

The eventual thermal process designed to sterilise the fish in can is more than adequate to cook the fish in order to make it palatable. Pre-cooking of fish prior to filling is carried out either to assist in the packing operation or when this occurs in the container it is designed to remove excessive aqueous cook-out liquor from the fish flesh. Such liquid often has a detrimental appearance in the finished product.

One use of pre-cooking is in the production of boneless mackerel fillets where the fish is conveyed to a cooking bath operating at around 90°C immediately after a caustic skinning operation. The cooking takes approximately 25 min, at the end of which a short spray cooling stage precedes the packing into cans. In the cooked form it is easy to separate the two fillets from either side of the fish skeleton (Figure 2.9). These may then be placed directly into cans or placed onto modified conveyors leading to automatic can filling machinery.

Large tuna may be up to 20 kg in weight and must be pre-cooked prior to preparation for insertion in the can. Cooking in steam at atmospheric pressure may take up to 4 h to complete and should target for achieving a backbone temperature of 70°C. They are then allowed to cool in chill rooms for 24 h, allowing the flesh texture to become firm and easier to handle in the trimming operation, during which the head, skin, spine and dark flesh which underlies the lateral line are all removed. The flesh which remains is then packed into cans as solid steaks to produce a premium product whilst the offcuts are packed as chunks or flakes.

In the case of shellfish, molluscs are pre-cooked in order to remove the meat from the shell, this operation is known as shucking and is normally achieved by the use of pressurised steam at 3 bar (30^5 Pa) absolute for a period of 30 s, followed by rapid reduction to 2 atm (202 kPa). Immediate quenching with cold water is required to reduce the evaporation which causes textural damage due to dehydration. In the case of crustacea such as crabs, pre-cooking is required in order to facilitate the extraction of the white meat from the claws and carapace prior to filling in the can. Shrimps

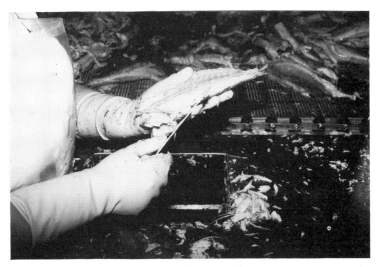

Figure 2.9 Removing backbone from skinned mackerel to produce mackerel loins. (Courtesy of International Fish Canners.)

and prawns are pre-cooked after removal of the head and shell from the tail, by immersion in a tank of hot brine. The time of cooking is up to 4 min and the meat becomes white and firm containing the characteristic curl which assists in subsequent size grading prior to filling into cans.

2.7 Storing prepared fish

In most fish canning operations once a fish has been prepared for canning the process is continuous. However, this may be disrupted by machinery breakdown or as in the case of smoking, the preparatory process may take place in a separate part of the factory or indeed on a separate site. This normally requires the storage of the prepared material for short periods of time, a maximum period of 20 min is a useful guideline, though this will depend upon the ambient temperature (higher temperatures allow less time delay). Prepared fish and shellfish if left standing for even short periods of time will tend to deteriorate faster than the raw material in store (2.3°C) due to the temperature of the fish being slightly higher as it will have absorbed heat from the atmosphere in the processing area, or as in the case of smoking from the preparatory process itself. As in the case of raw material the rate of spoilage may be reduced by bringing the temperature down to chill temperatures of 0–2°C.

Smoked fish to be used for canning should be chilled as quickly as possible after the smoking process unless it is to be used immediately in the packing operation. Ideally, such fish should be stored in a separate chill room due to the problems of cross contamination of smoke flavour to non-smoked raw material. Where the use of a separate chill store is impossible the problem may be reduced by storing the fish in plastic trays with lids. However, this will not guarantee the avoidance of tainting of other fish stored in the same room. Where prepared fish must be stored at the end of a day's production or because of a breakdown on the packing line, the fish should be moved to the chill room as quickly as possible and stored in clean plastic boxes. Depending on the state of preparation the fish should be iced top and bottom or be covered with a thin polythene sheet in order to reduce dehydration on the surface. In some situations the use of ice may act as a leaching agent. This may be reduced by placing the ice in polythene bags and resting the bag on top of the fish thus achieving both cooling and reduction of evaporation in one operation; however, it must be noted that for long-term storage such trays should be placed in a chill room.

Care must be taken not to store too great a depth of prepared fish as fish in the lower layers will lose fluid due to the pressure of the fish above. As with the storage of raw material prior to processing, the containers of prepared fish should be labelled clearly for identification and stock rotation purposes.

2.8 Chemical indicators of quality

Quality of fish and shellfish may be checked using chemical analysis in three separate groupings outlined below.

Firstly, the analysis of TVB-N (total volatile basic nitrogen) and TMA-N (trimethylamine nitrogen). These tests are carried out in order to obtain guidance regarding the freshness of the sample and may form a useful back-up to sensory analysis.

Secondly, the analysis for histamine. Canned fish have been implicated in several outbreaks of histamine poisoning, also known as scombrotoxin poisoning because of its frequent association with scombroid fish such as tuna and mackerel. In the UK, a survey showed that canned seafood accounted for 42% of the histamine poisoning outbreaks during the period 1976–1982 (Taylor, 1986). The histamine accumulates in the fish before thermal processing especially during long periods of unrefrigerated storage or transport. Histamine, being fairly thermostable, is not affected by the heat of the retorting process and is therefore found in the finished canned product even though the bacteria responsible for its presence have been destroyed. The E.C. 1991 Fish Hygiene Directive (Annex Chapter V, para 3) lays down limits for histamine content of not more than 200 ppm in any sample with not more than two samples containing between 100 and 200 ppm and a mean value of less than 100 ppm, for nine samples taken from one batch of fish.

The same regulations cover the third group which is the analysis for heavy metals, in particular mercury, lead and tin. In the case of lead, the advent of the welded seam has reduced the danger from the can itself, but it should be remembered that the fish chain does have a great ability to assimilate heavy metals from contaminated waters and so produce contaminated products.

In conclusion, the internationally demanding legal requirements of the European, North American and Japanese governments require that the handling of the raw material for fishery products is of a particularly high standard. The use of internationally accepted standards for quality systems such as ISO 9000 and BS 5750 are useful tools for ensuring the control of quality throughout the raw material chain as well as the complete process. It is beyond the scope of this book to cover this topic but the reader is urged to give this subject consideration.

References and Bibliography

Atkin, et al. (1982) Fish Handling and Processing. HMSO, London, UK.
Borgstrom (1965) Fish as Food (Vol. 4) Academic Press.
Burgess, G.H.O. et al. (1967) Fish Handling and Processing. HMSO, London, UK.

Hardy R. and Smith, J.G.M. (1976) The storage of mackerel. Development of histamine and rancidity. *J. Sci. Food Agric.*, **27**, 595–599.

Hardy, R., McGill, A.S. and Gunstone, F.D. (1979) Lipid autoxidation changes in cold stored cod. *J. Sci. Food Agric.*, **30**, 10.

Horner, W.F.A. (1992) *Fish Processing Technology* (ed. Hall, G.M.). Blackie, Glasgow, UK.

Huss, H.H. *et al.* (eds) (1992) *Quality Assurance in the Fish Industry. Developments in Food Science* (Vol. 30). Elsevier.

Jason, A.C. (1981) The storage of herring in ice, R.S.W. and at ambient temperature. *Adv. Fish Sci. Technol.*, 108–175.

Jason, A.C. *Torry Advisory Note* (No. 25) Torry Research Station.

Konagaya (1983) *J. Japanese Soc. Food Sci. Technol.*, **29** (6), 379–388.

Labuza, T.P. (1970) Properties of water as related to the keeping qualities of foods. *Proc. 2nd Int. Congress. Food Science and Technology*. Inst of Food Technology, pp. 618–635.

Labuza, T.P., Tannenbaum, S.R. and Karel, M. (1970) Water content and stability of low moisture and intermediate moisture foods. *Food Technol.*, **24**, 543–550.

Maga, J.A. (1987) The flavour chemistry of wood smoke. *Food Rev. Int.*, **3** (1 & 2), 139–184.

Putro, S. *et al.* (1989) Studies on stability of dried salted fish. In *Conference Proceedings, Food Preservation by Moisture Control*. Elsevier Science Publishers, London, UK, pp. 261–268.

Shenoy, A.V. and Pillai, V.K. (1971) *Fishery Technol.*, **8**, (1), 37–41.

Slabjy, B.M. and True, R.H. (1978) Effect of pre-process holding on the quality of canned Maine sardines. *J. Food Sci.*, **43** (4), 1172–1176.

Taylor, S.L. (1986) *CRC Crit. Rev. Toxicol.*, **17**, 2.

Warne, D., Foran, M. and King, M. (1987) Histamine control survey in canned tuna. *Infofish Marketing Dig.*, 2/87.

Yamashita, M. and Konagaya, S. (1991) Participation of cathepsin L into extensive softening of the muscle of chum salmon caught during spawning migration. *Bull. Japanese Soc. Fish.*, **56** (8), 1271–1277.

Yamashita, M. and Konagaya, S. (1991) A comparison of cystatin activity in the various tissues of chum salmon between feeding and spawning migrations. *Comp. Biochem. Physiol.*, **100A** (3), 749–751.

Appendix: Sources of machinery

• Complete fish canning lines:
  – Alsthom Atlantique Group, Nantes Cedex, France.
  – Cabinplant International As., Haarby, Denmark.
  – FJC-Projectos, Maquinas e Acessorios Para A Industria Lda., Lisbon, Portugal.
  – Ghizzoni Dante & Figlio, Felino, Italy.
  – Hermanos Rodriguez Gomez, SA, Vigo, Spain.
  – Irmaos Fischer SA Ind E Com., Brusque, SC, Brazil.
  – Jedinstvo, Zagreb, Croatia.
  – Jorgensen Food Engineering APS, Odense S, Denmark.
  – Mather & Platt (India) Ltd, Bombay, India.
  – Vettori Manghi & C SPA, Parma, Italy.
  – Talleres Metalurgicos Condor (TMC), Mendoza, Argentina.

- Fish graders:
  - Cabinplant International As., Haarby, Denmark.
  - Kronborg, Dybvad, Denmark.
  - Sort-Rite International Inc. Harlingen, TX, USA.
  - Stalvinnslan HF., Reykjavic, Iceland.

- Fish washers and scalers:
  - Machinefabrieken Rijn BV, Katwijk Zh, The Netherlands.
  - Nordischer Maschinenbau Rud Baader GmbH & Co Kg., Lubeck, Germany.
  - Cabinplant International As., Haarby, Denmark.
  - Irmaos Fischer SA Ind E Com., Brusque, SC, Brazil.
  - Machinefabrieken Rijn BV, Katwijk Zh, The Netherlands.
  - Mather & Platt (India) Ltd, Bombay, India.
  - Simnar Inc, Ontario, Canada.

- Fish headers, gutters and nobbers:
  - Constructions Mecaniques D'Armorique SA, Quimper Cedex, France.
  - Louarn SA Quimper Cedex, France.
  - Machinefabrieken Rijn BV, Katwijk Zh, The Netherlands.
  - Nordischer Maschinenbau Rud Baader GmbH & Co Kg., Lubeck, Germany.
  - Norden Seafood Machinery AB, Kalmar, Sweden.

- Freezers:
  - APV Baker Freezer Division, Thetford, UK.

- Defrosters:
  - Afos, Hull, UK.
  - APV Baker Freezer Division, Thetford, UK.
  - Cabinplant International As., Haarby, Denmark.

- Shellfish cookers and processing lines:
  - Farvis Ltd, Bristol, UK.
  - Franken BV Goes, The Netherlands.

- Smoking kilns:
  - Afos, Hull, UK.

3 Meat raw materials

R.J. HART

3.1 Introduction

Meat was one of the first foods to be preserved by 'canning', albeit in glass containers (Appert, 1810), and some early examples of meat originally preserved in metal containers for an 1824 expedition to the North West Passage still appear sound. These were assessed and found still to be edible in 1938 (Drummond and Macara, 1938), and were resealed in glass. Originally, the underlying principles involved were not understood; preservation was the aim, and it is likely that the quality of the preserved meat would not appeal to today's consumers.

The factors involved in the selection and sourcing of meat raw materials for canning have much in common with those involved in the choice of meats for other manufacturing purposes and, indeed, for the supply of meat for retail sale. The most important of these factors, along with price, are the identity of the meat (i.e. the species from which it has been derived), its composition (fat content, collagen content, etc.), its quality (particularly the functionality of the meat proteins) and its microbiological condition. Manufacturers and canners of meat products need to pay constant attention to all of these if their products are to be consistently high in quality, safe, legal and as described on the label.

Generally, producers of canned meat products are less likely to slaughter their own animals than are manufacturers of some other meat products (such as bacon). Thus, they may have less control over their raw materials. Often, they will be buying meat in frozen-block form (e.g. boxed forequarter and mechanically recovered meat (MRM)) and this presents its own difficulties in examination, sampling, etc.

3.2 Specifications and quality assurance

In most manufacturing processes, it is now widely accepted that quality assurance (avoiding mistakes before they have a chance to happen) is more cost-effective than quality control (detecting mistakes after they have happened). The production of canned meat products is no exception. Quality assurance with regard to meat raw materials involves a knowledge of the intended use, a specification for the meat, a monitoring system to establish whether the material supplied meets the specification, and a procedure (with defined responsibilities) to follow if it does not.

A knowledge of the intended use of the raw material will be likely to define much of its specification. Firstly, meat intended for human consumption must normally be inspected and approved by an appropriate authority. For certain meat products, the species and, perhaps, the precise cut of meat are laid down by law; if one wishes to make canned ham, for example, one is limited to pork leg meat. Other products may allow considerably greater latitude in the choice and specification of raw materials.

Meat is an inherently variable commodity. An appreciation of the basic principles of meat science, and of the major reasons for this variability, will help canners of meat products to avoid many potential problems. Although meat is considerably more variable than most other raw materials, the purchaser will, or at least should, have a specification. The specification should describe those properties of the material that the purchaser believes to be important to his operations, and should be concise, realistic and unambiguous. The specification forms part of the contract between purchaser and supplier and, as such, should be something that both parties believe to be achievable.

Although a good specification (preferably agreed with the supplier) is desirable, it is really only a 'wish-list'. Unless the supplier is totally infallible (and honest!) some form of inspection of the raw material, as delivered, will be needed to ensure compliance with the specification. The level and frequency of this inspection will vary with the degree of confidence between supplier and manufacturer, and with the perceived importance of each constituent part of the specification.

Finally, the knowledge that a consignment of meat has failed to meet its specification is of little value unless someone acts on it. A system of defined actions, in the event of non-compliance, as well as defined responsibilities, are essential components of the process of quality assurance.

Church and Wood (1992) give a full account of the factors affecting the quality of manufacturing meat and of the setting up of a system of quality assurance specifications and monitoring.

In this chapter, we shall look at the factors that are of most importance in deciding the specification of meat raw materials for use in canned meat products, and see what steps the manufacturer can take to ensure that the specification is actually met by the supplier.

3.3 Sampling procedures

Before any assessment can be made of a batch of raw material, it is vital that a representative sample be obtained. For visual assessment, one approach is to cut the block, using a bandsaw, into several smaller cubes. Four cuts (two pairs at right angles) can yield a total of 54 cut surfaces for inspection. The cutting plan is shown in Figure 3.1.

An alternative system that has been recommended (Church and Wood, 1992), particularly when chemical or microbiological analysis is needed, involves drilling into the block in the 'domino-five' pattern. An electric drill, fitted with a sterilised 2.5 cm wood-bit, is used to drill five holes approximately three-quarters of the depth of the meat block. The swarf from these holes is sampled into sterile polythene bags and retained for microbiological, chemical or other analysis. The domino-five drilling pattern is illustrated in Figure 3.2.

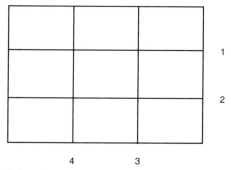

Figure 3.1 '9-cube' cutting pattern for examination of frozen blocks of meat.

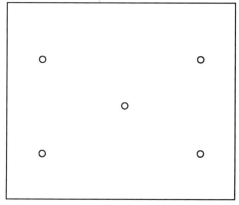

Figure 3.2 'Domino-five' sampling pattern for frozen blocks of meat.

3.4 Identity of meat

3.4.1 Species

Most people would have little difficulty in telling the difference between a steer and, say, a horse or a kangaroo. Somewhat fewer would be able easily to distinguish between a side of beef and a side of horse and, were the side to be further broken down into cuts, the job would be even more difficult. The difficulties of species identification are compounded when the meat is delivered by lorry, loaded with boxes of frozen meat.

Immunological tests are now widely available to distinguish between the common meat species and the most common adulterants. Enzyme-linked immunosorbent assays (ELISA) can usually detect between 1 and 5% of an adulterant species in a mixture and commercial kits are reliable, give rapid results and are reasonably cheap. One remaining drawback is that the analyst needs to know what to look for; a sample of meat (e.g. beef) might need to be analysed individually for several different potential adulterants (e.g. horse, kangaroo, buffalo). In addition, detection of cooked meats poses more of a problem than does that of raw meat; although an ELISA exists for raw horse meat, at the time of writing the corresponding test for cooked horse meat is still under development. A small amount of cooked meat continues to be used in products, such as some corned beef.

Electrophoresis (especially iso-electric focusing) can also be used for the detection of foreign species. It can reveal adulteration without the need for foreknowledge of the particular adulterant, but requires a more experienced analyst than does ELISA, and is still prone to the same limitations where cooked samples are concerned.

3.4.2 Age and sex

Meat generally becomes tougher (and somewhat darker) as animals age. This is due not so much to an increase in the total connective tissue content of the muscles as to changes in its structure. Collagen becomes more highly cross-linked (and, therefore, more difficult to soften or dissolve) as animals age (Bailey, 1968). In comminuted products, mechanical breakdown of the connective tissue tends to overcome this problem and allows the use of meat from older animals and/or tougher cuts. In the manufacture of many canned meat products, toughness of the raw material can be a positive advantage as it enables the meat structure to withstand the severe processing conditions encountered during cooking. Monitoring the age of animals from which meat has been derived is not possible with any precision at present; only indirect indications can be obtained from observations of toughness, colour and, perhaps, the solubility of the collagen.

The sex of meat animals can affect the quality of their meat in several ways, although the effects are often revealed indirectly. One specific example of the effects of sex involves pigs and boar taint. Meat from mature, uncastrated, male pigs (boars) can be affected by a stale, urine-like, odour, which is noticeable to a proportion of consumers. The active principle was shown (Patterson, 1968) to be 5α-androst-16-en-3-one (a fat-soluble steroidal compound); its effect becomes noticeable at levels above 1 μg/g in the fat (Patterson and Stenson, 1971). Skatole has also been implicated in boar taint. In the UK, the pork industry favours the use of entire males, slaughtered before sexual maturity; in Denmark and The Netherlands the practice has been to use castrated males to avoid the problem of taint. Boar taint may not be noticeable in uncooked meat, but suspect batches can be tested using a boiling test; this involves boiling a sample in water and smelling the odour; an alternative (Lawrie, 1991) is to heat a sample of the fatty tissue, using a hot soldering iron. Other, more sophisticated (and expensive), tests are also available, such as gas chromatography, coupled with mass spectrometry (GC–MS).

3.4.3 Other factors

Many of the remaining factors concerning the identity of meat raw materials are best approached via the relationship and trust between customer and supplier. It is not possible, for example, to analyse meat in order to establish whether or not it came from free-range, or organically reared animals (although there are tests for hormones and other veterinary residues in meat). Reputable suppliers should have no objection to supplying documentary evidence of compliance with specifications, and inspection visits will sometimes be appropriate.

3.4.4 Chemical composition

According to Lawrie (1991), on average, lean meat consists mainly of water (75%), protein (19%) and intramuscular fat (2.5%). Fatty tissues comprise mainly fat, water and protein, in that order (e.g. pork back fat, from a modern British pig, will be approximately fat (75%), moisture (16%) and protein (5%); (Royal Society of Chemistry, 1991). The proportion of these (particularly the fat content) will affect the contribution that a particular raw material can make to a product, bearing in mind any recipe considerations, whether legal or labelling. Fat content of meat is usually assessed subjectively as 'visual lean' (which means almost precisely what it says: the proportion of the meat that appears to be lean). This requires an experienced judge and, again, is much more difficult with frozen blocks than with fresh carcass meat. Samples taken from the drilling procedure described above can be analysed chemically for fat content.

Rancidity of fat can pose a problem in meat products, and this can be avoided if suitable control is exerted over the quality of the incoming raw material and its storage prior to use. The development of oxidative rancidity in fats is a two-stage process (Allen and Hamilton, 1989) and measurement of the peroxide value (PV) and thiobarbituric acid value (TBA) can assist in avoiding problems of rancidity that may otherwise be revealed in canned products. These measurements can also be made using the domino-five samples.

MRM (also known as mechanically separated meat, MSM), is used primarily in some comminuted products, such as frankfurters and pâtés. Although its status as meat, and the need to declare its presence in a product, continue to be subjects of discussion, it is one of the meat raw materials available to manufacturers and canners. MRM is generally lower in connective tissue than is hand-deboned meat, while poultry MRM may have a lowered overall protein content, due to water pick-up during chilling. In the UK, the BMMA has issued guidelines (BMMA, 1991) for the manufacture of MRM. In their opinion, MRM prepared following these guidelines should be regarded as meat, although due account should be taken, by manufacturers, of its actual protein content in calculating the apparent total meat content of products containing it.

Historically, MRM prepared by some methods was likely to contain elevated levels of calcium (from bone fragments); this was particularly the case in the USA but, even there, it is becoming less common. It may also be prone to fat rancidity, particularly if long bones are used. (The BMMA guidelines exclude these.) Other factors that should be specified in sourcing MRM include protein, fat, moisture and ash contents, PV, TBA and free fatty acid (FFA) content of the fat, pH and microbial condition (general or specific organisms, where relevant). Purchase from an approved supplier, possibly coupled with inspection visits, is also advisable.

3.5 Manufacturing quality factors

3.5.1 Functionality of meat proteins

Much meat product manufacture (Ranken, 1984) involves two basic principles:

(1) extraction of meat protein into salt solution, to provide a matrix capable of holding the product together, and to emulsify fat; and
(2) heat-setting of the extracted proteins to form a firm gel.

The protein gel provides structural integrity, retains moisture and fat in the product and, not least, is responsible for its eating quality. The major meat protein fraction responsible for all of these activities is the salt-soluble myosin. This accounts for about 11.5%, out of the total 19% protein content of lean meat (Lawrie, 1991).

Clearly, the more myosin that is available, the better it will be able to perform its task in the product. However, the manufacturer also has an opportunity to control its functionality through the use of different manufacturing techniques. The options vary with the type of product.

For highly comminuted products, like frankfurters and luncheon meats, the meat ingredients are extensively chopped in a bowl chopper or mill. For maximum protein extraction, it is desirable to add the salts (sodium chloride, plus phosphates, if used) as dry powders, and to chop the mixture for a time before the addition of any recipe water or ice, and further chopping. In this way, the protein is exposed to a very high salt concentration, resulting in a greater degree of extraction. High levels of protein extraction ultimately yield very strong, almost plastic, textures on cooking, the 'snap' of a frankfurter being a good example.

In canned ham manufacture, protein extraction is equally important, but must be achieved by less drastic means. Typically, the meat will be injected with the curing brine (a solution of sodium chloride, phosphates and sodium nitrite, to give the cured colour). If a high brine injection rate is to be used, a hydrocolloid such as carrageenan or methylcellulose may be added to the brine to improve its retention in the meat. The meat will then be cut into pieces (perhaps cubes of about 2.5 cm) and these will then be tumbled or massaged, to extract the myosin into solution. This procedure may take several hours, and will be likely to be carried out under vacuum, to aid the development of the cured colour, and to minimise the development of rancidity.

3.5.2 Curing of meat products with nitrite

Nitrite has two distinct roles in cured meat products. The first relates to food safety, involving the specific action of nitrite and its reaction products in inhibiting the outgrowth of spores of *Clostridium botulinum*. Such spores may survive the heat treatment involved in canning of cured meat products, but nitrite, in conjunction with the salt in the brine, suppresses their growth and the consequent production of toxin.

The second role of nitrite is in the formation of the bright pink colour typical of cured meat products. This involves the chemical reaction of the meat pigment, myoglobin, with nitrite to produce nitrosylmyoglobin. The mechanism of this reaction is rather complex, and is outlined in Figure 3.3.

Examination of Figure 3.3 shows the importance of reducing conditions, either to reduce the nitrite to nitric oxide, or to reduce nitrosylmetmyoglobin to nitrosylmyoglobin; (although not shown in Figure 3.3, metmyoglobin can also be reduced to myoglobin). Until comparatively recently, this reduction would have depended upon enzyme activity within the meat;

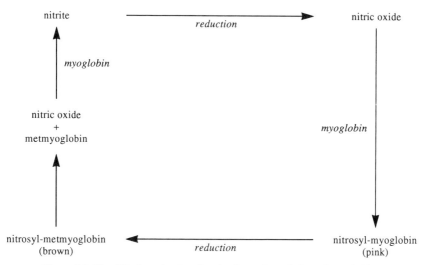

Figure 3.3 Simplified mechanism for the formation of nitrosylmyoglobin.

nowadays, however, a reducing agent such as sodium ascorbate is commonly added as a curing aid. Sodium erythorbate (or iso-ascorbate) is also sometimes used in the USA, and is likely soon to be permitted within the EU, for the same purpose.

Although nitrite is deliberately added to cured meat products, accidental contamination of meat with nitrite can cause unwanted pink discoloration. MacDougall and Hetherington (1992) found that 1–2 ppm of nitrite was sufficient to cause discoloration of pork, while similar results were obtained by Whitehead and Hart (1994, unpublished results) for chicken and turkey breast. Nitrite can also be produced by the action of bacteria on the nitrate present in meat or water supplies if brined meat is held, even at chill temperatures, for too long before further processing (Ahn and Maure, 1987).

3.5.3 The importance of meat pH

The functional properties (heat gelation, water binding and fat binding) of the myosin fraction of meat depend, like those of most other proteins, on pH and salt content, and on the concentration of the myosin itself. Proteins contain both positively (e.g. lysine and arginine) and negatively (e.g. aspartic and glutamic acids) charged amino acids. As the pH of a protein's environment is changed, the balance of its positive and negative charges also changes. This is shown schematically in Figure 3.4.

For each protein, there is a characteristic, intermediate pH where there is no net charge on the protein. This is known as the isoelectric pH (or isoelectric point, pI). Because there is no net charge on the protein

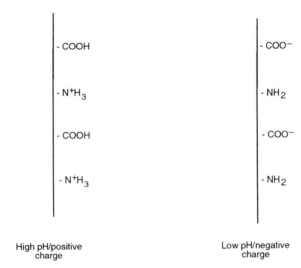

Figure 3.4 Effect of pH on the overall charge on protein molecules.

molecules, they no longer repel one another but may, instead, bond together, forming aggregates or precipitates. (A familiar example of this is the curdling of milk, where the low pH, brought about by the production of lactic acid by bacteria, causes precipitation of the casein.) Meat proteins also have iso-electric properties, and the pH of a piece of meat can affect its value, both as meat *per se*, and for processing into meat products, including canned meat products.

Above or below the iso-electric pH, individual protein molecules have a layer (or 'skin') of water molecules around them; these are attached via bonds known as hydrogen bonds. However, as the pH approaches the iso-electric pH and the protein molecules associate with one another, they lose their ability to bind this water. The water-binding capacity of the proteins, and thus of the meat, therefore decreases as the pH is lowered from neutral. This phenomenon is the basis of two of the most common faults in meat – DFD (dark, firm, dry) meat and PSE (pale, soft, exudative) meat. The former of these particularly affects beef, and the latter, pork. They can often both be traced to poor handling of the animals prior to slaughter, although PSE pork is sometimes also associated with certain genetic characteristics of the pigs, which makes them more susceptible to stress.

3.5.4 pH changes in meat after slaughter

During life, the pH of muscle is close to neutral (pH = 7). Following death, enzymes in the muscle begin to convert glycogen (the energy-storage carbohydrate of muscle) into lactic acid. This causes a drop in pH, typically to about 5.7 in normal meat. This is still above the iso-electric pH (about 5.5) of the meat proteins (Lawrie, 1991).

If animals are given inadequate food in the period prior to transport to the abattoir, their muscles will contain very little glycogen at the time of death. Little lactic acid will therefore be produced, and the ultimate pH of the meat will be high, perhaps up to about 6.8. At this pH, the proteins have a very high water-binding capacity, so the meat will appear dry and firm; it is also dark in colour, hence the term dark, firm, dry, or DFD. Although the high water-binding capacity might appear to be an advantage, because of its high pH, DFD meat is prone to very rapid microbial spoilage.

The PSE condition is also a consequence of the metabolism of glycogen. In this case, the pig's muscles may have had a reasonably high glycogen reserve on arrival at the abattoir but, perhaps as a result of short-term stress induced by poor handling or fighting among different groups of pigs, this is very rapidly converted to lactic acid and the ultimate pH is reached while the carcass is still warm. PSE is characterised by meat having a pH of less than 5.9 within 45 min of slaughter. The ultimate pH of PSE meat may, however, be similar to that of normal meat.

Typical pH changes for normal, DFD and PSE meat are shown in Figure 3.5.

Some breeds of pig (especially some continental breeds) are particularly prone to stress and, therefore, are likely to yield PSE meat. A test using the anaesthetic gas halothane can be used to indicate stress susceptibility, and the gene responsible has recently been identified. Pig-breeding companies are now able to control the incidence of the gene in, and the stress susceptibility of, their breeding lines (although it might appear desirable to eliminate the gene completely from breeding stock, such animals have desirable feed-conversion, weight gain and lean to fat ratio characteristics).

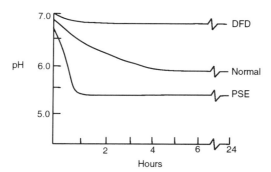

Figure 3.5 Post mortem pH changes for normal, DFD and PSE meat. (From Church and Wood (1992), reproduced by permission.)

PSE pork is pale in colour and suffers from excessive drip losses due to its poor water-binding capacity, in turn caused by the rapid fall in pH. Because of this, it gives reduced yields in cooked cured products, such as canned hams (Ranken, 1984). Because its ultimate pH is similar to that of normal pork, pH measurements of samples obtained frozen may not be very informative, but PSE pork can also be detected by its colour, using optical probes.

The incidence of DFD and PSE meat can be reduced by proper handling of animals prior to slaughter. Use of loading ramps, avoiding fighting by not mixing animals of different groups, provision of adequate drinking water and, above all, adherence to the best animal welfare and humane slaughter practices will all help to ensure that meat is of the best quality possible. Cruel, or even merely careless animal handling practices will result in poor-quality meat and economic losses, whether it is to be used directly as meat or to be further processed into meat products.

3.5.5 Chilling and freezing

Meat animals have a body temperature similar to our own, and this is highly favourable to the growth of spoilage bacteria. Carcasses are therefore chilled after slaughter, in order to reduce the rate of microbial growth; chilling also maintains the organoleptic quality of the meat.

From a bacteriological point of view, there are advantages in achieving this fall in temperature as quickly as can be arranged. However, too rapid chilling can cause problems of its own. When beef or lamb carcasses are chilled to below 10°C within 10 h of slaughter (i.e. before rigor is completed), certain muscles may suffer an irreversible toughening (Locker and Hagyard, 1963; Cook and Langsworth, 1966). This is known as cold-toughening, or cold-shortening. (Pork can also suffer from cold-toughening, but it is a less common problem.) The recent appearance in UK stores of 'traditionally matured' beef is evidence of the seriousness of the problem for the retail meat trade. The UK Meat & Livestock Commission has invested heavily in research and publicity aimed at persuading meat producers to take steps to avoid cold-shortening by chilling carcasses properly (i.e. sufficiently slowly), and by hanging the chilled carcass for a sufficient time (i.e. approximately 7 days at 0°C to +4°C, in the case of beef) to allow tenderisation to occur. 'Blueprints' for animal production and slaughter have been published by the Meat & Livestock Commission for both beef and pork (MLC, 1991, 1992).

Apart from this effect on texture, poor chilling (which, from this point of view, would be too slow chilling) can cause deterioration in colour of both meat and fat and microbiological problems, including growth of spoilage bacteria, pathogens, moulds and yeasts. Inadequate control of humidity during chilling can also cause severe evaporative losses from the meat.

Much of the meat intended for canning operations will have been frozen. Freezing of meat, like chilling, can cause problems of quality. Roughly 75% of lean meat is water and, as we have seen, this is retained in the meat mainly by the water-binding activity of the proteins. Frozen and thawed meat exhibits increased drip losses compared with those of fresh meat. As the meat is frozen, particularly if freezing occurs slowly, the water-soluble salts and sugars become concentrated in the remaining liquid water. The conformation (shape) of the proteins changes in response to this increased salt environment and this, in turn, alters the functional properties (such as water-binding) of the proteins. Once the original conformation of the protein is lost (a process known as denaturation), it is most unlikely that it will be recovered on thawing. Slowly frozen meat therefore loses excessive drip on thawing, and the remaining meat has inferior water-binding ability. In extreme cases, failure to pay attention to the factors affecting freezing rate can result in meat that has microbiologically spoiled before it has had a chance to freeze. In this connection, it must be stressed that freezing (and frozen storage) does not kill appreciable numbers of microorganisms. If meat of poor microbial quality is frozen well, it will be of poor microbial quality when thawed. But, equally, if meat of good microbial quality is frozen poorly (particularly if the freezing rate is excessively slow), it may also be of poor microbial quality after thawing.

Like most other commodities, frozen meat is usually held at −18°C. The approximate storage life of the most common meats (before a noticeable fall in quality occurs) is shown in Table 3.1 (Church and Wood, 1992).

A temperature of −10°C is low enough to halt virtually all microbial growth. However, some of the chemical and enzymic reactions that can occur in meat, although slowed, can eventually bring about quality deterioration. The most common of these is the appearance of rancid flavour notes, due to oxidation of the fat. This accounts for the comparatively short frozen shelf-life of pork; its fat is particularly unsaturated (soft) and is therefore particularly prone to the oxidation

Table 3.1 Approximate storage lives of common meats

Species	Frozen storage life[a] (months)
Pork	4–6
Beef	8–12
Poultry	6–8
Lamb	6–12

[a]These storage lives would be reduced if the storage temperature was higher than −18°C (Lawrie, 1991), or if the temperature were allowed to fluctuate.

reactions leading to rancidity. Although poultry fat is even softer than pork fat, the actual levels of fat in poultry are generally lower than in pork, reducing the impact of oxidation. Very prolonged frozen storage of meat (e.g. for several years) can result in changes in texture as enzymes in the meat break down the proteins.

However well frozen the meat may have been, poor storage conditions in the freezer can also lead to weight losses and/or a deterioration in quality. Unpackaged, or poorly packaged, frozen meat will lose moisture by sublimation in the very dry interior of a freezer. Weight losses (and, therefore, financial losses) can be quite severe and the dehydrated surface of the meat will acquire a leathery appearance, known as freezer-burn; there may also be a yellowing of the fat. As with the effects of slow freezing, this denaturation of the proteins at the surface of the meat is also irreversible. To avoid freezer-burn meat must be wrapped in tightly fitting, moisture-impermeable packaging. Vacuum-packaging is probably the best, as it also confers other advantages; the effective exclusion of oxygen delays the onset of rancidity, while the inhibition of the spoilage flora, by the elevated carbon dioxide levels in the pack, may confer some microbiological protection while the meat is being frozen or after thawing.

Problems with both chilling and freezing are difficult to put right if one is buying in boxes of frozen meat. This is another area where a good relationship and trust between purchaser and supplier are essential if specifications are to be met and problems in manufacture avoided.

3.5.6 Transport and delivery

The transport of meat (whether frozen or chilled) is often the weakest link in the chain. Even assuming that meat has been properly packaged, quickly frozen and stored for a reasonable length of time in an efficient cold store, its temperature may not be maintained during transport if the vehicle is poorly maintained or poorly loaded. Any such rise in temperature may allow the growth of spoilage bacteria or even food-poisoning organisms. The temperature of meat should, ideally, be continuously monitored during transport but should always be checked at the time of delivery. The temperature at the centre of a pack should always be equal to, or lower than that at the surface (Church and Wood, 1992). If it is higher than the surface temperature, this may indicate that the freezer or refrigeration unit has been turned off during a part of the journey, and has only been switched on again to give the impression that all is well. The transport and delivery temperatures of consignments of meat should form part of their specification; non-complying materials should generally not be accepted.

3.6 Physical condition of meat

Many potential faults in a consignment of meat can be revealed by visual inspection at the time of delivery, although a suitably trained and experienced person is needed to carry out the inspection. The weight of the consignment and visual lean are obvious factors to check; other things to look for include the following:

- Visible signs of microbial growth, suggesting poor hygiene and/or temperature control.
- Foreign bodies, such as labels, metal tags or fragments, etc., implying poor control of manufacturing practices by supplier.
- Unusual appearance, possibly due to freezer burn or wrong or mixed species. Unusually brown meat is likely to be old, or to have been temperature-abused during storage. A black dye (Black-PN) is used in the UK to stain unfit meat.
- Natural contamination, due to poor trimming, etc. (For example, failure to remove salivary glands would cause problems of enzymic hydrolysis of starch in some luncheon meats, due to the high activity of salivary amylases. Bone fragments and hide are other examples of natural contamination.)

Depending on the seriousness of the problem, faults revealed or suspected as a result of such visual inspection might trigger immediate rejection of a delivery of meat, or may indicate the need for confirmatory testing. Either way, the value of this inspection, even as a last line of defence, should not be underestimated.

3.7 Microbiology of meat raw materials

3.7.1 Spoilage bacteria

On aerobically stored fresh meat, the most common spoilage bacteria are the pseudomonads, the Enterobacteriaceae and *Acinetobacter/Moraxella* spp. (Lambert *et al.*, 1991). The pseudomonads, in particular, are responsible for the production of slime, discoloration and putrid off-odours. If the meat is vacuum-packaged, these Gram-negative bacteria (which are either aerobes or facultative anaerobes) tend to be replaced by a Gram-positive flora, dominated by lactic acid bacteria and *Brochothrix thermosphacta* (ICMSF, 1980). Both of these can be involved in the spoilage of fresh meat. *Bacillus* spp. produce spores that are heat-resistant; those of *Bacillus stearothermophilus* are so heat-resistant that they can cause spoilage even of canned products.

In practice, all meat is contaminated with a certain number of spoilage bacteria; problems only arise when their numbers are allowed to get out of hand, whether through bad practices at the abattoir or failure to maintain low temperatures during storage or transport.

3.7.2 Food-poisoning bacteria

The fundamental purpose of canning meat and meat products is to maintain safety while extending their shelf-life from the organoleptic point of view. From the safety angle, the pathogen of most pressing concern is *Clostridium botulinum*, which, under anaerobic conditions (such as those associated with the interior of cans), produces a highly potent toxin. Consumption of foods containing the toxin causes the condition known as botulism, and is often fatal. At a raw material level, there is little that can be done to ensure the absence of clostridia on meat; control of the risks from this particular pathogen ultimately depends on adequate temperature control during processing and/or storage.

Like *Bacillus* spp., *Clostridium botulinum* is a spore former; this makes it one of the most heat-tolerant of the common pathogens, so thermal processing of canned foods, if sufficient to eliminate the possibility of the spores of *Clostridium botulinum* surviving, is likely to eliminate the danger from other pathogenic bacteria. However, not all canned meat products receive a sufficiently severe heat treatment to ensure the destruction of *Clostridium botulinum* spores. Some canned hams, for example, receive a heat treatment only sufficient for pasteurisation. Their shelf-life is due, at least in part, to the presence of the curing salts used in their manufacture; nevertheless, some have a limited shelf-life, compared with products, such as corned beef, that receive a more intensive heat treatment.

As well as *Clostridium botulinum*, some other pathogenic bacteria produce toxins. Of these, the most common is *Staphylococcus aureus*; its toxin, though fairly heat stable, is destroyed by heating to 100°C for 30 min (Halligan, 1993), and is most unlikely to survive retorting.

There have been reports (Gounot, 1991) that, during comparatively mild heat treatment, vegetative (i.e. non-spore-forming) pathogens, such as salmonellae, can acquire heat-resistance through the formation of 'heat-shock' proteins. This may be of significance for the pasteurisation of canned hams and underlines still further the need to ensure that raw materials are, as far as possible, free of such bacteria.

3.8 Summary

There are many considerations in the design and running of a modern meat products canning operation. As far as the meat raw materials themselves are concerned, close attention to specification, and the consistency of suppliers in meeting that specification will pay dividends. However, if manufacturers are to achieve consistently high standards of safety and quality, they must:

- understand their product;
- understand their process;
- understand their raw materials, and the demands made on them by the nature of the product and process, and
- put in place a system to detect and deal with the occasions when raw materials are out of specification.

A knowledge of the behaviour of meat, and what can go wrong with it, will be invaluable in deciding raw material specifications. Relationships with suppliers, and a willingness and ability to check their conformance with specifications, are similarly important.

References

Ahn, D.U. and Maure, A.J. (1987) *Poultry Sci.*, **66**, 1957.

Allen, J.C. and Hamilton, R.J. (eds) (1989) *Rancidity in Foods*. Elsevier Applied Science, London, UK.

Appert, N. (1810) *The Art of Preserving Animal and Vegetable Substances for Many Years*. Patris & Cie, Paris, France.

Bailey, A.J. (1968) *Nature*, **160**, 447.

BMMA (1993) *Standard for Meat Raw Materials used in Meat Products, Minced and Diced Meat and Meat Preparations*. BMMA, London, UK.

Church, P.N. and Wood, J.M. (1992) *The Manual of Manufacturing Meat Quality*. Elsevier Applied Science, London, UK.

Cook. J.D. and Langsworth, R.F. (1966) *J. Food Sci.*, **31**, 497.

Drummond, J.C. and Macara, T. (1938) *Chem. Ind.*, p. 828.

Gounot, A.M. (1991) *J. Appl. Bacteriol.*, **71**, 386.

Halligan, A.C. (1993) *Micro-facts* (2nd edn), Leatherhead Food Research Association, Leatherhead, Surrey, UK.

International Commission on Microbiological Specifications for Foods (ICMSF) (1980) *Microbial Ecology of Foods, Vol 2: Food Commodities*. Academic Press, New York, USA.

Lambert, A.D., Smith, J.P. and Dodds, K.L. (1991) *Food Microbiol.*, **8**, 276.

Lawrie, R.A. (1991) *Meat Science* (5th edn). Pergamon Press, Oxford, UK.

Locker, R.H. and Hagyard, C.J. (1963) *J. Sci. Food Agric.*, **14**, 787.

MacDougall, D.B. and Hetherington, M.J. (1992) *Meat Sci.*, **31** (2), 201.

MLC (1991) *A Blueprint for Improved Consistent Quality Beef*. Meat & Livestock Commission, Milton Keynes, UK.

MLC (1992) *A Blueprint for Lean and Tender Pork*. Meat & Livestock Commission, Milton Keynes, UK.

Patterson, R.L.S. (1968) *J. Sci. Food Agric.*, **19**, 31.

Patterson, R.L.S. and Stenson, C.G. (1971) *Proc 17th Meeting Meat Research Inst.*, Bristol, p. 148.

Ranken, M.D. (1984) *Notes on Meat Products*. Leatherhead Food Research Association, Leatherhead, Surrey, UK.

Royal Society of Chemistry Analytical Methods Committee (1991) *Analyst*, **116**, 761.

4 Canning factory standards

A.W. TIMPERLEY

4.1 Introduction

General guidance on manufacturing conditions, and cannery standards, are available in Codex and various relevant legislative documents.

However, such guidance is always couched in non-specific terms, and it is the intention within this chapter to provide more specific practical advice for canners.

The chapter is therefore structured in its presentation of information, rather than being written in narrative form.

4.2 Factory environment

4.2.1 Location and surroundings

Process and manufacturing premises should be located in areas which are free, and likely to remain free, from flooding, smoke, dust, objectionable odours and other contaminants. Potential hazards from the outside environment, e.g. intermittent air-borne contamination, should be established prior to construction.

There should be adequate facilities for the disposal of effluent and/or for the establishment of an effluent treatment plant in such a location in relation to the prevailing wind and at such a distance as to avoid the possibility of contamination.

The immediate surroundings of the premises, ideally having a 1 m wide hard surface, should be well kept and free from refuse, rubbish, overgrown vegetation and waste materials.

Surrounding activities often present potential sources of contamination (e.g. agriculture, sewage plant, rubbish tips). Control of birds, rodents and insects are also important considerations and should be assessed. In addition to preventing the access of pests to the process area, it is important that the surrounding 'free areas' are kept free of food wastes, rubbish and spilled product.

4.2.2 Vehicles and roadways

All traffic entering the factory site should be considered to be a potential source of contamination. It is, therefore, important that this contamination which may be deposited on factory access ways is not conveyed into the process areas.

4.3 Factory structure

4.3.1 External walls

There are many types of external wall available, the main types are listed below:

4.3.1.1 Concrete. Concrete walls must have a smooth surface and be of adequate thickness to resist possible traffic impact.

4.3.1.2 Profiled metal sheeting. Cladding is to be profiled plastic-coated steel, long rib type or similar. It is essential that the top and bottom are adequately sealed with profiled fillers (see section 4.3.3). Cladding shall not be taken down to ground level because of the risks of physical damage and infestation.

4.3.1.3 Brick/block. When used in conjunction with profiled metal cladding, traditional brick and block cavity walls shall extend to standard door and lintel level above the ground. The cavity space should be at least 50 mm not including slab insulation (if this is required).

4.3.1.4 Composite panel. Panels are to be of adequate thickness for structural stability and insulation value. Large panels subject to high wind pressures will require a thicker section. If sheeting rails are to be avoided on internal surfaces thicker sections will be required to span room height.
Materials should be selected to keep maintenance to a minimum.

4.3.2 Access ways

The building should be constructed to protect against the entrance and harbouring of vermin, birds and pests. Access points should be protected by the following.

- Insect screens on all opening windows (removable for cleaning).
- Insectocutors.
- Screens to all air intakes and exit ducts to prevent access and soiling by birds.

- Air curtains or plastic strip barriers on all doorways that are routinely open during processing.
- Traps on drains.
- Rainwater downpipes should be protected, at the top and bottom, to prevent access by rodents, etc.
- Cavity ventilators to prevent rodent infestation.

Further information on pest-proofing (mesh sizes etc.) is given in section 4.3.3.

Where access points are provided for traffic, e.g. fork-lift trucks, it is advisable to protect the access surround against accidental damage.

Where traffic access ways are adjacent to pedestrian access then it is recommended that in addition to crash barriers to protect the pedestrians, the barriers should be extended to a height to protect against falling loads.

If the design is such that the exclusion of voids is impossible then provision must be made for the laying of pest control devices.

Particular measures must be taken in those areas in the building where the design allows a natural access for mice and rats, etc.

External walls should be protected from damage with crash rails or barriers.

Ductwork and other similar services passing through the walls or cladding should have 'flashing flanges' fitted to assist with weathering the opening.

All rainwater drainpipes, etc. should be sited unobtrusively and preferably externally. Drainpipes should continue to ground level and rodding access must be provided. Protection from traffic impact must be provided where necessary.

4.3.3 Pest-proofing

Pests will eat and/or contaminate ingredients, packing materials and finished product. This presents a health hazard and a risk of prosecution coupled with a potential for considerable financial loss due to fines, product loss and pest eradication measures. Rodents can cause internal and external damage to buildings by gnawing and also cause fires and breakdowns if they gain access to electrical cables. Birds can also cause damage to buildings by pecking at mortar and by erosion of building materials from acid in their droppings.

Every food manufacturing facility must have an effective pest control programme. Such a programme can only be implemented successfully if eradication measures have first been carried out by an appropriate expert and good cleaning practices are in operation. Proofing measures should be carried out prior to eradication to prevent re-infestation.

The preventative measures necessary to exclude pests from premises and prevent their spread within a building are described below and apply not only to new or renovated premises but also existing ones.

4.3.3.1 Foundations.   In some existing buildings the foundations are too shallow and will not prevent rodents from burrowing underneath. Some rodents can burrow over 1 m vertically but will cease if they meet with an impenetrable obstruction. It is recommended that a curtain wall is built against the existing outside walls or footings to a depth of at least 600 mm below ground level and have a bottom member turned outwards from the building for a distance of 300 mm to form an 'L' shape.

All points where cables, drains and services pass through foundation walls and floors must be sealed.

4.3.3.2 Drains and sewers.   Drains and sewers must be proofed and regularly maintained to prevent rodents gaining access and using them as harbourage or as a means of entry to buildings. Any defective drains must be located and repaired. Inspection chambers, covers, hatches and rodding caps must be inspected regularly and all disused lengths of drain either filled with concrete to the connection with the sewer or collapsed and the trench filled with dense hardcore. Any storm-water drains should be protected with top-hung flaps and maintained regularly to remove silt and leaves. Back inlet gulleys can be used to prevent rodents from entering and climbing the inside of rainwater pipes at ground level. If these are not fitted then rodent access can be controlled by means of wire mesh balloons fitted to the outlet from the gutter. These balloons must have a mesh size of 6 mm or smaller and should also be fitted at the top of any soil or ventilation pipes. Wire mesh should not be used at the bottom of downpipes because of the risk of blockage. External climbing of downpipes can be prevented by fitting flat or cone-shaped guards. These should be sited high enough to clear vehicular or pedestrian traffic but not above the level of any sills, mouldings or branch pipes which may provide alternative routes into the building.

4.3.3.3 Holes.   Rodents are able to squeeze through small holes in order to gain access to buildings. A small rat can squeeze through a 10 mm crack and a mouse through one of 6 mm. Small holes in brick, stone or concrete walls and floors should be filled with mortar. Large holes should be filled with brick or stone set in mortar. If this is impractical then concrete can be used. To prevent rodents from re-opening holes during the setting period of the concrete or mortar, 25% of rapid hardening cement can be used. Alternatively, holes can be filled with crushed chicken wire prior to concreting. This should be done early in the day to ensure that the concrete has set before nightfall.

4.3.3.4 Internal pipes and ductwork. All pipes and cables passing through walls and floors should be built in to prevent pests from using them as runways. An example of a pipe sealing sleeve which offers complete protection against the ingress of pests, water and gas is shown in Figure 4.1.

Underground ductwork used for heating, water and other services can allow pests to move around within and between buildings. Where ductwork carries pipes or cables from one part of a building to another they should be proofed at each floor level and access provided for inspection cleaning and treatment.

4.3.3.5 Walls.

4.3.3.5.1 External walls. Rodents can climb rough brickwork or stone walls. This can be prevented by the application of a smooth coating of cement and painting it with a hard gloss finish. This coating should be applied below any dock barrier and a minimum of 2 m either side of any sliding doors when they are fully open. Where composite metal wall panels are used particular attention must be paid to sealing them effectively at the top and bottom junctions. Profiled metal capping strips should be welded to corrugated metal walls panels to prevent rodents from gaining access to the inner hollow core between the outer metal panel and insulation (Figure 4.2).

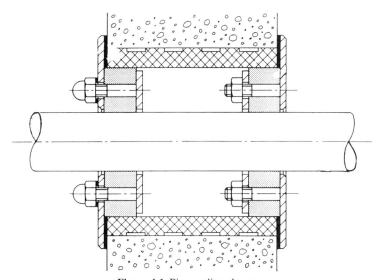

Figure 4.1 Pipe sealing sleeve.

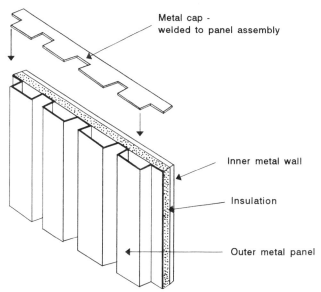

Figure 4.2 Metal capping strip on corrugated wall panel.

4.3.3.5.2 Cavity walls. Cavity walls provide excellent harbourage for rodents and allows them access between different parts of a building. Rodents often gain access via air bricks or ventilators and these should be proofed with metal mesh having openings of 6 mm or less. Internal ventilators should be constructed from metal or proofed with metal mesh if of plastic construction. Any damage to cavity walls must be repaired immediately.

4.3.3.5.3 Partition walls. Partition walls constructed from either hollow blockwork or composite panels must be sealed at the top and bottom to prevent rodents from entering the inner hollow core. This can be accomplished by laying a solid block course to cap hollow blockwork walls or welding a capping strip to composite panels.

4.3.3.5.4 Movement joints. Movement and expansion joints should be filled with a suitable packing and/or sealant material and the joint covered with metal angle or cover strip to prevent rodent access to the joint.

4.3.3.6 Beam filling. All spaces between floor joists or rafters should be filled in order to prevent rodents gaining access to the tops of the walls.

4.3.3.7 Doors. Pest-proofing of doors is a problem in food factories because of traffic movement, both pedestrian and vehicular, and sometimes external doors are left open for ventilation purposes. All external doors should be self-closing and fit closely in the opening with no gaps exceeding 6 mm but preferably being less than 3 mm. Exposed wood is vulnerable to rodent attack and is therefore an unsuitable material for doors, frames and thresholds, metal and some plastics (e.g. UPVC) being the preferable alternatives. All external door frames and thresholds should be sealed at the junctures with the walls and floors and kept in good repair. External doors should not open directly into food production areas. If doors are to be used at night, it is good practice to position lights 9–12 m from the door to attract insects away from the door area. Sliding and concertina doors should have all gaps between the door and the frame sealed with brush strips. Roller shutter doors should fit closely at the base and have a rubber strip fitted to ensure no gap exceeds 6 mm. All doors which have to remain open for vehicle entry and/or loading can be proofed by installing 'rapid roll' PVC doors or heavy-duty PVC strip curtains with the correct overlap, as specified by the manufacturers. The use of air curtains can be effective against insects but should not be used as the only proofing measure.

4.3.3.8 Windows.   All openable windows should be proofed with 10 mesh monofilament nylon mesh mounted in a removable frame of metal or PVC to facilitate cleaning. Birds may perch or nest on any horizontal surfaces, such as external window ledges, and this can be discouraged if all ledges are sloped at an angle of 60°.

4.3.3.9 Roofs.   All roofs should be kept in good repair, regularly inspected and any missing or damaged slates or tiles replaced. All holes formed at junctions with the eaves must be sealed either by fitting templates cut to shape or by the application of a suitable sealing material which cannot be pecked out by birds. Any ventilation openings should be proofed with 10 mesh monofilament nylon mesh mounted in a removable frame of metal or PVC. Exhaust fans should be fitted with shutters which are self-closing when the fan is idle.

4.4 Production area

4.4.1 Internal walls

Internal partitions are, in general terms, any continuous vertical structure that divides a building into rooms or compartments. Considered in the context of a food production area this generalisation should be condensed to include only solid walls which may be of load-bearing or non-load-bearing quality. It is worth noting, however, that hollow walls, e.g. timber stud walls, will be encountered in many existing facilities. The inherent voids found within such a structure makes this form one to be avoided wherever possible and if finance permits it is preferable to remove hollow walls completely and replace them with solid structures.

Walls will provide the space separation of a building. This separation is not only physical, providing security, but also thermal and acoustic providing fire and sound barriers. It will also act as an anchor point for the attachment of machinery and services. Thus, far from being 'just a wall' the installation of an internal partition must be examined and specified according to the duty it is expected to perform.

4.4.1.1 Load-bearing walls.

4.4.1.1.1 Brick/block. New installations will be designed specifically for the application required and will vary on the type and size of the block. In general, all 'new' load-bearing internal walls will be constructed from high-density concrete blocks. These are available with a 'fair-face' finish (allowing a coating to be applied directly) or rough cast as a 'key' for a render finish. Where a surface finish is to be applied directly onto the block then a fair-faced block with flush pointing is recommended.

4.4.1.1.2 Foundations. A check should be carried out to ensure that any existing floor slab can sustain any new imposed load. It must be noted that if such a foundation is excavated through an existing floor slab great care must be taken to reinstate the damp-proof membrane damaged during excavation.

4.4.1.1.3 Damp-proof course (dpc). Ensure that damp proof courses are inserted in all new walls. In existing walls a suitable membrane must be inserted if none exists (such as a chemical injection system).

4.4.1.1.4 Material composition. The composition of existing masonry walls varies enormously dependent on their function and the date when they were constructed. Whatever the material it is generally feasible to render the wall in readiness for the application of a specialist coating material such as those detailed later in section 4.4.1.3.

4.4.1.2 Non-load-bearing walls.

4.4.1.2.1 Brick/block. When constructing a non-load-bearing wall aerated blocks are usually used. These have low impact resistance and load-carrying capacity but do provide a good thermal and acoustic barrier.

4.4.1.2.2 Composite panels. The use of composite panels as a pre-fabricated building material has developed rapidly from the original concept of the cold store. The panels are of sandwich construction with skins formed of either Plastisol, PVC-coated sheet steel or glass-reinforced plastic (GRP). The inner core is usually bonded to the skin with adhesive. Within the laminate, the thickness, type and position of each layer can be specified according to the requirements of the job. For instance, the core can be varied to give different fire ratings and acoustic properties. All the PVC and fibre-reinforced plastics (FRP) (but not polypropylene) have been used as the facings for composite panels. Where a long panel is desirable FRP is the most suitable as it is available in up to 16 m lengths. A Class 1 spread of flame is generally required in manufacturing areas. Particular attention must be given to providing a hygienic seal to all joints.

Fires within food production factories constructed with composite panels have highlighted the potential fire problems associated with these materials. Special consideration should be given to fire ratings when specifying the use of composite panels. The core materials used in composite panels varies according to supplier/contractors, but polystyrene is widely used. This melts at about 80°C and then 'flows' causing a self-generating effect in a fire. As the core melts the rigidity of the wall or ceiling panel is lost and the panel collapses. Once started the fires tend to spread progressively through the sandwich, it being virtually impossible to dampen the fire within the skins. Other types of core generally available are:

- Styrene or Styrofoam (extruded), melts at 75°C,
- Polyurethane (foam injected or laminated), melts at 120°C,
- Polyisocyanurate (Nilflam) class 1 surface spread of flame (to BS476: Part 7: 1987) reacts at 140°C to form a carbonaceous layer retarding flame spread. Affected by loading (compresses or delaminates).

During a fire plastic insulating materials, particularly polyurethane, generate very high volumes of toxic fumes and smoke creating severe problems on escape routes.

The melting of core materials can be slowed or even prevented by the addition of incombustible boards clad on to the core, such as plasterboard or superlux. The outer surface of these can be finished with an identical surface cladding to the normal panels. However, these boards will not give structural integrity to the system and hence only 30 or 60 min ratings can be achieved.

Mineral wool (not fibreglass) such as Rockwool, which is a spun fibre of basalt rock, is now being offered as a core material for composites. This material was developed as cavity insulation and is now produced in lamella strips bonded and sandwiched together at a mass of 180 kg/m^3 (three times the weight of plastic foams). It is completely non-combustible but it is more expensive than plastic foams. It has an insulation value $K = 0.39$ W/m/°C (half the value of foams). It is also liable to sweating and hence is not suitable for chill and frozen stores.

4.4.1.3 Finishes. The choice of a coating to be applied will depend on the particular area. For example, in wet processing environments a coating system must be impervious to moisture and withstand the cleaning process, which may employ high-pressure spraying and/or harsh cleaning chemicals. In dry and possibly dusty environments the coating system must be free from pits and have a hard, smooth antistatic surface which is easily cleanable.

Relevant Directives or Regulations for specific processing environments must be consulted for requirements concerning the colour of the finish. For example, The Meat Products Directive, 92/5/EEC, states that walls must be covered with a light-coloured coating.

For all processing areas a hygienic, durable, and easily cleanable coating is required.

Any coating system must allow for differential expansion of the building structure and, therefore, all movement joints must continue through the coating system.

4.4.1.3.1 Liquid coatings. Ordinary liquid-based paint systems comprise a primer, one or more undercoats followed by one or more finishing coats. Some paint systems combine one or more of these functions. All paints contain a binder, or medium, which hardens. Other ingredients contained in various paints include: pigments, stainers, extenders, driers, catalysts or hardeners, thinners or solvents, gelling agents and, in some water-thinned paints, emulsifiers.

- *Emulsion paints*: Emulsion paints are bound with an emulsion of vinyl, acrylic and polyurethane polymers. They dry rapidly in varying light conditions but drying is impaired by high humidity and/or low temperature. Emulsion paints are suitable for walls and ceilings in 'dry' areas but must be regarded as cleanable rather than washable unless a further coating is applied to seal the surface. Toxicity and taint hazards are low with no lead being contained. Most emulsion paints contain low levels of fungicide or bactericide which are incorporated purely to keep the paint stable and should not be confused with fungicidal paints which are described below.
- *Oil-based, one-pack epoxy and polyurethane paints*: These paints are solvent-based and present high risks of taint during the first few days after application. Further risks of taint may be present for some weeks from the by-products of drying, particularly in poorly ventilated areas. These paints will withstand regular wet cleaning and are suitable for use in areas where periodic condensation occurs but will not withstand frequent hosing down. Polyurethane paints give good resistance to wear and may not require a special primer as they are fairly alkali resistant.

- *Two-pack epoxy and polyurethane paints*: These paints are usually solvent-based and, in the case of epoxy paints, normally present no taint hazard after approximately 3 days. The paint film may contain small amounts of unreacted amine which presents a toxicity hazard. Polyurethane paints may contain traces of unreacted isocyanates which presents both taint and toxicity hazards. Both of these paint systems offer good resistance to alkaline conditions, animal fats, vegetable oils and some organic acids with polyurethane paints having better water resistance. For good water resistance, epoxy paints must be heat cured by heating the area after application. Drying of these types of paint involves a complex chemical reaction which is temperature dependent and may take seven days at 18°C to attain their full chemical resistance. If the temperature in the area falls below 10°C the curing rate slows dramatically or may cease completely. Before using epoxy or polyurethane paint systems the paint manufacturer must be consulted to ensure that no ketonic solvents are contained within the particular product. If any paints containing 'ketones' are used in the vicinity of fresh meat, fish or poultry they are liable to develop powerful off-flavours and odours and make the food inedible.
- *Chlorinated rubber paints*: These paints are solvent-based and although the solvents used are very powerful they normally present no taint hazard after 3 days. Obviously, very good ventilation is essential, as drying is by solvent evaporation, but these paints will dry at low temperatures and in atmospheres which would retard the drying of other types of paint. Primers for these types of paint may contain lead salts and, therefore, present a toxicity hazard. Chlorinated rubber paints will withstand total immersion and frequent hosing down making them suitable for use in wet areas and on the non-product contact surfaces of equipment involved in wet processes. These types of paint, however, have poor resistance to animal fats, vegetable oils and organic acids and are being replaced in favour of acrylated rubber paints, which have the same properties as chlorinated rubber paints but contain chlorine free solvents.
- *Fungicidal and mould-resistant paints*: In areas where high levels of humidity or condensation occur regularly it may be necessary to apply a fungicidal paint system to control the growth of moulds. Some paint systems available rely on leaching of chemical substances from within the paint to control mould growth. These types of paint are not recommended as there will always be a potential taint hazard. Non-leaching fungicidal paints are available and have been tested and approved for application in food production areas. It is recommended therefore, that only paint systems with approval from a recognised body, such as the Ministry of Agriculture Fisheries and Food

(MAFF), be used. It is most important to ensure that the surface to which a fungicidal paint is to be applied has been prepared correctly. The surface should be treated with a biocidal wash prior to painting to prevent subsequent mould growth under the paint system affecting its adherence.

● *Water- versus solvent-based paints*: Legislation on the Control of Substances Hazardous to Health (COSHH) means that precautions must now be taken to protect personnel from the vapours given off during the application and subsequent curing of solvent-based paints. These precautions include the use of air supplied breathing equipment or cartridge masks. The trend in favour of using water-based paints is, therefore, increasing rapidly because of the ease of application, speed of drying and low odour. These paints considerably reduce the risks of taint and toxicity hazards, with minimum disruption to production.

4.4.1.3.2 Reinforced liquid coatings. These systems, based on glass fibres mixed with an epoxy resin can be applied directly to a substrate as a final finish. These 'thin coat' systems not only provide a smooth finish, which is easy to clean, but also give good resistance to impact damage, abrasion and a wide range of chemicals. They can also withstand cleaning with low-pressure steam, up to 110°C, provided care is taken to avoid localised overheating resulting in a loss of bond with the substrate due to differential expansion. It should be noted, however, that these systems produce a considerable mess during application. They are sensitive to environmental conditions during application, require skilled labour to install and take 4–7 days for full curing. During this time the area has to be fully ventilated to avoid the potential of taint. These systems are difficult to repair if they become damaged.

4.4.1.3.3 Cladding sheet. Although it is preferable to form the internal finish as an integral part of the wall structure in some instances the use of cladding sheets can be considered. Great attention to detail is essential when installing cladding systems to prevent infestation and/or mould growth. It is strongly recommended, therefore, to employ a reputable, experienced contractor for the installation of a cladding system.

4.4.1.3.4 Composite panels. These panels are normally used in areas where acoustic and/or thermal insulation properties are a consideration. Their construction details, facing materials and properties are very similar to those described within section 4.4.1.2. It is worth noting that any panels in which wood is used as a construction material should be avoided. If painted metal faced panels are used, especially in wet processing areas or where aggressive chemicals are likely to come into contact, then the integrity of the paint finish should be checked frequently.

4.4.1.3.5 Tiles. Ceramic wall tiles may be specified for application in areas where frequent washdown occurs, where abrasion and/or heat resistance is required or where aesthetics are a consideration. They should be fully vitrified, glazed, light in colour and have a Group 1 classification for water absorption in accordance with BS6431: Parts 11: 1983 (EN87). All external corners should be suitably protected. If ceramic tiles do become damaged they are readily replaced locally to restore the integrity of the surface. Solid bed fixing is essential, ensuring that the whole back of the tile is in contact with the adhesive and that no voids exist behind. Sufficient time must be allowed for the tile adhesive to set prior to grouting, to avoid any disturbance of the tiles. Epoxide resin grout material of a light colour should be used and all joints must be completely filled. After completion of the grouting the tiled surface should, ideally, not be subjected to service conditions for at least 7 days.

Any fixing or grouting material used must comply with the mould-resistance requirements of BS5980: 1980 and possess Class AA water resistance.

4.4.2 Floors

The floor is considered to be a most important part of the process area because it forms the basis of the entire operation. It is worthy of high initial capital investment because failure of the floor can result in lengthy disruptions of production and large financial losses whilst repairs are made. There seems to be more problems with floors than with any other part of the factory structure. When considering the floor, all the layers which make it up must be given careful attention because the integrity of the flooring (topping) depends upon them, in particular the structural slab, the membrane, the screed and movement joints, as well as taking into account drainage.

4.4.2.1 Structural floor slab.   In both new and old structures the substrate (floor slab) should be capable of withstanding all structural, thermal and mechanical stresses and loads which will occur during service. It should remain stable whilst protected by the flooring and be provided with all necessary movement joints to enable it to do so. Failure of the substrate to remain stable will invariably affect the stability of the flooring. In particular, movement in the substrate, however caused, will often be reflected in the flooring.

4.4.2.2 Membranes.   Good flooring design requires that all water- or corrosion-resistant floorings should be laid on a waterproof and acid-resistant membrane. This does not necessarily apply to solid ground floor construction but with a wet operation water can penetrate and affect the slab due to the porosity of concrete. It is, however, particularly important in the design of suspended floors where, for example, deflection due to heavy moving loads may cause cracks or fissures through which corrosive liquids might pass to damage the structural concrete, even when tiles are both bedded and jointed in a chemical resisting cement. It is considered essential that membranes should be installed in all suspended floors even for dry operations because the floor will probably require washing down and there may be a change in use in the future. The membrane plays a very important part in the flooring system and must be considered at the design stage as the siting of drainage points and the grouping of services are also involved. The life of an industrial floor very often depends on the efficiency of this membrane.

4.4.2.3 Screed. It may be necessary to interpose a screed between the structural floor slab and the flooring itself for various reasons, e.g. the finish of the slab may not be smooth or flat enough to accept the flooring or it may not be possible to form the required falls in the concrete slab. The mix for a screed is generally made from cement and fine aggregate or fine concrete and is applied to a hardened base. Screeds may be bonded or unbonded to the base and should be laid in as large an area as possible at one time to minimise the possibility of curling.

4.4.2.4 Movement joints. Movement joints in floors are an essential requirement to prevent damage, not only as the result of temperature changes but also from many other factors such as changes due to drying shrinkage, moisture absorption, deflection and vibration. The stresses due to these factors may result in loss of adhesion of the flooring, cracking or bulging. All movement joints in the subfloor must be carried through the flooring whether it is synthetic resin or tiles.

4.4.2.5 Drainage. It is widely recognised that one of the most important aspects in the design of a floor is that of drainage to ensure that spillages, whether deliberate or accidental, are directed rapidly away from the surfaces to minimise possible damage. Whenever possible the layout and siting of equipment should be finalised before the floor is designed to ensure that discharges are fed directly into drains. Equipment should not be sited over drainage channels as it may restrict access.

Satisfactory drainage can only be obtained by providing adequate falls to drainage points. Normally, a fall of 1 in 60 is adequate and should be the aim, but other factors such as the surface texture of the flooring and the type of operation to be carried out have to be taken into consideration.

4.4.2.6 Flooring.

4.4.2.6.1 Concrete. Ordinary concrete is not generally considered to be suitable as a flooring material for most food processing areas despite the fact that it provides a seamless finish. Whilst concrete is resistant to chemical attack from alkalis, mineral oils and many salts it is attacked by acids, vegetable and animal oils, sugar solutions and by some salts. In addition, concrete is porous and has a tendency to crumble under impact or when abraded. The properties of concrete can, however, be improved by various means making it suitable as a flooring material for food storage, access and some processing applications. The addition of a polymer to the mix will not only improve the compressive and flexural strength but improve resistance to penetration of liquids and provide a surface largely free from dusting.

4.4.2.6.2 Ceramic tiles. Ceramic tiles (if properly laid and grouted) are available with a range of slip-resistant surfaces and are suitable as a durable and hygienic flooring material. The absolute need for hygiene dictates that only fully vitrified tiles are used because of their very low water absorption.

4.4.2.6.3 Resin. As an *in-situ* floor finish, resin-based seamless floors hold the prospect of achieving high standards of hygienic conditions, coupled with acceptable durability under severe conditions. Resin-based finishes are not the whole floor only the topping and accordingly much of their durability is dependant upon the concrete substrate. Given the proper base concrete, the choice of seamless floor finish can be made either from various resin-based systems (epoxy, polyurethane, polyester or methacrylate) or from polymer modified cementitious systems.

4.4.3 Ceilings

The ceiling should be smooth and easy to clean. Finishes must be selected to minimise flaking and mould growth, especially in areas prone to high humidity. Ideally, ceilings should be of the suspended, walk-on type where all supporting members and services are physically separated from the processing area and services taken down vertically to equipment.

4.4.4 Lighting

Lighting may be a combination of natural and artificial. Artificial lighting is more desirable as, if properly arranged, it provides even illumination over, for example, inspection areas. Lighting levels should be adequate, at working height, for a particular area, e.g. 500 lx at work points and 700 lx in areas where inspection and quality control procedures are carried out. Any glass tubes or lamps in a processing area must be protected by covers, usually of polycarbonate material, to not only protect the glass but contain it in the event of breakage. Suspended lighting units must be easily cleanable and prevent the ingress of moisture. Ideally, recessed lighting flush with the ceiling is recommended but maintenance may be difficult.

4.4.5 Ventilation

Adequate ventilation is most important in areas where large quantities of steam and moist air are involved. This is necessary for the comfort of personnel and to reduce the possibility of microbial and visible mould growth, corrosion and attack on internal finishes. Extraction systems should be sited above certain equipment to ensure that problems are dealt with at source. Any air inlets to processing areas should be screened to prevent access by insects, and these screens must be cleaned regularly. If a slight overpressure is required in certain processing areas it may be necessary to install microbiological air inlet filters on any air-conditioning system. The flow of air within a processing area should, in general, be in the opposite direction to the production flow.

4.5 Factory layout

4.5.1 Separation of processes

Premises should be designed to provide separate physical areas for various storage and processing operations, whilst still ensuring good product flow from raw materials through to the storage of finished product with no backtracking. Correct separation of processes will reduce the risk of product contamination and spoilage from chemicals, foreign bodies, microorganisms or other sources.

Separate areas should be provided for the following purposes:

- Storing stocks of unused empty cans or other containers.
- Storage of ingredients used in the make-up of products.
- Storage and preparation of raw meat, poultry and fish (see current EC regulations).
- Storage and preparation of vegetables or other materials.
- The manufacture, filling, closure and sterilisation of the foods.
- Storage of freshly processed cans until sufficiently cooled and dry.
- Post-process can transport and labelling.
- Cartoning and palletising operations.

- Storage of packaging materials such as cartons, wrapping materials, etc.
- Accumulation of waste materials from the food preparation processes.
- Storage of by-product materials.
- Storage of finished goods.
- Lockable storage for cleaning and other chemicals.
- Engineers' store and workshop.

It is most important to ensure that unprocessed and processed containers are separated so that unprocessed containers cannot, under any circumstances, become mixed with, or mistaken for, those which have been processed.

4.5.1.1 High specification areas.   It is very important that the contamination of vulnerable raw materials is avoided during the preparation processes. Any raw material which is susceptible to increased microbiological contamination, such as raw meat, fish or poultry, or which can cross-contaminate other raw materials should be considered as a vulnerable raw material. Areas used for the preparation of such materials should, therefore, be designed and constructed to a high standard to permit cleaning and disinfection processes to be carried out easily and effectively to prevent the build up of contamination. Separate rooms should be provided for the preparation of specific raw materials, e.g. the cutting and boning of raw meat. A separate facility is required for removing the outer packaging from all raw materials; specifically raw meat intended for processing, which is received packed in cartons, must be removed from the cartons in a completely separate area. Discarded cartons must be removed from the unpacking area at regular intervals.

4.5.2 Separation of personnel

The separation of personnel may provide an essential part of the separation of processes with regard to avoidance of microbiological cross-contamination, as is the case for pre- and post-process container handling operations. Processing areas in which operations of high microbiological risk are being undertaken should be limited to essential personnel. Processing areas should not be used as thoroughfares. Identification of personnel in different areas may be achieved by colour-coded clothing (see also section 4.7.2).

   Certain personnel may be exempt from access restrictions between areas. These may include maintenance, hygiene and technical support personnel, quality-assurance auditors and management. However, if such personnel move between high- and low-risk areas, they must change their protective clothing and wash their hands.

4.6 Services

Service pipes should be routed outside the process area, where possible, and pass through walls and/or ceilings local to the point of usage. Overhead pipes should not pass over vessels or production lines in order to prevent possible contamination from condensation, leakage, lagging or dust.

Pipe insulation must be crevice free, with sealed joints, and have a durable and easily cleanable outer surface.

4.6.1 General water supply

The provision and maintenance of a satisfactory supply of potable water in a cannery has important public health implications. It is important that all water used in the making up of products, or likely to come into contact with the product or packaging, is at least of the highest standard for drinking water laid down in the EU directive relating to the quality of water for human consumption (80/778/EEC) or the equivalent WHO standard. Mains water supplied to the factory should be of that standard and the responsibility for ensuring that this is the case rests with the water supplier. It should be recognised that water of potable quality may be unsuitable as an ingredient in certain products. Water used as an ingredient, therefore, should be chemically tested at appropriate intervals, both with respect to public health and to product quality considerations.

In the canning factory, water in the distribution system should be sampled from appropriate outlets. It would be considered to be of the EU standard if coliforms were not detectable in 100 ml in 95% of samples taken nor in any two consecutive samples of that series. The total aerobic plate count should be less than 100 organisms per ml of water after incubation for 3 days at 20–22°C. However, in practice, it is important that limits should be established for the water in the factory and that any significant variation from these should be investigated immediately. Coliform and total aerobic plate counts should be performed at least once a month at different points in the factory and total aerobic plate counts at least once a week. If water is derived from a private source or receives further treatment on arrival at the premises, samples should also be taken as the water enters the distribution system. Water supplied from a private source is generally more susceptible to variations in microbiological loading with environmental changes. If the water is chlorinated in the factory, residual free chlorine estimations should be carried out, at least twice a day. Once an adequate dosing regime has been established, the frequency of microbiological testing may be reduced.

4.6.2 Water for cooling purposes

The main requirement for container cooling water is that it should be free from microorganisms which might gain access to the cans during the cooling process. In general, the total aerobic plate count should be checked daily and the count should contain no more than 100 organisms per ml of water after incubation at 20–22°C for a minimum of 3 days. All cooling water should be obtained from a source of potable quality.

Normally water for container cooling is recirculated and will receive a disinfection treatment, usually chlorination, and this treatment should provide the water with a residual disinfecting property at the point of use. If the water contains high levels of organic impurities filtration and/or periodic draining and refilling may be required to remove gross debris. It should be noted that a build up of impurities within the water or changes in pH may affect the efficiency of the disinfection treatment.

If non-potable water is circulated within the factory, e.g. for steam generation or fire control, it should be completely separated from pipes carrying potable water and the pipes clearly identified to prevent any cross-connection.

Although chlorination is the most commonly used disinfection system for water chlorine dioxide and bromine compounds may be used; but, as with chlorine, there are certain hazards associated with their use, and advice should be sought from the suppliers prior to installation.

4.6.3 General steam supply

Steam for general service, i.e. not in direct contact with the food product, should be dry saturated, clean and free of non-condensables. Superheated steam should generally be avoided but some superheat may be used to prevent undue condensation in large distribution systems. Condensate should be removed from pipelines and items of processing equipment through properly sized steam traps.

4.6.4 Potable steam supply

Potable steam, for culinary use, is steam which is in direct contact with the food product or food contact surfaces, and is used as a heating medium and ingredient in the product. Clean, dry saturated steam is essential and the following list of requirements should be met.

- Boiler feed water treatment chemicals must be suitable for direct food use.
- Materials of construction, including seals and gaskets, must be compatible with the steam and any descaling or cleaning solutions.
- Final steam filters which are capable of removing all particles above

5 μm must be used and should be fitted prior to any steam injection point. A line-size strainer should be fitted upstream of the filter to improve the life and performance of the filter element.

• Equipment must be suitably rated for pressure and temperature and should be hygienically designed and self-draining.

• Dry steam is most important in order to avoid excessive condensate mixing with the product. Carry-over of boiler feed water and pipeline condensate should be avoided.

4.6.5 Other services

Other services, such as air supplies, must be fitted with adequate water and oil traps and, if in direct contact with food product, suitably filtered to remove microorganisms and odours.

4.6.6 Effluent

Any drainage system must be of suitable construction for the particular effluent, adequate in size, cleaned regularly, and be capable of operating efficiently at the maximum load imposed by the process and cleaning operations. The flow of effluent should always be directed away from high-risk areas. Different types of effluent, e.g. process and domestic, may need to be kept separate. Disposal of process effluent must meet the requirements of the appropriate authorities and advice should be sought from them.

4.7 Personal hygiene

A high standard of personal hygiene is necessary in ensuring minimal risk of food contamination. The management is responsible for ensuring that all personnel are aware of and understand the relevant factory regulations. These regulations should be printed in a company booklet or other document and given to the employee when engaged. Regular training programmes should be conducted to stress the importance of personal hygiene and behaviour and to issue any updates on legal obligations. A list of basic points related to personal hygiene is given below. This list should be used for guidance only and companies should conduct a critical review for their particular circumstances.

Personal hygiene requirements for personnel working in production areas are listed below.

(1) Protective overclothing, footwear and headgear issued by the company must be worn. When considered appropriate by management, a fine hairnet must be worn in addition to the protective

headgear provided. Hair clips and grips should not be worn. Visitors and contractors must comply with this regulation. Protective clothing must not be worn off the site (for more details see section 4.7.2).

(2) Personnel must wash their hands thoroughly before commencing work, after using toilets or urinals and on returning to the production area after leaving for any reason. Ideally, non-perfumed bactericidal soap should be used and non-hand-operated taps should be installed at all sinks. Disposable hand towels or hot-air driers should be used to reduce the possibility of recontamination. Fingernails should be kept short and clean.

(3) Beards and moustaches must be kept short and trimmed and a protective cover worn when considered appropriate by management.

(4) The wearing of make-up, false eyelashes, false fingernails, and nail varnish should be prohibited.

(5) The wearing of watches, jewellery and other adornments (except plain wedding bands and possibly 'sleeper' earrings) should be prohibited.

(6) Personal items must be left in lockers situated outside the production area.

(7) The consumption of food and drink must be prohibited. Spitting and the chewing of gum must also be forbidden. Any drinking water should be supplied from foot/elbow-operated drinking fountains and clearly marked as drinking water only.

(8) Smoking, taking of snuff and any use of tobacco must be prohibited. If smoking is permitted at all, designated areas should be provided which are physically separated from production areas. Hands must be washed thoroughly before returning to production areas.

(9) Superficial injuries, e.g. cuts, abrasions, etc., on any exposed part of the body must be covered by a clean waterproof dressing. It is recommended that any such dressing be distinctively coloured to assist in recovery should it become detached. Furthermore, if metal detectors are fitted in the production line prior to filling a metal strip should be contained in the dressing.

(10) Personnel suffering from heavy colds, bowel disorders, vomiting, discharges from the eyes, nose or ears or having skin infections, septic lesions, boils, etc., should be excluded from work connected with handling food until pronounced fit by a competent medical officer. This also applies to personnel who have been in contact with any person suffering from an infection which is likely to be transmitted by food and personnel returning from foreign travel where there has been a risk of infection (see also section 4.7.1).

4.7.1 Health control

Prior to commencing employment all prospective personnel should complete a detailed medical questionnaire to provide information regarding previous illnesses which may have a bearing on their fitness to work with food. This information should be passed to an experienced medical officer who will decide whether a medical examination is required before employment.

The detection of infection of personnel depends to a great extent on their cooperation in reporting illness to management, who can then obtain medical advice. However, it is a legal requirement that food handling personnel who become aware that they are suffering from, or become the carrier of, certain types of infections (typhoid, paratyphoid, any other *Salmonella* infection, or amoebic or bacillary dysentery, or any staphylococcal infection, including infected cuts) that are likely to cause food poisoning are required to inform the food manufacturer who must inform the relevant Health Authority immediately.

Periodic checks should be carried out by a responsible person to ensure that personnel are free of any septic cuts or lesions on the hands or exposed parts of the body, and that any uninfected cuts or skin lesions are properly protected by waterproof dressings. This is especially important for personnel in the post-processing area.

4.7.2 Protective clothing

Protective clothing must be worn by all personnel in processing areas. Such clothing is designed to protect the food from contamination by the personnel and to protect the wearer's own clothing. The protective clothing should be washable or disposable, clean, in good repair, laundered regularly and changed when soiled. All protective clothing should be light coloured and may be colour coded if segregation or easy identification of personnel is required, for example in post-process can handling areas. Protective clothing should never be worn outside the processing area. Engineers and other personnel who normally work outside processing areas should change their clothing on entry to processing areas.

Coats should cover the arms and be of the loose-fitting smock type for comfort. Clothing should be fastened with secure metal press studs or velcro-type fastening. Trousers should have an elasticated waist and a velcro-type fly. Pockets should be avoided on the outside of protective clothing to prevent objects falling into the food.

Headgear must be worn correctly and completely contain the hair, or an additional hairnet must be worn. If personnel have beards, then beard masks may be required. Footwear should be hygienic, kept clean and ideally be of the safety type.

4.7.3 Sanitary accommodation

Separate sanitary accommodation must be provided for each sex and meet the standards required by legislation. All sanitary accommodation must be constructed with smooth, impervious internal surfaces and fitted with hygienically designed equipment which is easily cleanable and capable of being disinfected. Rooms containing water closets and/or urinals must be kept clean, well lit, properly ventilated and must not communicate directly with food rooms. All doors leading to sanitary accommodation must be self-closing. Adequate hand wash-basins must be provided adjacent to the toilets and supplied with hot and cold water, or warm water only at a suitably controlled temperature. A suitable hand-cleaning preparation should be provided along with single-use towels or other hygienic means of hand drying. Taps should be foot, knee or electronically operated. Additional hand washing facilities must be provided on entry to processing areas.

Prominent notices must be displayed in the sanitary accommodation instructing personnel to wash their hands after using the facility.

4.7.4 Staff amenities

Adequate separate facilities should be provided for the changing and storage of outdoor clothing, preferably adjoining the sanitary accommodation. Suitable facilities should be provided for meal and other breaks and for smoking (when permitted).

4.8 Equipment

4.8.1 Hygienic design

Manufacturers have, for many years, been mainly concerned with the operational requirements of the equipment and have ignored to a large extent the hygienic aspects.

Purchasers of equipment, as well, have not realised the importance of hygienic design until after the equipment has been commissioned and problems have arisen. It is then often too late to make any necessary modifications which may be difficult, if not impossible, and certainly costly. In most instances the choice of equipment has been based on cost and delivery.

The importance of hygienic design has long been recognised by some major food processors who have produced their own standards and guideline documents which have not been generally available. Various organisations, have, however, been producing guideline documents. In 1967, the UK Food Manufacturers' Federation, together with the Food Machinery Association published an excellent booklet on the Hygienic Design of Food Plant with reference to tanks, pumps and pipework. The Campden Food and Drink Research Association, also in the UK, has, in conjunction with an industrial working party of manufacturers and users of equipment, been producing guideline documents on hygienic design since 1982 and is continuing to do so. Since the end of 1992 The European Hygienic Equipment Design Group (EHEDG) has been publishing guideline documents on the hygienic design and operation of food plant.

In June, 1989, however, an EU Directive (89/392/EEC) relating to machinery was adopted; within it there is a section concerning essential health and safety requirements for agrifoodstuffs machinery. This states that machinery intended to prepare and process foodstuffs must be so designed and constructed as to avoid any risk of infection, sickness or contagion and then lists a number of hygiene rules relating to materials, design and sanitation. A harmonised European Standard is being produced as a consequence. In the USA there is a National Standard for Food, Drug and Beverage Equipment (ASME/ANSI F2.1-1986) which is quite detailed and specific. The first section of this standard covers all equipment with respect to materials of construction, sanitary design and construction, as well as safety. Subsequent sections are related to specific products. In addition, the 3-A Sanitary Standards Organisation produce hygienic design standards for equipment used in the processing of dairy products.

In two American documents entitled *Sanitary Design* by Milleville and Gelber which were published in *Food Processing*, seven basic principles for hygienic design of equipment were outlined. Although these have been quoted by several authors they are still considered to be generally acceptable and are worthy of being repeated.

(1) All surfaces in contact with food must be inert to the food under the conditions of use and must not migrate to, or be absorbed by, the food.
(2) All surfaces in contact with food must be smooth and non-porous so that tiny particles of food, bacteria, or insect eggs are not caught in microscopic surface crevices and become difficult to dislodge, thus becoming a potential source of contamination.
(3) All surfaces in contact with the food must be visible for inspection, or the equipment must be readily disassembled for inspection, or it must be demonstrated that routine cleaning procedures eliminate the possibility of contamination from bacteria or insects.
(4) All surfaces in contact with food must be readily accessible for

manual cleaning, or if clean-in-place techniques are used, it must be demonstrated that the results achieved without disassembly are the equivalent of those obtained with disassembly and manual cleaning.

(5) All interior surfaces in contact with food must be so arranged that the equipment is self-emptying or self-draining.

(6) Equipment must be so designed as to protect the contents from external contamination.

(7) The exterior or non-product contact surfaces should be arranged to prevent harbouring of soils, bacteria or pests in and on the equipment itself, as well as in its contact with other equipment, floors, walls or hanging supports.

Additionally, as suggested by a CFDRA Working Party the following general principles should also be applied.

(8) In design, construction, installation and maintenance it is important to avoid dead spaces or other conditions which trap food, prevent effective cleaning and may allow microbial growth to take place.

(9) The requirement of guarding machinery to ensure safety in operation may easily conflict with hygiene requirements unless considerable care is taken in design, construction, installation and maintenance.

(10) Noise suppression is important in providing acceptable working conditions. However, many noise reducing materials can give rise to microbiological or infestation problems unless care is taken in their selection, installation and maintenance.

(11) It is important that the equipment itself is so designed, installed and maintained that it does not cause product contamination. Examples of possible contamination are lagging which may break up, or insufficiently secured nuts and bolts. Such hazards should be designed out of the system.

Austenitic stainless steel continues to be the main material of construction for food processing equipment and it is considered that it will be for the foreseeable future. The type AISI 304 is most commonly used in environments where fluids do not contain any chlorides. If chlorides are present they can lead to locally high concentrations and result in corrosion such as pitting. In this case the molybdenum-containing type AISI 316 or possibly titanium may be the better choice. Hard plastics are also used as a material of construction but it must be ensured that the material is approved for food contact and is inert to cleaning chemicals. Polypropylene, for example, is not resistant to attack by low levels of sodium hypochlorite, a commonly used disinfectant. Plastics are more easily abraded than stainless steel and this affects their cleanability. Conveyor-belts are a common source of contamination, especially if the belting has a carcass of an absorbent material such as canvass or cotton. Polyester is a material now widely used for the carcass of belting because it is stable and non-absorbent. Certain materials must be avoided; these include zinc, lead, cadmium, antimony, plastics containing free phenol, formaldehyde or plasticisers and under most circumstances, wood. Copper must be avoided especially if brine is present.

The internal design is obviously one of the most important factors in the hygienic design of equipment. The finish of product contact surfaces can affect cleanability because rougher surfaces can provide a better mechanical key for product residues. A maximum surface roughness value of 0.8 µm Ra is suggested for the surface finish which is a not too exacting requirement when it is known that sheet stainless steel, as supplied directly by the steel mills, has a value of less than 0.5 µm Ra. There should be no internal crevices or 'dead spaces' in which product can be retained or from which product residue cannot be readily removed during cleaning. Internal radii should be as generous as technically possible with a minimum of 5 mm and at least 25 mm for tanks, hoppers, etc. There should be no metal to metal joints in product contact areas because they are uncleanable and can retain very high numbers of microoganisms. All permanent joints should be continuously welded and the weld ground and polished to a surface roughness value similar to that of the surrounding metal. Where this is not possible a gasket of suitable material should be used but arranged to give a flush, continuous, crevice-free surface. Non-toxic solders may also be used to seal joints but it must be ensured that they are not attacked by the cleaning chemicals. Exposed screw threads must be avoided in product areas because they are difficult to clean as are countersunk screws and socket head cap screws. Any fastener in or above product areas must be secure to avoid the possibility of product contamination.

Whilst special attention to the hygienic design of all the equipment in a process line may be unnecessary, although it facilitates cleaning, it is vital to identify those parts of the line which are critical control points. In a canning operation poorly designed post-process can handling equipment can result in leaker infection which is the commonest form of spoilage encountered in the canning industry and has been associated with a number of serious food-poisoning incidents. The hygienic design of post-process can handling equipment is, however, an area which is beyond the scope of this chapter and is well covered in Campden Food and Drink Technical Manual No. 8.

Attention should also be paid to the external design of equipment to ensure that it may easily be kept clean. External surfaces should, therefore, be smooth and uncluttered so that spillages, dust and debris cannot accumulate. In particular, electric motors should be fitted with cowls or enclosed such that dust and debris cannot become trapped in the cooling fins. Lids should be fitted to hoppers and vats to protect the contents from foreign body contamination. Hinges, if fitted to lids, must be of a simple design, such as the hook-on type, to facilitate cleaning. Horizontal flat surfaces should be avoided, wherever possible, to aid drainage and horizontal tie bars on frames should be of circular cross-section or if of square section, turned through 45° to minimise the accumulation of debris. The ends of all tubular or hollow section material must be sealed completely. It must be ensured that painted surfaces, which should be avoided above the product area, are not liable to flake and must be suitable to withstand, not only product spillages, but also cleaning chemicals. Gearboxes or geared motors should not be mounted above product areas but if this is unavoidable, then drip trays must be provided to avoid possible product contamination.

It is mandatory that all moving parts of machinery are guarded to satisfy safety requirements but these often conflict with hygiene requirements. Guards must be such that they do not increase cleaning problems and must be easily removable where necessary for cleaning but fitted with suitable safety devices. All fasteners used to retain removable guards should be captive to avoid the possibility of product contamination. Permanent open mesh guarding may be fitted but it must be ensured that it is possible to clean behind it.

4.8.2 Installation

The installation of the equipment should be given careful consideration if cleaning and maintenance problems are to be avoided. A minimum of 1 m should be allowed all round equipment but preferably at least 2 m. Equipment supported by legs should be at least 200 mm off the floor to allow for cleaning underneath. Heavy equipment may have to be mounted directly on the floor or on a plinth in which case the base must be completely sealed with a suitable compound. There must also be adequate space left above equipment for cleaning and a minimum of 0.5 m is suggested. Larger clearances around and above equipment may be required for maintenance purposes and this must not be overlooked at the planning and layout stages. As mentioned previously, attention to the supply of services to the equipment must be given in order to avoid cleaning and other problems.

Major problems are often caused by insufficient thought being given to the linking of different items of equipment in a line. This can lead to the 'hold-up' of product caused by unsatisfactory transfers and often compounded by the fitting of deflectors or chutes; organoleptic, taint or microbiological problems may result.

Further reading

Catell, D. (1988) *Specialist Floor Finishes: Design and Installation.* Blackie and Son Ltd, Glasgow, UK.

DoH (1994) *Guidelines for the Safe Production of Heat Preserved Foods.* HMSO, London, UK.

Guidelines for the Design and Construction of Floors for Food Production Areas (Technical Manual No. 40). The Campden Food and Drink Research Association, UK, 1993.

Guidelines for the Design and Construction of Walls, Ceilings and Services for Food Production Areas. The Campden Food and Drink Research Association (in press).

Hayes, P.R. (1992) *Food Microbiology and Hygiene.* Elsevier Applied Science, London, UK.

Hygienic Design of Food Processing Equipment (Technical Manual No. 7). The Campden Food and Drink Research Association, UK, 1983.

Hygienic Design of Liquid Handling Equipment for the Food Industry (Technical Manual No. 17). The Campden Food and Drink Research Association, UK, 1987.

Hygienic Design of Post Process Can Handling Equipment (Technical Manual No. 8). The Campden Food and Drink Research Association, UK, 1985.

Imholte, T.J. (1984) *Engineering for Food Safety and Sanitation.* Technical Institute of Food Safety, Cristal, MN, USA.

Jowitt, R. (ed) (1980) *Design and Operation of Food Plant.* Ellis Horwood Ltd, Chichester, UK.

Katsuyama, A.M. and Strachan, J.P. (eds) (1980) *Principles of Food Processing Sanitation.* The Food Processors Institute, Washington, DC, USA.

Melville, H.P. and Gelber, P. (1964) Sanitary design. *Food Proc.,* **36** (10), 93.

Melville, H.P. and Gelber, P. (1965) Sanitary design. *Food Proc.,* **37** (4), 170.

Shapton, D.A. and Shapton, N.F. (eds) (1991) *Principles and Practices for the Safe Processing of Foods.* Butterworth Heinemann, London, UK.

The Principles of Design for Hygienic Food Processing Machinery (Technical Memorandum No. 289). The Campden Food and Drink Research Association, UK, 1982.

Troller, J.A. (1983) *Sanitation in Food Processing.* Academic Press, New York, USA.

Standards

BS 5980: (1980) *Specification for Adhesives for use with Ceramic Tiles and Mosaics.* British Standards Institution, London, UK.

BS 6431: Parts 11: (1983) *EN87. Ceramic Floor and Wall Tiles.* British Standards Institution, London, UK.

ASME/ANSI F2.1 (1986) *Food, Drug and Beverage Equipment.* The American Society of Mechanical Engineers, New York, USA.

European Community Directives

Council Directive, 80/778/EEC (1980) Relating to the quality of water intended for human consumption. *Off. J. European Communities,* **L229**, 11–29.

Council Directive, 89/392/EEC (1989) Relating to machinery. *Off. J. European Communities,* **L183**, 9–26.

Council Directive, 91/493/EEC (1991) Laying down the health conditions for the production and the placing on the market of fishery products. *Off. J. European Communities,* **L268**, 15–34.

Council Directive, 92/5/EEC (1992) Amending and updating Directive 77/99/EEC on health problems affecting intra-community trade in meat products and amending Directive 64/433/EEC. *Off. J. European Communities,* **L57**, 1–26.

5 Cans and lids

T.A. TURNER

5.1 Introduction

Metal cans have dominated sectors of the food and beverage markets for many years because of their cost effectiveness, durability and the overall protection they provide for their contents. The past 20 years have seen dramatic changes in can-making technology and in the materials used to make cans and closures. Can manufacture has become increasingly a high technology business.

Food cans can be made from steel, in a variety of forms, and from several aluminium alloys, using a number of different manufacturing routes. This chapter reviews the various can-making methods, the metals used in can manufacture and the organic coating systems used in their protection, all of which will be seen to be closely interrelated.

5.2 Metals used in can manufacture

Containers for heat processed foods are made from steel, in a variety of forms, and from aluminium. The former is substantially more common than the latter for reasons of cost and performance.

5.2.1 Steel

Steel, usually in the form of tinplate (hence the misnomer, tin can), is by far the most common metal used in the manufacture of heat processed food cans. Over 50 billion such cans are made each year. The gauge and, where tinplate is used, the level of tincoating varies considerably with container size and the product to be packed. Typical ranges are:

- Nominal gauge, 0.15–0.30 mm
- Tincoating weight, 0.5–15 gsm

The generic name for steel-based materials is tin-mill products, a name derived from the equipment used in their production. In fact tinplate and various tin-free steels are produced on essentially the same equipment.

Tin-mill products are available in a wide range of specifications relating to

- Gauge
- Single or double reduction
- Temper
- Continuous or batch annealed (CA or BA)
- Continuous or ingot cast

A specification is selected to suit the product to be packed and the manufacturing route for the container.

The manufacture of steel-based strip products is shown in simplified form in Figure 5.1. The essential steps are seen to be as follows:

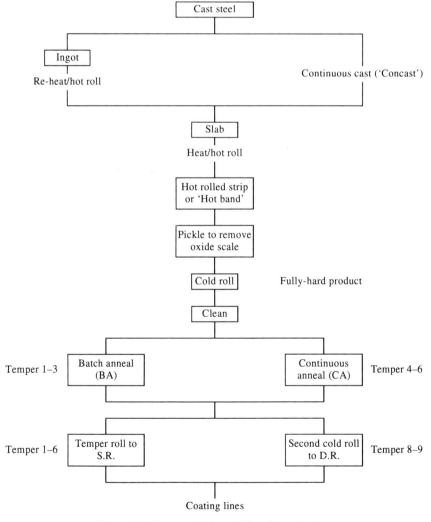

Figure 5.1 The manufacture of tin-mill products.

(1) Refined low carbon steel, a typical composition for which is shown in Table 5.1, is cast to ingot or continuously cast into a slab. In practice, the length of the slab is limited only by the supply of molten steel from the furnace tundish.

(2) In the case of ingot cast steel, the ingot is reheated to uniform temperature and then rolled into a slab; once in slab form the steel is hot rolled into a strip.

(3) In strip form, the steel has a significantly thick iron oxide 'scale' which is removed by mechanical flexing of the strip followed by passage through acid tanks (commonly sulphuric or hydrochloric acid). This process is called 'pickling' and is followed by oiling to facilitate subsequent rolling.

(4) The next stage involves cold reduction to nominal gauge, which in the case of single reduced plate is close to the final gauge. Typical cold reduction can result in a 10-fold reduction in thickness.

(5) Cold reduction produces a material which is fully hard and virtually unusable by virtue of its crystalline structure which renders it very brittle.

(6) The next important stage is annealing which traditionally necessitated holding the coils of steel at elevated temperatures (around 580–600°C) in an inert atmosphere for a prescribed length of time (typically 60 h incorporating 8–10 h at peak temperature). More recently continuous annealing that allows less time for crystal growth, has been introduced, this can be carried out in the coil as a continuous process in a matter of minutes.

(7) The two processes of annealing produce different products. Batch annealing produces steel within the temper range 1–3 whilst continuous annealing produces higher tempers of 4–6. In each case the precise level is dictated by chemistry. The annealed product can then either be light-temper rolled to produce the surface finish required or be subjected to further cold reduction to produce DR materials of temper 8 or 9. The latter processes produce the final gauge.

Table 5.1 Steel grade CP (low copper content)

	% max
Carbon	0.13
Manganese	0.60
Phosphorus	0.02
Sulphur	0.05
Silicon	0.02
Copper	0.08
Aluminium	0.08
Nitrogen	0.01
Plus traces of arsenic and nickel	

(8) At this stage the strip is ready for final finishing:
 – oiling in the case of blackplate
 – electrolytic tinning in the case of tinplate
 – electrolytic deposition of a chrome/chromium oxide layer in the case of electrolytic chrome coated steel (ECCS), commonly referred to as tin-free steel (TFS).

A summary of these coating processes is given in Table 5.2. The above is intended to give the reader a broad understanding of the steel-making process and a familiarity with common terminology used in the can-making industry. More information on steel and strip manufacture and on the metallurgical properties produced by the various manufacturing routes can be found elsewhere (Hoare *et al.*, 1965; Bodsworth and Bell, 1972; McGannon).

5.2.2 Tin-free steels (TFS) and blackplate

Blackplate, defined as uncoated mild steel, has been considered for the manufacture of food cans but is likely to be suitable only for a very limited range of products even when fully lacquered. This is because it readily rusts and generally has poor chemical resistance.

Tin-free steel (ECCS) has found fairly wide usage, typical examples being draw–redraw containers and fixed (non-easy open) ends for processed food cans. The extremely abrasive surface of TFS material necessitates overall lacquering prior to fabrication of containers or components to avoid tool wear. This aspect is dealt with later.

In addition to differences in chemical composition, steel-based products are used in a wide range of strengths (tempers) and ductility, these differences arising from the detailed chemistry and from the particular choice of manufacturing route (see below).

In an increasingly high technology business, the importance of these production variables and the resultant variation in the characteristics of the steel, especially strength and plastic anisotropy can be of vital importance.

Table 5.2 Coating operations[a]

Blackplate	Tinplate	ECCS (TFS)
Oil	Clean	Clean
	Electroplate	Electrolytic deposition
	Flow brighten	of chromium
	(heat to melting	Electrolytic deposition
	point and quench)	of chromium oxide
	Chromate passivation	Oil
	(300/311)	
	Oil	

5.2.3 Aluminium

Aluminium in can-making gauges is used less extensively than steel for food can manufacture, although of course aluminium foils are used extensively. Today, commercial applications largely concentrate upon shallow drawn containers for such products as paté and fish. A typical manufacturing route for aluminium alloys, the composition of which is given in Table 5.3 is shown in Figure 5.2.

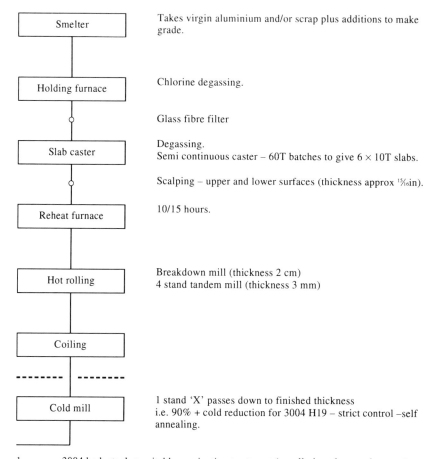

Smelter	Takes virgin aluminium and/or scrap plus additions to make grade.
Holding furnace	Chlorine degassing.
	Glass fibre filter
Slab caster	Degassing. Semi continuous caster – 60T batches to give 6 × 10T slabs. Scalping – upper and lower surfaces (thickness approx ⅟₁₆in).
Reheat furnace	10/15 hours.
Hot rolling	Breakdown mill (thickness 2 cm) 4 stand tandem mill (thickness 3 mm)
Coiling	
Cold mill	1 stand 'X' passes down to finished thickness i.e. 90% + cold reduction for 3004 H19 – strict control –self annealing.

1.   3004 bodystock + suitable passivation treatment (usually based upon chromate)
2.   Tab stock decreased + DOS
3.   End stock 5182
        Degreaser chrome/phos surface treatment + leveller.

Variants – Thickness after hot rolling approx 6 mm – intermediate annealing (batch anneal) undertaken during cold rolling schedule.

Figure 5.2 Typical manufacturing route for aluminium container stock.

Table 5.3 Composition of a number of aluminium alloys

Alloy type	Use	Added % (range)[a]		Added % (max)[a]					
		Mn	Mg	Si	Fe	Cu	Cr	Zn	Ti
3004	Body stock	1.0–1.5	0.8–1.3	0.3	0.7	0.25	—	0.25	—
5182	End stock	0.2–0.5	4.0–5.0	0.2	0.35	0.06	0.1	0.25	0.1
5052		0.1 (max)	2.2–2.8	0.45	0.45	0.1	0.15–0.35	0.1	—
5042	Tab stock	0.2–0.5	3.0–4.0	0.2	0.35	0.15	0.1	0.25	0.1
5082		0.15	4.0–5.0	0.2	0.35	0.15	0.15	0.25	0.1

[a]Unless indicated otherwise, other ingredients up to 0.05% per element/total 0.15%.

Aluminium in foil gauges (<0.1 mm) is used extensively in trays for a variety of products including ready-meals, snacks and reheatable trays.

5.2.4 Mechanical properties

Mechanical properties of the various metals described above are important in the contexts of both container fabrication and the container's strength necessary to satisfactorily withstand filling/closure, retorting, and distribution through the retail chain.

After conversion into containers, aluminium alloys can achieve an ultimate strength comparable to that of the lowest temper steel. However, steel and the commonly used aluminium alloys are very different in terms of strength, strain hardening, tensile elongation and the reaction to exposure to lacquer curing temperatures (200°C approx.) Typical properties for 3004 H19 aluminium alloy and steel in three tempers are summarised in Table 5.4.

Table 5.4 Mechanical properties of steel and H19 aluminium alloys

	3004 HI9	T2BA	T4CA	DR8BA
0.2% proof stress N/mm^2	285	235	315	550
UTS	295	350	400	580
Tensile elongation (%)	3	35	25	2
Strain hardening coefficient	0.04	0.18	0.15	0.04

In the manufacture of draw–redraw (DRD) and drawn and wall-ironed (DWI) containers, grain size and plastic anisotropy are also important. Planar anisotropy, the asymmetric reaction to deformation during drawing or stamping associated with rolling direction and grain orientation, manifests itself as 'earing' (see Figure 5.3) and needs to be kept to a minimum to avoid excessive material wastage due to trimming.

The degree of plastic anisotropy is highly dependent upon chemical composition, in particular aluminium and nitrogen content, hot rolling conditions, the degree of primary (and secondary) cold reduction and the method of annealing.

The following properties are measured as routine by steel and can makers:

• Strength and tensile elongation by tensometer
• Plastic anisotropy
• Grain size and distribution by microscopy
• Hardness by superficial hardness testers

5.2.4.1 Influence of temper and gauge.
Steel-based products are commonly used in gauges between 0.15 and 0.30 mm for cans and components

Figure 5.3 Drawn cups showing earing due to planar anisotropy.

and in tempers between 2 and 9, although thinner gauges, particularly DR material, are becoming more readily available.

Typical examples include:

	Temper	Gauge (mm)[a]
DWI 2-piece food can	T.2–T.4	~0.30
DRD 2-piece food can	DR8–DR9	0.16
Welded food can bodies	DR8	0.14–0.16
Food ends	T.5–T.7	0.20–0.21
Easy open end	T4/T.5	0.24

[a]Dependent upon container/component diameter.

5.3 Methods of container manufacture

The soldered three-piece tinplate can, standard up to about 1970, has been progressively replaced by

- Three-piece welded cans
- Two-piece cans made by either the drawn and ironed (DWI) route or by the draw–redraw approach (DRD)

One further three-piece method exists involving adhesive bonding of the side-seam, this method is dealt with briefly below.

This section describes the various can-making processes and reviews the factors which dictate the choice of the manufacturing route and the economics associated with the various options available. Brief mention is made of some key can-making equipment and processes used. The following is a brief description of the various can-making processes and serves to clarify the terminology used in the industry.

5.3.1 Three-piece can manufacture

Three-piece cans comprise a cylinder, today normally made by the welding route, and two ends. The essential steps in manufacture are as follows: cut up coil into rectangular sheets; apply protective lacquer (when appropriate), externally decorate (when appropriate); slit the sheets into rectangular blanks; form a cylinder and a side-seam; form flanges each end of the cylinder; fit makers ends, test, palletise and despatch to the filling lines. Such a can is commonly referred to as an open-top can (see Figure 5.4 which shows additionally the construction of the double seam closure of the ends). The formation of the welded cylinder is shown diagrammatically in Figure 5.5.

The side-seam as mentioned above is today normally resistance welded and this has been a development away from soldering. The change from soldering was on the basis of eliminating lead from the can contents and the factory atmosphere since the most commonly used solder was 98% lead and 2% tin. An alternative solder was 100% tin which was normally avoided other than for baby food and soft drink cans because of cost. In addition to the technological considerations, welding uses less metal in the

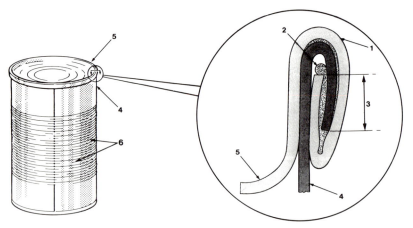

Figure 5.4 Open top (three-piece) food can and details of the double seam construction. (1) End curl; (2) lining compound; (3) seam lap; (4) can wall; (5) end counter-sink; (6) body heads.

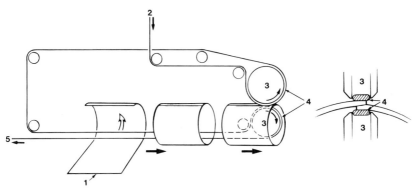

Figure 5.5 Stages in formation of a welded cylinder. (1) Blank rolled to cylinder shape; (2) copper welding wire loom; (3) welding rolls (electrodes); (4) copper wire contacts; (5) used wire to scrap or for recycling.

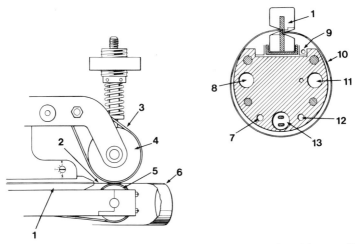

Figure 5.6 End of welding arm showing welding rolls and cross-section of the arm. (1) Z-bar; (2) side seam; (3) welding wire; (4) and (5) upper and lower welding rolls; (6) welded cylinder; (7) lacquer feed-pipe; (8) cooling water feed; (9) duct for nitrogen shroud (when required); (10) can wall; (11) cooling water return; (12) lacquer return pipe; (13) channel for welding wire.

side-seam in that modern welders require an overlap of only approx 0.5 mm.

The minimum diameter that can in practice be resistance welded is limited to 52 mm. This is because the diameter of the cylinder needs to accommodate the welding current-carrying rolls, which are supported by the welding-arm (see Figure 5.6). The welding-arm not only mechanically supports the welding roll but also conducts the welding current (~3500 A),

cooling water tubes and the side-stripe lacquer supply in most instances.
The need to be able to remove the welded cylinder means the arm and the
services it carries can be supported only from one end.

Welded cans are made almost exclusively from tinplate although in
principle TFS can be welded provided the edges to be joined are first
cleaned of chromium oxide, which is necessary for two reasons. Firstly the
contact resistance between chromium oxide and the sacrificial copper wire
electrode used in the resistance welding process is too high and secondly
the abrasive wear of machine parts is excessive. Edge-cleaning of TFS has
been attempted but is generally regarded as an unattractive operation in a
production environment.

Whilst TFS cannot be conveniently resistance welded, it can be readily
welded by laser fusion. Thus the development of laser welding, of which
brief mention is made below, will permit the welding of TFS without the
need to edge-clean.

5.3.1.1 Laser welding. Resistance welding is really only viable with
tinplate although technically TFS can be welded if the lapped edges are
cleaned free of chromium oxide. Basically the requirement is low contact
resistance between tin (on the tinplate surface) and the copper welding
wire.

An alternative approach is laser welding whereby the edges to be joined
are butted together, without overlap, and a focused laser beam is used to
fuse the touching metal surfaces to form a bond (see Figure 5.7). A
comparison of the types of weld produced by resistance and laser welding is
shown in Figure 5.8.

Currently a few such machines exist but they are at a fairly rudimentary
stage in their development. Laser welding has the following advantages:

- TFS (without edge-cleaning), tinplate and aluminium can be welded
- Butt welding uses less material than resistance welding, plus the cost
  of the disposable welding wire is eliminated

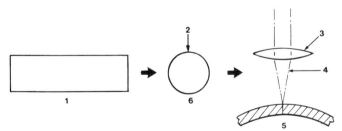

Figure 5.7 Principles of laser welding. (1) Tinplate blank; (2) butt joint; (3) lens; (4) laser
beams; (5) section at weld point; (6) unwelded cylinder.

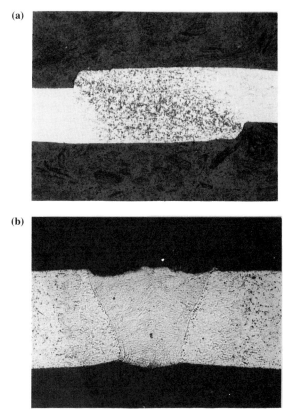

Figure 5.8 Comparison of the structure of (a) resistance (overlap × 100) and (b) laser (butt × 200) welds.

- Laser weld are smooth, aesthetically more pleasing and are more easily protected
- Smaller diameters can be welded than is possible with resistance welding.

Currently, however, welding speeds are limited to about 35 m/min compared with 70 m/min by resistance welding. In addition the laser fused weld area is extremely hard resulting from the formation of 'martensite' during fusion and subsequent rapid cooling.

Irrespective of the method of welding, the side-seam normally requires protection of the exposed iron via a side-striping operation internally and sometimes externally. Further description of this process is given below.

5.3.1.2 Side-stripe application. A number of methods have been devised for applying the side-stripe protection to the welded cylinder. These include the spraying of lacquers in both liquid (solvent-based) and powder form and the application of liquid lacquers by miniature roller coaters. Similarly various methods of side-stripe lacquer curing systems are employed including hot-air, gas-flame impingement and induction heating. Curing times are typically a few seconds.

5.3.1.3 Cement/adhesive side seams. Driven by the ability to use cheaper materials, a number of companies have developed alternative technologies (A-seam, Mira-seam, Toyo-seam) for the manufacture of three-piece cans from TFS. The use of adhesively bonded side seams for food cans has been limited principally to Japan, although some were made in the UK in the 1970s.

In brief, the process involves cylinders made from lacquered TFS to which a longitudinal strip of nylon is applied. The cut edges of the blank are overlapped to form a cylinder and the nylon fused to form a bond. An advantage of this process, other than the ability to use TFS, is that the seam does not require further protection as the fused nylon covers the cut edge.

5.3.2 Two-piece can manufacture

There are essentially two methods for manufacturing two-piece cans:

- Draw–redraw (DRD)
- Drawn and wall-ironed (DWI), sometimes called drawn and ironed (D&I)

although recent tooling developments are beginning to make the difference between these two methods less distinct (see section 5.4.2). The two fundamental metal-forming operations, drawing and ironing, are now explained.

5.3.2.1 Drawing. In the context of can-making, the process is one of cup formation, where the diameter is reduced at essentially constant metal thickness, by drawing metal from a flat sheet via a punch through a circular die (see Figure 5.9). In practice, some metal thickening occurs but in general terms the surface area of the cup is equal to the surface area of the blank from which the cup is made.

5.3.2.2 Redraw. The diameter of the cup can be further reduced and its height increased by one or more redraw operations. The extent of reduction in diameter via redraw operation is governed by fairly rigid theoretical considerations which are outside the scope of this book.

Figure 5.10 shows the draw–redraw operation to form a DRD can body, including the formation of a stronger base in the body-maker, and Figure 5.11 shows the stages in the manufacture of a DRD can.

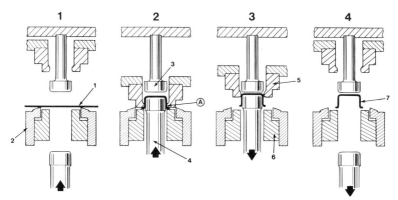

Figure 5.9 Typical tooling arrangement for a drawn can or cup. (1) Metal sheet or coil; (2) blanking tool (cut edge); (3) knock out pad; (4) ram/punch; (5) draw-die; (6) draw-pad; (7) drawn cup.

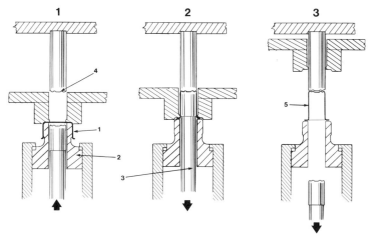

Figure 5.10 Typical redraw tooling arrangement. (1) Draw cup; (2) redraw sleeve; (3) punch; (4) base tooling; (5) redrawn container.

The first stage in the manufacture of a DWI or DRD container is the formation of a cup, the basic tooling arrangement for which is shown in Figure 5.9. It will be apparent that a finished single-drawn container, with the introduction of base profile tooling, can be produced with the same basic tooling assembly.

Whilst Figure 5.9 shows the formation of a flange which needs to be subsequently trimmed, the tooling can be so designed to eliminate the flange as in the first stage of the DWI process. The latter approach is referred to as 'through-draw'. Stages 1 and 2 show the formation of the

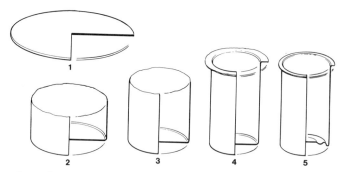

Figure 5.11 Stages in forming a DRD body. (1) Circular blank; (2) cup; (3) first redraw; (4) second redraw; (5) form base and trim flange.

blank which becomes clamped between the draw-die and the draw-pad. The pressure holding the blank is carefully balanced against the force exerted by the ram to shape the cup whilst allowing the metal to flow controllably through point (A). (This area of the tooling can be designed to produce a cup without a flange.)

Stages 3 and 4 show the fully formed cup with the draw-die separating with the cup positioned under the knock-out pad to allow ejection after withdrawal of the bottom ram/punch.

Redraw tooling for a second (and in this particular case final) redraw is shown in Figure 5.10. It can be seen that a cup has been placed over the redraw sleeve prior to being forced through the draw-die by the 'punch'. The working faces of the tooling are essentially the same as in the previous first draw/cup stage (Figure 5.9). At the top of its stroke the cup is forced into the base panel die.

5.3.2.3 Ironing.   Ironing is wall-thinning produced by forcing a redrawn cup on a punch through dies which create a gap that is less than the thickness of the metal. In a can-making process two, three or even four dies, to produce progressively smaller gaps, may be used to reduce wall thickness by up to 70%.

The volume of metal remains constant from the blank to the finished can and this fact dictates the essential economics of the DWI process for the manufacture of cans from steel and from aluminium.

Figure 5.12 shows the stages in the manufacture of a DWI can and it can be seen that the essential steps are the formation of cups from coil using vertical multi-toolpack presses. These cups are fed into wall-ironing machines where they are redrawn and ironed to form cylinders. It should be noted that the top of the can is allowed to thicken to facilitate flange formation and to assist stripping of the untrimmed can from the punch at the end of the ironing process.

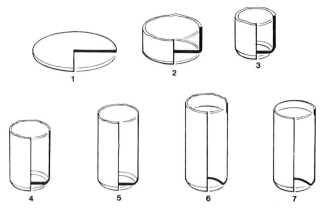

Figure 5.12 Stages in forming a drawn and ironed DWI body. (1) Circular blank; (2) cup; (3) redraw; (4) first ironing stage; (5) second ironing stage; (6) third ironing and dome forming; (7) trimmed body.

Table 5.5 Summary of steps in the manufacture of two-piece cans

DWI	DRD
Unwind coil	Coil lacquer or cut to sheets and lacquer
Lubricate	
Blank disks and form cups	Blank disks and form cups
	Redraw (once or twice)
Iron walls and form base	Form base
Trim body to correct height	Trim flange or form flange
Wash and treat	
(passivate)	
Decorate (optional)	
External protection	
Internal protection	

After trimming the container to the correct height, it is washed and dried ready for the down-line operations listed in Table 5.5.

Figure 5.13 shows a typical toolpack comprising a single redraw die and three ironing dies.

The frictional considerations of drawing and ironing have important impact on the can-making process. The very high friction between metal and tooling and the extreme pressures produced in the ironing process necessitate flood lubrication and restriction of the process to tinplate and aluminium. In the former case the tin coating also behaves as a lubricant.

Attempts have been made to extend the wall-ironing process beyond tinplate and aluminium but these have failed to reach commercialisation.

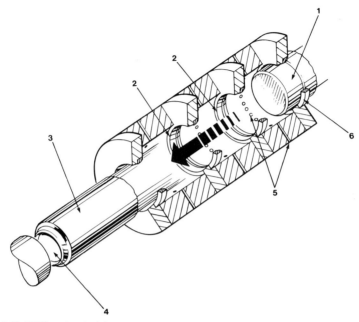

Figure 5.13 DWI toolpack. (1) Cup on punch; (2) ironing dies; (3) ironed/untrimmed can; (4) dome tooling; (5) coolant ports; (6) redraw die.

5.3.3 Can ends

Can ends are of two basic types:

- Fixed (non-easy open)
- Easy open

In the case of food cans, fixed ends, i.e. those which need to be opened using a can-opener, are far more commonly used than easy open ends which are opened by removing a scored panel area (see Figure 5.14). This is in marked contrast to cans for beverages which up to 1990 at least have been closed with pouring aperture aluminium easy open ends (see Figure 5.15).

5.3.3.1 Fixed ends. Ends for tinplate or TFS food cans are invariably made from steel, again either tinplate of TFS, and may be found, oval/irregular or rectangular to suit the shape of the container.

The end/body closure provides a hermetic seal via a double seam, the construction of which is shown in Figure 5.4. It will be seen that the seam construction involves a gasket material (lining compound) comprising

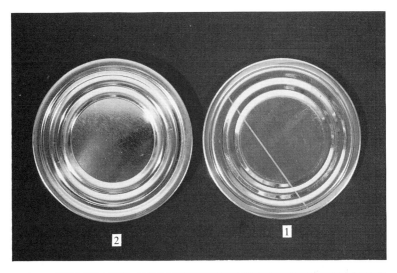

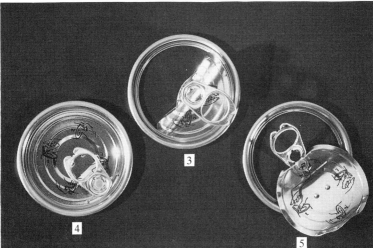

Figure 5.14 Fixed or non-easy ends (top) and full aperture easy open ends for food cans (bottom). (1) Lining compound; (2) expansion beads; (3) tab; (4) score areas; (5) panel removed.

essentially a solution of latex in hexane although water-based compounds are used for some applications.

The end is constructed to resist can internal pressure generated during retorting and importantly to recover its original profile on cooling. The latter property provides an indication of can spoilage, manifested as a bulged end, during storage.

The overall strength of the end is provided by the gauge and temper of

Figure 5.15 Two types of pouring aperture easy open ends for beverage cans. Left: Detached tab; right: ecology or stay-on tab.

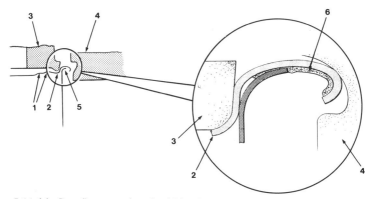

Figure 5.16 (a) Can flange and end within double seamer tooling; (b) detail showing formation of the double seam. (1) Expansion beads; (2) counter-sink; (3) chuck; (4) seaming roll; (5) flange; (6) lining compound.

the metal used in its construction and by the depth/shape of the countersink. Resistance to distortion by internal pressure is provided by one or more circumferential expansion rings (see Figures 5.14 and 5.16). Figure 5.16 also shows the tooling and initial formation of the double seam.

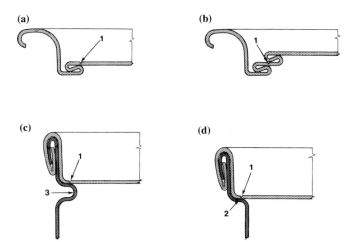

Figure 5.17 Single and double safety folds on full aperture easy open food ends. (A) Single safety fold; (B) double safety fold; (C) single safety fold with guard-bead; (D) single safety fold with necked-out body wall to provide guard. (1) Score; (2) necked-out guard; (3) internal guard bead.

5.3.3.2 Easy open ends. In order to provide convenience some cans are sold with easy open full aperture ends which are made normally from tinplate or, for some products, aluminium. The opening feature is produced by introducing a circumferential score close to the double seam and a tab which permits the panel contained within the score to be removed (see Figure 5.14).

Once the panel is removed the can contents can be poured (or otherwise removed) from the container. The removal of the panel leaves a torn surface on the panel and around the aperture which some designs seek to overcome by the introduction of safety-folds, either single or double (see Figure 5.17), with or without the introduction of guard beads.

The score can be placed internally or externally and normally requires repair either by spraying lacquer or oil or by electrophoretic lacquer application. The use of TFS is generally avoided because of unacceptable tool wear during the scoring and rivet-forming operation.

5.4 Selection of a can-making route

The following factors will influence the choice of the most suitable can-making route within a particular geographical area

- Products to be packed
- Food preservation method
- Numbers of cans to be made

- Variety of specifications
- Availability and price of raw materials

All the above need to be considered in any territory where significant investment in can-making is planned.

5.4.1 Product(s) to be packed

For food cans, where the contents are to be heat processed in the pack, both three-piece welded and two-piece (DRD or DWI) are relevant. If other than in-can heat processing is to be considered, e.g. aseptic packaging, then new rules begin to apply and a whole new range of containers and closures becomes available to the packer.

5.4.2 Size of the market and the manufacturing unit

The size of the market and of the manufacturing units required to serve that market will greatly influence the choice of the can-making route. Two important considerations are the capital cost and versatility of the equipment. Where the manufacturing unit is to be small and/or variety of can sizes and specifications large, welding is normally the preferred option. However, the need to provide lacquered sheets for some specifications must not be overlooked in considering the total manufacturing unit.

Where the manufacturing unit is large and variety is small, the DWI route will offer advantages in container cost but at the expense of high capital investment. Typical developed markets include petfood and beverage cans where units producing 1 billion (10^9) cans per annum are commonplace.

Between these two extremes is the position of DRD which has advantages in terms of material utilisation over three-piece manufacture, with less flexibility in terms of product/specification variety but with the advantage of significantly lower capital cost by comparison with DWI.

	Capital cost	Versatility
Welding	Low	High
DRD	Medium	Poor
DWI	High	Poor

These are broad generalisations and the choice of process may be further refined by, for example, the ability to purchase precoated coil, the availability of appropriate quality steel or aluminium and by the choice of tinplate of TFS. These subjects are further developed below.

5.4.2.1 Which two-piece method? The strength of the can wall is clearly an important property governing filling, seaming of the closure, storage and resistance to abuse. This property is controlled principally by wall-thickness.

It will be obvious that if the same nominal can size is made by the DRD and DWI routes, then for the same nominal wall thickness, the ingoing gauge of metal will be substantially different. The example of the 0.5 kg can (typical diameter 73 mm, height 110 mm) illustrates the situation well.

Process	Ingoing gauge (mm)	Blank diameter (mm)	Wall (mm)	Base (mm)
DRD	0.18	179	0.18	0.18
DWI	0.30	154	0.13	0.30

Based upon the price structure of steel, which is related to gauge and area and not tonnage, the traditional rules suggest that

- High height/diameter ratio (tall cans) are favoured by DWI
- Low height/diameter ratio (squat cans) are favoured by DRD

In strict metal-forming terms and for like metals, these rules are generally applicable but other factors complicate the situation

- DWI necessitates the use of tinplate whereas DRD cans can be manufactured from prelacquered TFS (both types of container can be made from aluminium).
- DWI demands more costly equipment and hence greater volumes are required to justify the capital investment.
- The economics can be complicated further by partial wall-ironing of DRD cans.

5.4.2.2 Partial wall-ironing. When taller cans are made by the DRD route it is possible to include an ironing die in the second redraw operation to reduce the wall thickness by up to approximately 20%. This requires sophisticated tooling but naturally improves the metal utilisation in the DRD process by allowing the use of a smaller blank ('cut-edge').

5.5 Mechanical properties of containers and ends

5.5.1 General

Food containers need to have sufficient strength and robustness to permit handling, filling and processing, storage and distribution without undue damage. The filled and closed containers also need adequate strength to withstand the temperature and pressure conditions used in the in-can sterilisation process.

The mechancial strength properties of (filled) containers are measured in terms of:

- Axial strength: resistance to buckling from top load
- Panelling resistance: resistance to external pressure/in-can vacuum
- Peaking resistance: resistance to in-can pressure

In practice, axial strength and panelling become closely inter-related in modern can body design. Peaking performance is accommodated via the design of the end(s) countersink depth and by the introduction of circumferential (expansion) beads.

5.5.2 Axial strength

If the three-piece can body, for example, is regarded as a perfect cylinder it can be assumed that axial strength is largely independent of metal gauge and temper within the range of loads that would be normally applied. In practice the can body does not have perfectly uniform and parallel sides and variations in symmetry and the presence of small imperfections have an effect on axial strength.

5.5.3 Panelling resistance

During the retorting process the external pressure generated in the retort is counter-balanced to a degree by the internal pressure generated within the can. The container specification is such that this differential pressure can be accommodated. In the extreme, the external pressure will cause the side walls of the container to collapse inwards. Cooling subsequent to in-can heat sterilisation of the can contents produces a vacuum within the can, which varies with products and filling conditions. This vacuum will exacerbate any tendency for collapse to occur.

Resistance to panelling is a function of gauge and strength of the side wall. Container diameters and height/diameter ratio will also have an effect. The tendency for panelling to occur can be substantially reduced by the introduction of circumferential beads into the side wall (see Figure 5.4). A great deal of fundamental work has been carried out to optimise the depth, number and spacing of such beads. However, the most significant factor determining resistance to panelling is bead depth.

Introduction of such beads, whilst reducing the panelling by increasing hoop strength, significantly reduces axial strength. The physical properties of beaded and unbeaded 0.5 kg cans made from steel with a wall-thickness of 0.17 mm are as follows.

	Axial strength (lb)[a]	Panelling (psi)[b]
Unbeaded	1800	14
Beaded	900	26

[a]1 lb $\approx$ 0.45 kg.
[b]1 psi $\approx$ 6.9 kPa.

In unbeaded containers increased gauge compensates for imperfections in the can symmetry and increases its resistance to mechanical abuse, this abuse subsequently reducing axial strength.

In beaded containers, the can designer is in greater control and can manipulate the various combinations of metal gauge, temper and beading configuration with greater certainty. This is of course of great importance as the manufacturer seeks to reduce container costs by lightweighting, i.e. the use of thinner and stronger metals. As a general guideline beading is normally required for steel gauges below 0.20 mm and is essential for sound economics in two-piece food cans. The beads are introduced after the body maker, and in the case of two-piece cans, before internal lacquer protection is applied.

5.5.4 Peaking resistance

During the processing cycle, the contents of the filled container, including gas in the headspace and elsewhere, expand and generate an increased pressure within the can. Some release of the pressure can be accommodated by the concentric expansion beads designed into the end(s). Gauge and strength of the metal as well as detailed design of the end are important. There are, however, limitations to the use of very strong materials such as double-reduced tinplate and to some extent to the minimum gauges that can be utilised. These limitations are related to 'shape', rippling, warp or buckling, typically found in DRD materials and to producing adequate double-seams without splitting of the metal.

Distortion of the end during processing/sterilisation is acceptable provided it is not so great as to prevent the end resuming its original profile on cooling. Peaked ends are associated with can spoilage, either microbiological or from evolution of hydrogen gas resulting from chemical attack of the container by the contents.

5.5.5 Measurement of mechanical properties

A range of performance tests ensures that the mechanical strength of containers is always sufficient to withstand the loads imposed during the filling, seaming and processing operations, and subsequently during palletisation, storage and distribution.

The application of external overpressure in a sealed chamber measures the resistance to panelling during processing, while internal pressure is used to examine the expansion characteristics of can bases and ends, and determine the maximum pressure permissible prior to permanent failure.

Compression test equipment measures the maximum axial load-supporting capability of the cans, and pendulum impact tests are used to check resistance to, and effect of, damage.

At the design stage, these tests are related to measured properties of the container and material, and allow prediction of the behaviour of novel, or lightweighted products. Further performance checks during production ensure process control and product consistency.

5.5.6 Secondary processes

The chapter so far has concentrated upon the primary processes involved in the manufacture of the can body or body cylinder and only passing reference has been made to the secondary processes such as coating/lacquering, flange formation, necking, beading, etc. The latter have significant impact upon can-making costs and represent an area where significant development continues that will affect the economics of the future.

5.5.6.1 Beading of food cans. Fundamentally the cost of a container and its axial strength are dictated by wall thickness. Panelling resistance can be improved substantially by introducing body beads into the side wall of the can and thus introducing increased 'hoop-strength'. Bead designs incorporate variation in the depth, contour, number and frequency. However the major factor influencing hoop-strength is bead depth.

5.5.6.2 Flange formation. Flange formation at each end of three-piece cylinders and on the open-end of two-piece can bodies is essential for the formation of the universal double-seam closure (see Figures 5.4 and 5.16). The flanging operation can be by a die process or by spinning; the latter is becoming increasingly the standard for the industry.

5.5.6.3 Necking. Originally all cans had straight walls whilst today diameter reduction to facilitate the use of smaller diameter and hence cheaper ends is commonplace for beverage cans. Parallel developments are taking place, notably in Europe, in food cans where the introduction of a stacking feature is seen as an additional benefit.

The necking operation can be carried out in a number of ways; by die-necking (single or multiple), by flow/roll-necking or most commonly by spinning in which case the flange can be produced at the same time. Spin-necking has the advantage over die-necking of using substantially lower forming loads and hence facilitating the use of thinner metal.

5.6 Coatings

A large proportion of food cans and ends have an internal and sometimes an external protective coating. In addition they may be externally decorated, in which case the external coating(s) may provide both a decorative and protective function.

5.6.1 General classification

Broadly speaking, surface coatings can be categorised as follows:

- Protective internal coatings: lacquers or sanitary enamels
- Pigmented external coatings: simple (white) coatings
- Clear external coatings: varnishes

These definitions are not absolutely watertight and for example, external varnishes for draw–redraw cans are often referred to as external lacquers and indeed the basic chemical compositions are very similar.

These various coatings, whether protective or decorative, are generally applied as liquids comprising, in the simplest terms, a solution or dispersion of one or more resins/polymers in a solvent which may be organic or a mixture of water and organic co-solvent. In practice the formulation may be quite complex and involve a blend of resins, several solvents, plasticisers, catalysts to promote curing and additivies to enhance flow and produce surface lubricity (waxes).

Such materials may be applied before or after fabrication of the container, dependent upon the method of manufacture, by roller coater or by spraying. More information about methods of application are given elsewhere.

Alternatively, surface coatings can be applied as powders, either thermoplastic or thermosetting, and subsequently fused onto the surface. As a means of reducing solvent effluents to the atmosphere, powders have advantages (being theoretically 100% solids) but their use has been limited by the high cost of manufacture and a rather high average particle size. Powder coatings are applied by spraying normally with an electrostatic assist.

For some very special end-uses, laminates, i.e. metal to which polymer films, such as polypropylene, have been adhesively bonded, are used. The use of this type of construction can be expected to increase in the future.

5.6.2 Protective internal coatings

Lacquer or (sanitary) enamel is the name given to those coatings which are normally applied internally to ensure compatibility between product and container. Broadly speaking lacquers can be regarded as being of two types, viz. oleoresinous and synthetic. The former are based upon natural products (fossil gums and drying oils) mixed with other resins. The latter are carefully synthesised products, which may additionally contain certain natural raw materials.

5.6.2.1 Oleoresinous products

These were amongst the earliest lacquers to be used in the canning industry and they are still in use, largely because of their low applied cost. Typical ingredients would include natural gums (rosin) and other resins with drying oils such as tung oil or linseed oil. In general terms they would not be regarded as high performance materials in that they lack process resistance and have poor colour characteristics. They are nevertheless suitable for a wide range of vegetable products such as green beans, butter beans when sulphur absorbing chemicals such as zinc oxide are incorporated in the formulation.

5.6.2.2 Synthetic products. Synthetic materials have replaced oleo-resinous types and there is now available a wide range of lacquers designed to give specific performance with different products and for use in different can-making processes. There are few comprehensive texts relating to modern container coatings, largely because of the confidential nature of the formulations. However, the reader's attention is drawn to two texts dealing with the basic chemistry of resins and modern coating types and methods of application. Some of the more common types and their uses are now described.

5.6.2.3 Epoxy lacquers. Epoxy resins, produced from the condensation reaction between epichlorohydrin and biphenol A (diphenylol propane), form the basis of a wide range of protective and decorative materials as well as adhesives (Scheme 5.1).

These materials are available in a range of viscosities and molecular weights and are used in conjunction with other synthetic resin materials of which the following are common examples:

- phenolic
- ester
- polyamide
- amino (urea or melamine).

5.6.2.3.1 Epoxy-phenolic. Traditionally regarded as the mainstay of the food can industry, epoxy-phenolic lacquers combine high degrees of

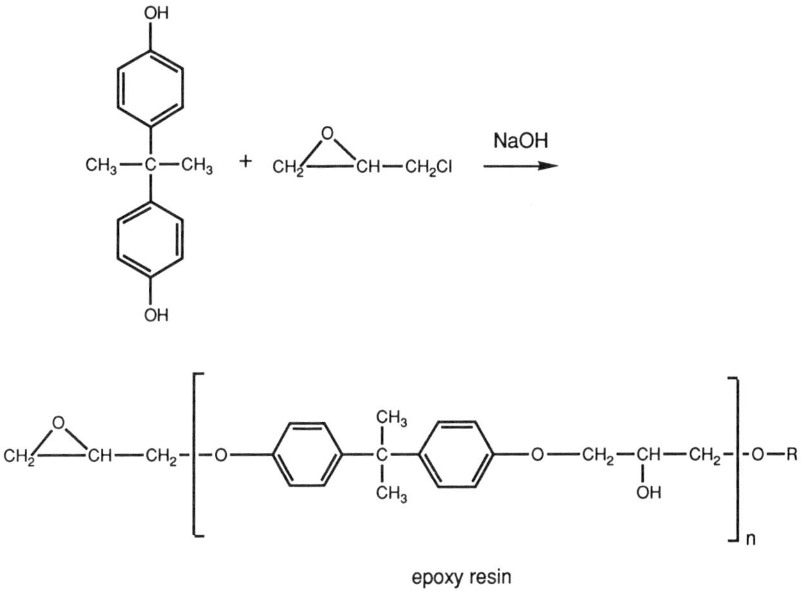

epoxy resin

Scheme 5.1

flexibility and adhesion with chemical resistance. The emphasis on flexibility or chemical resistance can be adjusted by the ratio of epoxy and phenolic content, the former giving flexibility and the latter chemical resistance.

Epoxy-phenolic lacquers, normally gold in appearance, are used for a wide range of acidic and non-acidic foods as well as for non-food products. They are sometimes used in a pigmented form (aluminium powder or zinc carbonate) to mask or absorb sulphide staining, they are also the base lacquer type for meat-release lacquers, in conjunction with waxes and aluminium pigmentation.

5.6.2.3.2 Epoxy-amino. Blending with animo resins, such as urea formaldehyde or melamine formaldehyde, produces coatings of high chemical resistance, which are nearly colourless (Scheme 5.2). Consequently they are used commonly for decorative purposes, where their lower stoving temperature is an additional advantage, and for internal protection of beverage cans.

Both resins are usually alkylated (commonly butylated) to varying degrees and cross-linking occurs with epoxy resin via methylol groups.

5.6.2.3.3 Epoxy ester. Epoxy resins esterified with certain fatty acids give rise to a family of lacquers and varnishes with excellent flexibility and

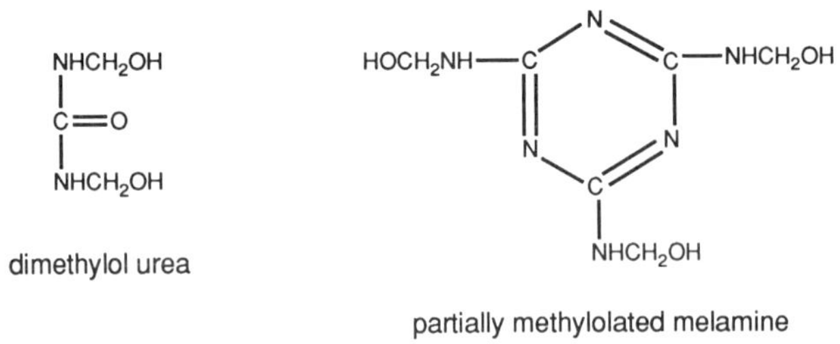

NHCH$_2$OH
|
C=O
|
NHCH$_2$OH

dimethylol urea

HOCH$_2$NH—C

C—NHCH$_2$OH

NHCH$_2$OH

partially methylolated melamine

Scheme 5.2

colour. Their main use is in external/decorative varnishes for printed (food) cans.

Epoxy polyamide. When used in conjunction with polyamides, epoxies give rise to rapid curing systems normally requiring two-pack formulation, i.e. mixing of the ingredients immediately prior to use.

Polyamide resins are formed by the reaction between an organic acid and an amine; the generic reaction is as in Scheme 5.3. A well-known and typical polyamide is nylon 6.6 produced from the reaction between adipic acid and hexamethylene diamine.

$$R\begin{array}{c}—COOH\\ \diagdown COOH\end{array} + R^1\begin{array}{c}—NH_2\\ \diagdown NH_2\end{array} \longrightarrow R\begin{array}{c}—COOH\\ \diagdown CONH \cdot R^1 —NH_2\end{array}$$

Scheme 5.3

In can coatings, however, polyamides with greater functionality/reactivity are used, e.g. to cross-link epoxy resins. In such cases polyamides formed for example from the condensation reaction between dilinoleic acid and diethylene triamine are used. The reactive amino group combines via the opening of the oxirane ring of the epoxy resin (Scheme 5.4).

$$CH_2—CH—CH_2 + H_2N—R \rightarrow —CH_2—CH—CH_2—NH—R$$
$$\overset{\displaystyle O}{\diagup \diagdown} \qquad\qquad\qquad\qquad\qquad | $$
$$\qquad\qquad\qquad\qquad\qquad\qquad\qquad OH$$

Scheme 5.4

5.6.2.3.5 Vinyl lacquers. There exists a family of vinyl-based lacquers ranging from low viscosity/low solids solution vinyls, to mid-range vinyl alkyds used in decorative coatings up to the higher solids dispersion organosols.

Solution vinyl lacquers are solutions of co-polymer resin; vinyl chloride and vinyl acetate, occasionally with the introduction of small percentages of maleic anhydride, in mixtures of ketonic and aromatic hydrocarbon solvents. Vinyl resins may also be blended with other resin groups such as epoxies, phenolics and alkyds.

The essential qualities of vinyl products are adhesion, high flexibility and a complete absence of taste, the latter makes them particularly suitable for beer and soft drink internal spray lacquers. Generally speaking they can be dried (or cured) at very low temperatures and indeed on tinplate it is essential to keep below around 180°C to avoid catalytic decomposition by available iron. Common uses include deep drawn caps, decorative finishes and dry food packs.

Solvent resistance is generally very poor, particularly in the case of air-drying/unmodified vinyls, which actually re-dissolve in their own solvents. Resistance to steam sterilisation is also fairly limited.

Of increasing use in the manufacture of drawn food cans and ends are organosols. Organosols are dispersions of high molecular weight polyvinyl chloride (PVC) resins in hydrocarbon solvents with the inclusion of a suitable plasticiser, e.g. dioctyl phthalate and resin additives. Commonly polyesters and acrylic resins are used as adhesive promoters to metal, and phenolic or amino resins are used to introduce some degree of cross-linking and hence chemical resistance. Being dispersions they can be produced at much higher solids (50–70%) at relatively low viscosities than is possible with solution vinyls (Scheme 5.5).

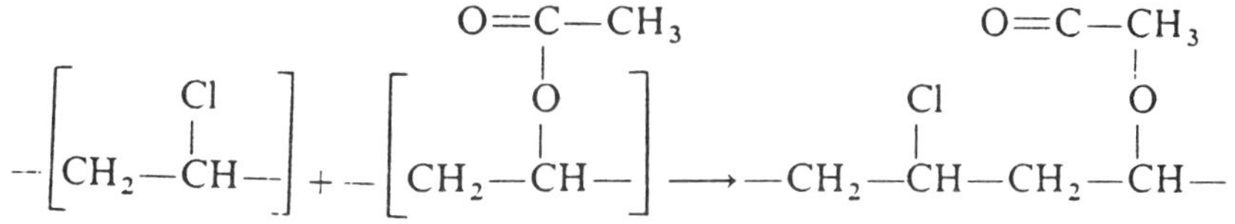

$$\left[\begin{array}{c} Cl \\ | \\ CH_2-CH- \end{array} \right] + \left[\begin{array}{c} O=C-CH_3 \\ | \\ O \\ | \\ CH_2-CH- \end{array} \right] \longrightarrow \begin{array}{c} Cl \\ | \\ -CH_2-CH-CH_2-CH- \end{array} \begin{array}{c} O=C-CH_3 \\ | \\ O \\ | \\ \end{array}$$

Polyvinyl chloride + polyvinyl acetate ⟶ Vinyl chloride–vinyl acetate co-polymer

Scheme 5.5

Organosols have all the desirable vinyl properties of absence of flavour, flexibility and adhesion but in addition they have better process resistance and hence can be more widely utilised. In the context of process food cans they have reasonable chemical resistance and resistance to sulphide staining but they are prone to absorb food colourants. They can be applied at low viscosity but with high solids either unpigmented or pigmented with aluminium.

Their drying performance is quite different from other lacquers and is a three-stage process. The first stage involves solvent evaporation, the second involves fusion of the PVC particles into a coherent film and finally a cross-linking reaction occurs.

The third common category of vinyl lacquers/coatings are the vinyl alkyds (see below), which are used principally for deep drawn white coatings and as a size-coat to promote adhesion between other coatings and the metal substrate. The drying of these materials reflects their chemical composition in that they dry partly by solvent evaporation and partly by oxidation/heat polymerisation.

5.6.2.3.6 Phenolic lacquers. Phenolic lacquers were one of the earliest types of material to be synthesised by the reaction of phenol with formaldehyde (Scheme 5.6). The reaction under alkaline conditions with excess formaldehyde results in *ortho-* and *para*-substitution into the aromatic ring of the phenolic. Subsequent heating allows polymerisation to occur via a series of methylene bridges and via ether links. Such materials found wide usage because of their extremely good chemical resistance and resistance to sulphide staining. However their use requires very careful control of the thin films applied and of the stoving temperatures 190–195°C. Under stoving limits chemical resistance whilst excessive stoving increases the brittleness of the film. Poor flexibility characteristic of phenolic lacquers limits their use to three-piece bodies and ends.

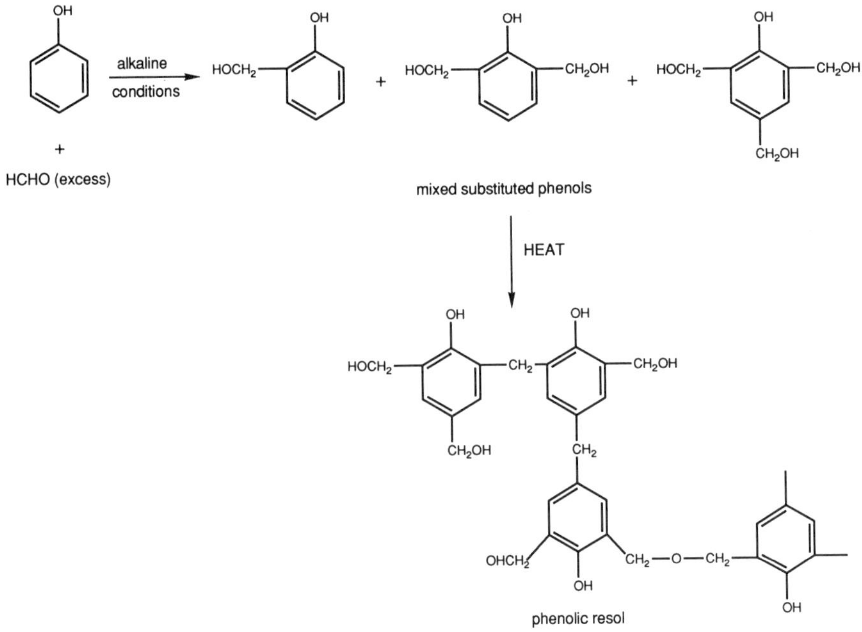

Scheme 5.6

5.6.2.3.7 Acrylic lacquers and coatings. The most common usage of acrylics is the manufacture of pigmented and clear decorative coatings where high temperature resistance and/or resistance to steam sterilisation is required. A typical example would be decorated solid meat packs where high stoving of the meat-release lacquer (applied last) to effect maximum lubricity is required. More recently internal white lacquers have been formulated as alternatives to white vinyls, which have relatively poor heat resistance.

5.6.2.3.8 Alkyds and polyesters. Alkyds formed by the esterification reaction between glycerols, such as glycerol and pentaerithrytol, and phthalic anhydride are suitable only for external decorative coatings and inks because of the taste characteristics introduced by the oil content. Alkyds are readily modifiable with other resins such as vinyls to give a range of products with very wide properties in terms of adhesion, gloss and flexibility.

Closely related and finding increasing usage are other types of polyesters which are oil-free and based upon, e.g. isophthalic acid; they are used singly or in combination with other resin types such as phenolics. Pigmented polyesters with good colour retention on stoving are used for drawable white lacquers and varnishes, whilst in combination with phenolic materials they are sold as cheaper alternatives to epoxy-phenolic lacquers.

5.7 Functions of can lacquers/enamels

Container coatings provide a number of important basic functions:

- Protect the metal from the contents
- Avoid contamination of the product by metal ions from the packages
- Facilitate manufacture
- Provide a basis for decoration
- Barrier to external corrosion/abrasion

5.7.1 Internal corrosion protection

The reaction between containers and contents manifests itself in a variety of ways

- Dissolution with evolution of hydrogen, solution of metal ions and in extreme cases perforation of the container (normally associated with acidic products)
- Conversion of the metal surface by ingredients of the product, typically the formation of iron and tin sulphides resulting from the

interaction of the metal surface and sulphur compounds deriving from the degradation of protein during the high temperature/pressure cooking process.

The above broad generalisations can be further subdivided to describe the types of interaction between product and container, as follows:

- Tin sulphide staining
- Iron sulphide staining
- Selective and severe tin dissolution
- Acid attack leading to hydrogen evolution, high metal content and ultimately perforation
- Staining by natural and artificial colourants
- Beneficial tin dissolution

The corrosion mechanisms of the above are dealt with elsewhere and here we will concern ourselves only with product and lacquer selection aspects with respect to different containers and components.

Always there is a need to strike the correct compromise of price, performance, container specification (beaded/unbeaded) and product. In the case of tinplate cans, the tincoating level is also an important consideration. Table 5.6 summarises some typical product/lacquer combinations for three-piece welded cans.

5.7.2 Protection of the product

Internal corrosion and product contamination are in many cases complementary processes. In the latter case, product contamination does not

Table 5.6 Some examples[a] of three-piece welded tinplate can body specifications for a variety of food products

Lacquer specification	Tincoating	Products
None (plain tinplate)	High ($\sim$11.2 g)	White fruits: grapefruit, pears, peaches and pineapple Vegetables: asparagus, tomatoes, artichokes
Single-coat epoxy-phenolic or phenolic	Low ($\sim$2.8 g)	Meats: chicken, fish, duck Vegetables: green beans, peas, spinach
Two coats: oleoresins plus phenolic	High (11.2 g)	Gherkins, concentrated grapefruit juice, strawberries, red plums, damsons, beetroot in vinegar
Epoxy with meat-release additive (wax)	Low-medium (5.6 g)	Solid meat packs: ham, tongue, luncheon meat

[a]These are examples of general specifications in commercial use and serve to demonstrate differences in pack requirements. Other specifications are used which may vary in detail from the examples chosen here.

always result in a deterioration of the nutritional qualities but frequently the organoleptic qualities are affected.

Thus, for example, dissolution of iron by beer or soft drinks affects the flavour at quite low levels and consequently packers specify very low levels of iron and aluminium in beverage cans. With few notable exceptions (e.g. lemonade), tin pick-up is not a problem in carbonated drinks.

Generally speaking food products, as opposed to beverages, are more tolerant of metal pick-up levels and only in the case of tin is there a recommended guideline level of 250 ppm. Some food packers set levels of their own, e.g. for iron, although in practice for acidic products in particular, high levels of iron dissolution could inevitably result in unacceptable levels of hydrogen evolution and 'hydrogen swells'.

Other metals of concern are lead (note: British Standard BS3252 (1960) dictates <0.08 w/w lead in electrolytic tin coatings), where in most cases lead is limited to 0.2 ppm, chromium and copper. In all cases the can maker/canner would be looking to achieve levels between 'none-detectable' and subparts per million (Jowitt, 1986).

The reader is directed to alternative literature for further specialist information on the subject of metals in food and beverage packaging.

Examples of requested levels (i.e. customer expectations) for metals in carbonated drinks currently are for iron 0.3 ppm and 1 ppm after 6 months storage for beer and soft drinks, respectively, and for aluminium 2 ppm.

Some special and extreme interactions between tin and product exist. In the case of white fruits, relatively high levels of tin dissolution are required (i.e. 'free tin') to maintain colour and taste. Other products such as asparagus, beans and pasta products in tomato sauce also have this requirement although this is very much a matter of taste. Products packed in plain cans in the UK are packed in lacquered cans in other countries.

5.7.3 Facilitating manufacture

Most metal-forming processes require some form of lubrication. In the case of wall-ironing, it is provided in the 'bodymaker' by oil–water emulsions and in the case of tinplate containers, the surface tin facilitating the ironing process.

Other metals such as tin-free steel cannot be worked economically either with or without lubricant because the surface of such material is so hard and abrasive. The manufacture of draw–redraw cans and food can ends from TFS necessitates the use of prelacquered steel or coil. Very flexible vinyl materials are commonly used for DRD can manufacture and these lacquers incorporate internal lubricants (e.g. waxes).

5.7.3.1 Drawn containers. In the simplest terms, DRD cans cannot be made from uncoated TFS and such containers are normally not an economic proposition when made from tinplate (or aluminium?). Such containers (DRD/TFS) are made from either precoated coil or precoated sheet in order to protect the expensive tooling and can handling systems from the abrasive wear by the chromium oxide layer on the plate.

Two other properties are required by the coated plate:

• Flexibility/lubrication
• Product compatibility

High flexibility normally is associated with loosely cross-linked/high molecular weight materials such as vinyl organosols and certain polyesters. However, these are not necessarily the first choice for chemical resistance where the selection would be epoxy-phenolic and phenolic lacquers. By and large the surface coating manufacturers have responded with good compromises and this, in combination with high film weights, provides one solution for most products. Some products cannot, however, be satisfactorily packed in as-made containers and a secondary 'repair' spray lacquer is applied. Such products would include highly acidic packs.

Lubrication is also an important factor. In addition to flexibility, the lacquer is normally internally lubricated by the addition of waxes, such as polyethylene and paraffin types, which migrate to the surface when the lacquer is stoved.

The final consideration is method of application. Two methods are possible, coil coating and sheet-fed coating. The former offers the advantage of facilitating coil feeding of the presses used to make cans as well as producing a smoother film, by reverse roller coating, which is beneficial to the metal-forming operation. Coil-coated steel can of course be cut to sheet for sheet-fed press operations.

The inference of this is that viscosity control is extremely important to ensure good smooth application of the plate. The availability of coil-coated plate is a matter of concern since, whilst fairly widely available in the UK, there is relatively little capacity for can coatings in Europe and other territories. This is expected to change in the future.

5.7.3.2 Ends.   The arguments concerning tooling design also apply to the manufacture of ends from TFS. However, the metal-forming operations are less severe and this permits the use of a wider range of coatings; this range would include organosols applied at lower film weights than for DRD.

There tends to be a wider range of specifications for ends than for DRD cans and today the bulk of ends are manufactured from sheet-coated TFS or tinplate. Broadly, however, the following rule applied. For acid products, organosols are preferred at the expense of some lack of resistance to natural colour staining, for example from tomatoes and other 'red' fruits. For non-acid products lower film weights of epoxy-phenolic or polyester phenolic or even oleoresinous lacquers are used. In the future we can expect to see lacquer rationalisation perhaps accompanied by the availability of coil-coated TFS.

5.7.4 Base for decoration

Coatings, usually pigmented with titanium oxide or other pigments and applied in thick films >10 μm, are used to provide the background for printed decoration. These materials frequently need to be formulated to allow subsequent forming operations.

5.7.5 External corrosion and abrasion resistance

Both tinplate and other steel-based products visibly rust. Aluminium containers discolour and are highly prone to acid attack as in the case of secondary corrosion in the soft-drink can, notably in hot climates. External protective coatings (varnishes) are applied as a means of providing abrasion resistance and as a barrier to external corrosion.

The above categories are not sharply defined and frequently a material may be required to perform more than one function. Unless very considerable cost penalties are to be borne, the formulation of a coating performing more than one function is invariably a compromise. Typical examples include the highly flexible vinyl organosols used for deep (DRD) containers which have limited stain resistance to, e.g. sulphide or natural colours. A second example is the formulation of a whole family of epoxy-phenolic lacquers where the percentage of phenolic ingredient (which has high chemical resistance but limited flexibility) is varied to suit the needs of flexibility from the epoxy ingredient and chemical resistance of the phenolic.

5.8 Methods of lacquer application

Three basic coating processes are in common use:

- Sheet coating by roller coater
- Coil coating by reverse roller coater
- Spraying

Further information on the various processes can be obtained elsewhere (Anon., 1900; Anon., 1900) but particular advantages and uses of each method are outlined below.

5.8.1 Roller coating in sheet form

This process is essential for sheet coating of tinplate for welding cans since the process allows for stencilling, i.e. the provision of plain margins (see

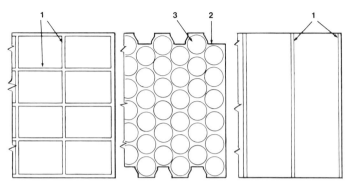

Figure 5.18 Various sheet lacquering lay-outs (stencil lacquering). (1) Unlacquered margins/
areas; (2) scrolling to optimise metal utilisation; (3) spot lacquer for ends or DRD disks.

Figure 5.18) which permits resistance welding of the side seam. Plate for
sheet-fed DRD lines is also prepared in this way.

5.8.2 Coil coating

This process can only be justified for applications where very large volumes
of material of essentially the same specification are required. Capital cost is
high, as is the cost of stoppages to effect either substrate or coating
changes.

Typical applications are TFS for DRD cans in the US although its use for
food can ends is anticipated. In addition to cost considerations, lacquering
in the coil permits the use of reverse roller coating which produces a more
uniform film ideal for drawn can manufacture. Stencilling necessary for
welding cannot be achieved in the coil process.

5.8.3 Spraying

Spraying is used for made-up containers (DWI) and as one means of
applying side-stripe protection on welded cans. Wider descriptions of the
processes are available in other texts where printing and decorating are
also covered. Mention in this chapter is made primarily to indicate the type
of processes used and how their availability and the materials to support
them can affect the choice of can-making route.

Broadly speaking the following rules apply:

- Welding: requires availability of, or access to, sheet-coated (stencilled)
  tinplate sheets
- DWI: requires the skills and materials necessary to operate spraying
  machines

- DRD: requires either sheet roller-coated plate (all-over lacquer for TFS or spot lacquer for tinplate), or
- coil-coated coils or sheets from coil-coating operations.

In a green-field site, the need to purchase sheet lacquering equipment as well as can-making equipment may influence the choice between DRD and DWI.

5.8.4 Electrocoating

Electrophoretic deposition of protective coating films has been well established in the automotive industry for many years. More recently it has been developed as an alternative for applying protective films to finished can bodies, such as DWI and DRD cans made in tinplate or aluminium. No machines are known to be in commercial production but the position can be expected to change. The advantages of the process are seen to be

- Lower materials usage; thinner, more uniform lacquer films
- Lower solvent emissions to the atmosphere
- Higher standards of process monitoring and quality control

Details of the process, the equipment and materials necessary are given elsewhere.

5.9 Container corrosion: theory and practice

Both the internal and external corrosion of heat processed food containers are of concern to the can-maker, the packer and the ultimate consumer.

5.9.1 External corrosion

In the case of tinplate, which is the dominant material used for heat processed containers, external corrosion results in either the formation of rust or localised staining and detinning associated with contact with aggressive alkaline compounds. These effects can be minimised by good control in the packer's plant and in distribution, e.g. over-cooling of cans after processing can initiate external rusting. Excessive use of chlorine in cooling water can also cause the corrosion of tinplate. These together with the prevention of boiler-water 'carry-over' should be avoided in cannery practice. The over-wrapping and storage of processed cans are also areas where good canning practice needs to be implemented if external corrosion is to be prevented.

Bright or labelled cans should never be stored 'wet' or warehoused where temperature and humidity can fluctuate to such an extent as to allow the cans to 'sweat'. In areas of high humidity, this phenomenon can occur when temperature differences of 7°C occur between the temperature of the cans and the surrounding atmosphere. Where shrink-wrapping is employed, external rusting is minimised when cans have been packed dry.

Aluminium is, by and large, less problematical in terms of external corrosion in that its use is restricted mainly to shallow-drawn containers for food and pâté. External corrosion in the case of processed food containers manifests itself principally as staining.

5.9.2 Internal corrosion

Both steel and aluminium present specific difficulties in terms of internal corrosion. Thus, with the notable exceptions of products requiring 'available tin' for organoleptic reasons, most cans are internally lacquered to limit the interaction between container and contents. For products requiring tin, only the welded tinplate is an option as, by and large, unlacquered DWI tinplate cans do not give satisfactory pack performance.

Internal corrosion and the mechanism by which it proceeds varies with the nature of the product and the type of can. Dissolution of the component metals of the container results as corrosion progresses. The consequence is that the container may either swell or perforate resulting in commercial spoilage. In addition to this type of corrosion, other forms of attack occur resulting in either staining of the container or the product or changes in the colour and flavour of the product. The most common in this category is the formation of iron and tin sulphide.

When reviewing internal corrosion there are two significant aspects to be considered. The first is the effect of internal corrosion on the commercial acceptance and marketability of products and secondly, and more importantly, is its effect upon public health.

We consider first the case of plain tinplate containers which have been traditionally used for a number of acid and non-acid products. In these cases, the internal corrosion which has occurred has been considered of benefit to the palatability and visual acceptance of the product. When these products are packed into plain cans the residual oxygen in the can, derived from the atmosphere or the product, either trapped in its tissues or absorbed on its surface, or both, acts as a depolariser. Dissolution of tin occurs without hydrogen formation. The oxygen is rapidly used up in the can when the next stage in the corrosion process occurs. Here other inorganic or organic depolarisers become involved when the tin continues to dissolve. Hydrogen is usually evolved only when considerable detinning has occurred exposing appreciable amounts of steel.

The reaction is then an electromechanical one with the tin affording anodic protection to the steel (see section 5.9.3). The rate at which the reaction occurs is dependent upon the composition of the steel, the residual oxygen content of the can when closed, the presence of other depolarisers or corrosion accelerators, e.g. anthocyanin pigments and nitrates, and the temperature of storage. The storage temperature has a considerable effect on corrosion and generally it is recognised that the rate of corrosion almost doubles with an increase of 10°C.

While the acid content of a canned food has a definite effect on its corrosivity, its effect is seldom directly proportional to its concentration as measured by titration or pH value. A product's tendency to promote or inhibit corrosion depends more on the nature of the types of acid present.

Certain trace metals can also influence the type and rate of corrosion. 'Excess' copper is an example; its presence may cause swells in plain cans and perforation in lacquered cans. When present in sufficient amounts in acid products, the corrosion is normally accompanied by the 'plating out' of the copper onto the metal surface of the container. Corrosion involving plating out normally occurs when the copper levels are at about 4–5 ppm. However, in products such as canned apple juice and soft drinks, corrosion has occurred where levels as low as 0.5–2 ppm of copper have been present.

Nitrates, which are natural constituents of many foods, have been known to greatly accelerate corrosion in acid products packed in tinplate containers. Below pH 5.4 nitrates act as de-polarisers. However under certain conditions the corrosive nature of nitrates is influenced by the presence of other depolarising substances such that their corrosivity can be greatly increased or decreased. As a consequence it is very hard to predict the corrosive action that may result merely by observing the nitrate content of the product. Equally, because the nitrates are broken down into other products during corrosion, the amount of nitrates in a product, after corrosion has occurred, will not indicate the original nitrate content of the product. However, it is good manufacturing practice to get as low a figure as possible and especially in the case of acid products to pack at initial levels of less than 8 mg/litre measured as nitrate nitrogen.

There are also toxicological consequences of nitrates in water supplies. Methaemoglobinaemia, the conversion of blood haemoglobin to methaemoglobin, results in the loss of the transportation of oxygen to the body tissues. The conversion process can be affected by the presence of nitrate, which may in turn derive from nitrate arising in food or water. Infants are particularly susceptible to methaemoglobinaemia which could result in cyanosis and death. For this reason the WHO has recommended a limit of 45 mg/litre measured as nitrate ion in water supplies (equivalent to 11 mg/litre as nitrate nitrogen).

Although the result of corrosion detracts from the internal appearance of the plain container, the corrosion has in part been considered beneficial to the flavour and colour of certain products. Dissolution of tin in the container produces a reducing effect which protects against oxidative taints and also imparts the characteristic 'bite' to products such as citrus juices, white fruits and subacid products, e.g. beans in tomato sauce. It is considered that only when the tin concentration reaches several hundred parts per million can metallic tin actually be tasted. The presence of dissolved iron in the product is indicated at smaller quantities, e.g. 50–60 ppm, indicating that corrosion is far advanced.

The colour of the product is also favoured by the reducing action of the tin and in addition to the products already mentioned, some vegetable packs, e.g. mushrooms, asparagus, potatoes and carrots have also been traditionally packed in plain containers.

In those products which contain anthocyanin pigments, however (e.g. 'coloured' fruits), the reducing action of the tin has an unfavourable effect and the colour changes produced by the reduction of the pigments would result in a commercially unacceptable product. This effect is overcome by the use of lacquered containers for this range of products.

Aesthetically undesirable corrosion effects occur frequently, resulting from reactions with tin and iron; these are classified under the heading of sulphiding. Thermal degradation of certain organic sulphur compounds in foods can result in the formation of stannous and ferrous sulphides where these metals are exposed. In the case of stannous sulphide, the result is a fixed blue–black discoloration of the tinplate. In the case of ferrous sulphide the result is the formation of a black loose deposit usually associated with the headspace and in those products where the pH is above 6.0. To protect tinplate against sulphiding, special lacquers which afford good coverage and sulphur absorbent properties, such as the inclusion of zinc oxide or zinc carbonate, are used.

In the case of acid products, the presence of sulphur dioxide and sulphur can also present serious corrosion problems. They are reduced to hydrogen sulphide at tin and iron, producing severe odour and flavour problems in canned soft drinks and wines. By acting as depolarisers they can also enhance the rate of metal dissolution and sulphur dioxide has been the cause of rapid detinning problems in plain cans. Very small quantities, as little as 2 mg/litre, have been known to greatly reduce the shelf-life of tinplate containers.

Where lacquered containers are used, small areas of tin and iron may be exposed at pores or scratches in the lacquer. The beneficial action of sacrificial detinning is rapidly lost and the iron is soon able to corrode freely. Failure of this container for acid products is generally associated with the time taken for the onset of hydrogen swell formation, the continuing corrosion process then resulting in can body perforation. The commercial significance of this therefore is to produce containers with the minimum of metal exposure by providing good lacquer coverage. As previously mentioned, those products which are discoloured by contact with tin have of necessity to be packed into fully lacquered containers.

It is important to note that whilst aesthetically undesirable, the effects of corrosion resulting in either colour or flavour changes in the product or producing a visual defect in the container, do not significantly affect public health.

Where container corrosion is implicated in its effect on public health, this is more often than not associated with the dissolution of trace metals, and tin and lead in particular. At present, the recommended limit for tin in foodstuffs is 250 ppm. For most canned foods the lead limit is 2 ppm (reducing down to 1.0 ppm) but for baby foods it is 0.5 ppm and soft drinks 0.2 ppm (in the UK only). In practice, the move from soldering to welding ensured that levels of lead above 0.2 ppm will not result from the interaction between container and product.

In the case of tin, it is internally plain containers which obviously come under scrutiny where tin dissolution progresses with storage time. The rate of pick-up is relatively high initially, with a gradual tailing-off on storage. Considering the volume of cans produced there is little evidence of illness arising directly from the ingestion of canned foodstuffs containing high concentrations of dissolved tin. Very high levels are needed to be present in the product before a definite metallic taste is detected. It is likely that the product would be rejected prior to consumption from either the colour or odour of the product or the visual appearance of the container. However, it is believed that where illness has been caused it has resulted in vomiting probably produced by irritation of the mucous membranes of the gut by the tin. High levels of tin have been associated with high nitrate levels in the water used in the production of the canned products.

Should legislation change with regard to the reduction of the limit of tin concentrations permissible in canned foodstuffs then there are two possibilities which might arise. The first would be a drastic reduction in the shelf-life of many products at present packed in plain containers. The second, and probably the more likely result, would be the increased use of fully lacquered containers. This would result in slight but probably not commercially unacceptable changes in the colour and flavour of some products and would of course alter the basic corrosion mechanism in the container. The use of tin bearing lacquer systems to provide controlled amounts of tin going into solution, in an attempt to provide the desirable colour and flavour changes in the product, has been resisted.

When soldered cans were the norm, the use of fully lacquered containers played an important role in limiting the amount of lead pick-up in the container. Whilst soldered food cans are still manufactured, their number is reducing and by the year 2000 all are likely to be welded or of a two-piece construction. Thus lead pick-up is not discussed further.

5.9.3 Theory

When considering the corrosive interaction between a metal container and its contents, it is important to realise that we are considering electrochemical reactions involving electrodes (container and lid/closure) and electrolytes (products). The precise reaction that occurs will be influenced by numerous factors, including the number and type of metals present, the type of product and the presence or absence of air within the pack. There are, however, some general rules which apply universally.

5.9.3.1 Rules governing corrosion in metal cans.   (1) Anodes are areas of the can which dissolve or oxidise, i.e. electrons are lost. Similarly cathodes are the areas where reduction reactions occur, i.e. electrons are gained. Thus the reaction will involve the flow of ions in the product and electrons in the metal of the container. At any moment in time, the anodic current is equal to the cathodic current, the significance of this statement is further explained in the context of 'pitting' corrosion.

The reader must also recognise that the surface of the metal container, e.g. one made from tinplate, is not a simple one and on micro-scale it will contain areas of tin and of exposed iron and other metals. Whilst the anodic dissolution of metal, for example, is obvious, the cathodic counter-reaction is often less obvious.

(2) The reactions occurring at anodes and cathodes will in effect also obey Faraday's Law. The weights of various metals which dissolve are related to current which flows and the electromechanical equivalent of the metal incurred. Thus if we consider a detinning reaction (tin being in this situation anodic), then if the amount of tin dissolved is known, the total current flow (coulombs) can be determined as can the amount of oxygen reduced at the cathode.

$$Sn \rightarrow Sn^{2+} + 2e^-, \text{anodic reaction}$$

$$\left\{ \begin{array}{c} \cdot 2H^+ + 2e^- \rightarrow H_2 \\ 2H^+ + \tfrac{1}{2}O_2 + 2e^- \rightarrow H_2O \end{array} \right\} \quad \text{cathodic reactions}$$

5.9.3.2 Pitting corrosion.   'Pitting' or localised corrosion, which in the extreme may lead to perforation, is localised electrochemical attack where the balanced electrode currents are related to very unbalanced areas of anode and cathode. A good example would be an unlacquered tinplate container with a lacquered aluminium end with a product pack which renders the aluminium end anodic. We have a situation where the unlacquered tinplate surface of the can body is large and cathodic and the imperfections in lacquering of the aluminium end render very small surface

areas of the end anodic. Since the anodic and cathodic currents are balanced and equal, it follows that the cathodic current density on the tinplate is very low and the anodic current density on the exposed aluminium very high. Hence solution of the aluminium will occur locally at a very high rate leading to 'pitting' and ultimately, perforation.

5.9.3.3 Cathodic reactions. Whilst the results of anodic reactions are fairly obvious, e.g. metal dissolution with hydrogen evolution or sulphide staining, those of cathodic reactions are less obvious and sometimes ignored. However, a thorough understanding of these cathodic reactions will lead to an increasing understanding of the factors controlling shelf-life and minimising can corrosion. Anodic corrosion can be cathodically controlled.

Common cathodic reactions include the reduction of oxygen and nitrate, reduction of sulphurous compounds (sulphur dioxide, sulphur and sulphur-containing proteins in e.g. meat, fish and some (leguminous) vegetables). The latter group gives rise to the characteristic black sulphide staining with tinplate containers.

Limitation of the corrosive anodic reactions and hence long shelf-life are promoted by packing conditions that limit the availability of cathodic reactions.

5.9.3.4 Choice of container materials and their effect on corrosion. Tinplate remains the dominant material from which food cans and ends are made although the use of tin-free steel for fixed (non-easy open ends) and draw–redraw bodies is increasing. A second trend is that the levels of tincoating are reducing, to be compensated for by progressively more effective protective lacquer systems. Thus whilst tin weights exceeding 10 gsm were once commonplace, today tin weights as low as 1–2.5 gsm are used, the limit being frequently dictated by the ease of resistance welding rather than electrochemical performance. The use of higher tincoatings is retained for unlacquered containers where tin dissolution is required for organoleptic reasons or for very acidic products such as red plums, beetroot and gherkins in vinegar and concentrated grapefruit juice.

5.9.3.5 Tinplate containers. In general terms, acidic products are more corrosive to tinplate than non-acidic ones although no strict relationship exists between pH and rate of corrosion. Acidic detinning (tin dissolution) has been studied in depth and whilst the number of publications is great and their review outside the scope of this publication, it can be concluded that the basic rules of corrosion (described above) apply. Since acidic fruits represent a high proportion of the world's packaged foods, an explanation of the suitability of plain tinplate containers is relevant and serves to further explain the corrosion mechanism.

Stage 1: On packing the temperature is high and oxygen in the pack is rapidly reduced and rapid detinning also occurs.

$$Sn \rightarrow Sn^{2+} + 2e^-, anode$$
$$O_2 + 2H_2 + 4e^- \rightarrow 4OH^-, \qquad cathode$$
$$H^+ + e^- \rightarrow [H], \qquad hydrogen\ absorption\ by\ the\ steel$$

Stage 2: After a few weeks much of the oxygen will have been consumed and less 'vigorous' cathodic reactions occur, e.g. reduction of natural or synthetic dye-stuffs in the product or traces of nitrate. This results in lower cathodic 'driving current' and hence more controlled detinning.

Stage 3: Progressively further reduction reactions will begin to cease leaving only the small cathodic reaction concerning the generation of atomic hydrogen. The latter will occur slowly and further detinning will be limited by the rate of hydrogen absorption by the steel.

It is this sequence of events which renders the plain tinplate container suitable for many acid products. If, however, the tincoating weight is too low to afford adequate protection for the underlying steel and/or there is an excess of oxygen, then corrosive failure can occur even after Stages 1 and 2 have been reached. These failures are the result of iron dissolution and hydrogen evolution, the latter giving rise to hydrogen swells.

$$Fe \rightarrow Fe^{2+} + 2e^- at\ the\ anode$$
$$2H^+ + 2e^- \rightarrow H_2 \qquad at\ the\ cathode$$

Anodic dissolution ultimately may give rise to perforation and the ingress of oxygen which greatly affects the rate of corrosion. Leaking product will then attack other containers externally until catastrophic/cascade corrosion of stored packs occurs.

5.9.3.6 Corrosion limiting packs. As a general rule, packages presenting large areas of anode and small areas of cathode do not rapidly corrode because there is little cathodic reaction/current to drive the corrosion reactions. In some case the anodic reaction is limited by the nature of the corrosion product. A typical example of the latter is the formation of tin sulphides in meat and fish packs where the insoluble deposit of tin sulphide limits further attack at the corrosion site. Similar situations occur with iron sulphide.

5.9.3.7 TFS. Tinplate cans and ends are generally regarded as 'safe-systems' as far as most food products are concerned. The replacement of the tinplate end by a lacquered TFS end generally produces no problems provided the lacquer system has adequate integrity. TFS cannot be used in an unlacquered condition because of its lack of resistance to corrosion and because its hard surface produces unacceptably high tool wear.

5.9.3.8 Aluminium.   In some countries, food such as fish in oil and pâté, are packed in all aluminium containers with extremely satisfactory results. By and large, products containing brine are to be avoided as such products have produced rapid and dramatic corrosion of containers. This corrosion has exhibited itself in the form of container and/or end perforation in many cases within 24 h.

Corrosion has also led to the bleaching of red coloured fruits, e.g. fruit salad and fruit cocktail packs, as a result of traces of aluminium, exposed via imperfections of the lacquer coating, dissolving in the product.

5.9.3.9 Testing for corrosion performance.   Clearly when we come to pack the product in a particular container specification we expect a long shelf-life. A thorough understanding of the mechanisms by which corrosion occurs is valuable in producing suitable container specifications and removes the risk of unexpected failure with new products.

Container and lacquer specification are tested exhaustively. Most researchers would agree that there is no substitute for packing actual products for realistic periods of time but storage at elevated temperatures is a reliable guide and provides a good indication of the likelihood of success or failure. Chemical reactions (ionic) occur more rapidly at elevated temperatures but specifically cathodic reactions involving diffusion occur significantly more rapidly.

Constantly the researcher seeks improved and instrumented means of predicting pack performance and of understanding the complex reaction which can occur between container and contents. Methods for studying container corrosion include:

- Optical and electron microscopy supplemented by X-ray analysis
- Atomic absorption spectroscopy for (trace) dissolved metal analysis
- X-ray diffraction for plate and corrosion product identification
- Auger electron, X-ray photo-electron and infrared spectroscopy can be particularly helpful in the study of pitting corrosion and general surface analysis
- Various electrochemical techniques such as ac impedance for predicting the protective qualities of lacquer systems in various substrates.

5.10 Recycling

Technical, economic and political factors influence the extent to which materials can be or are recycled. The political factors relating to materials and energy conservation, whilst important, are considered outside the scope of this text.

5.10.1 Technical factors

In the case of aluminium and steel (in its various forms) as used in the can-making industry, there is little doubt that both metals can be recycled from a technical standpoint. Each can be collected and remelted to provide a reusable product.

The sources of scrap are essentially two-fold:

- In-plant can and end making scrap in the form of clean or at worse lacquered skeletal waste resulting from stamping of discs (DWI or DRD bodies and from end manufacture)
- Recovery from the used container stream (domestic waste and collection schemes)

The situation for steel is different from that for aluminium; the latter can be simply remelted and, with minor addition, re-used for can-making. In the case of steel, the presence of tin and the aluminium, for example from easy open ends associated with steel beverage cans, necessitate certain modifications to the recycling process. Tin *per se* is not a problem in that it can be removed, normally by solution in caustic soda, or diluted with other sources of tin-free scrap. Aluminium is certainly a problem if tin recovery is contemplated in that it reacts violently with caustic solutions. Steel- and aluminium-based scrap can be readily separated magnetically and the normal arrangement is to pulverise the scrap prior to separation.

5.10.2 Economics

A significant factor in the economics of recycling is the market value of the metal since the price per ton provides a motive for recovery. On a tonnage basis, aluminium is more valuable whilst the higher density of steel presents advantages in terms of the volume of material to be transported. Further advantage to steel can recycling occurs when the market price for tin is high, unfortunately this market price fluctuates.

Pressures for the conservation of materials and energy sources and for the reduction of land-fill sites, will provide a further driving force for recycling. Recycling schemes for both steel and aluminium are well established in various parts of the world. In 1988, 30% of all tinplate sold in Europe was recovered and recycled; this equates to some 10 billion cans. In the US and Australia around 50–60% of all aluminium beverage cans are recycled.

Bibliography

Bodsworth, C. and Bell, H.B. (1972) *Physical Chemistry of Iron and Steel Manufacture.* Longmans, London, UK.

McGannon, H.E. (ed.) *Making, Shaping and Treating of Steel.* United States Steel Corporation.

Hoare, W.E., Hedges, E.S. and Barry, B.T. (1965) *The Technology of Tinplate.* Edward Arnold, London, UK.

Proceedings of the 1st International Tinplate Conference, London, UK.

US Patent No. 155272, US Steel Corporation and European Patent No. EP 0–043–182.

Nippon Steel D.A.P. Blackplate.

Printing Ink Manual, W. Heffer, Cambridge.

Pilley, K.P. (1977) *Lacquers, Varnishes and Coatings for Food Cans and for the Metal Decorating Industry.* Arthur Holden Inks Ltd. (now ICI Coatings).

Metal Decorating from Start to Finishes. NMDA, USA.

Food Additives and Contaminants Committee Report on the Review of Metals in Canned Foods (FAC/REP/38), HMSO, London, UK.

Jowitt, F.W. (1986) *SME Conference*, Chicago, IL, USA.

6 Filling operations

A.S. LEWIS, R. HEROUX, F. NOLTE and
P. ROBINSON

6.1 Introduction

Can filling is a critical part of the canning operation.

The majority of meat and fish products are machine filled, but hand filling is still common in countries where labour costs are low, particularly for high value or fragile products or where there are particular requirements of presentation.

In general, products will consist of two components – a solid and liquid component – but some meat and fish products are filled as a paste or slurry, and salmon is filled as a 'cylinder' of raw fish to which only salt is added.

Careful control of any filling operation is essential to ensure the following:

(1) Optimum presentation to the consumer.
(2) A consistent product weight, to ensure compliance with statutory regulations and to improve the effectiveness of any subsequent screening (dud detection operation).
(3) The maintenance of a uniform headspace. Inadequate headspace may result in underprocessing where rotary retorts are in use, or in 'flippers'. Excessive headspace may accelerate product deterioration and/or can corrosion during storage, or result in oxidative discoloration (scorch) of exposed solids in the headspace during thermal processing.
(4) The avoidance of flange contamination that may act as a potential source of seam interference which could result in product droops.

Where there are two components – a solid and a liquid component – or multiple components, the operation is more complex.

Each component of the fill must be effectively controlled to ensure uniformity of composition. Besides meeting consumer expectations, this guards against underprocessing of these mixed heating packs, and ensures any compositional or other statutory requirements are met (for example, meat contents or drained weight).

Brine, oil, sauces and gravy also help displace air from between solid particulates. Unless these liquids are filled with multihead rotary vaccum fillers, sufficient distance should be left between filler and clincher/seamer to allow entrapped air to escape.

6.2 Hand filling

6.2.1 Meat products

Hand filling is generally employed for meat products which, due to their physical configuration, are susceptible to damage (if mechanical means are employed) or, if the desired out turn is not able to be achieved by the use of a mechanical filler.

Canned ox tongues illustrate the first category (i.e. physical configuration). With the larger sized cans, the ox tongues are normally packed whole. This is achieved through the skill and experience of the operative who positions the tongues in the can, so that distinct layers are formed. A gelling agent, such as agar agar, is deposited between the tongue layers to minimise the incidence of voids in the pack and facilitate the maintenance of product integrity during subsequent slicing operations.

The second category (i.e. product damage limitation) will include products such as 'canned sliced beef in gravy'. The slices of beef are submitted to thermal processing prior to the filling operation and are, therefore, easily broken or shattered by any subsequent mechanical abuse.

The third category (i.e. presentation on out turn) is ably illustrated by 'canned brisket beef'. The beef briskets are cured, heat treated and trimmed to specification, prior to the filling operation. The briskets are cut into usable pieces by skilled personnel using templates. The muscle blocks are sliced in such a way that the muscle fibres are vertical, or at a minimum of 45° (scarf joins are employed) when filled into the cans.

The muscle pieces, together with the interleaved fat layers, are positioned into a mould. The contents of the mould are manually filled into the can. The muscle orientation is critical to the subsequent slicing operation and the correct positioning of the fat layers achieves the required presentation on out turn.

In France, a canned product designated as 'Pied Pacquet' requires a hand filling operation.

The same consideration also apply to fish products, though the interrelationship between low labour costs and the high cost of imported mechanical equipment is also a key factor in many developing countries.

6.2.2 Fish products

Anchovy fillets, brisling, smoked oysters and mussels, and tuna slices are examples of products that are hand filled to ensure optimum product presentation when the can is opened. For many of these types of products fill control is achieved by count rather than weighing.

Delicate high value products such as prawns are also filled by hand, the fill-in weight being controlled using counter-poised weighing scales or, less frequently, electronic scales.

Sardines, too, are hand filled in countries such as Morocco and Portugal, mainly because wage costs are perhaps a minor consideration.

Most hand-filling operations are undertaken on semi-automatic lines where fish and cans are presented to the packer, and full cans conveyed away.

A typical line for sardines might consist of:

• a cardan conveyor for transporting the nobbed and salted sardines to the individual packing stations, and a second for removing the empty plastic boxes;
• a variable number of packing stations on each side of the line; or
• diagonal racks for the placement of the plastic boxes at the packing station.

The plastic boxes with nobbed and salted fish travel to the filling stations on a conveyor positioned centrally in the packing line. The individual packing operators take a plastic box down, placing it on a shelf in front of him/her.

He/she then takes an empty can from the infeed can track, packs it and places the filled can on the other track which conveys the can to the exhauster.

Cabinplant International are one of several manufacturers producing such equipment (Figure 6.1).

Count rather than checkweighing is again used to control fish fills.

6.3 Mechanical filling – general considerations

A wide variety of semi- or fully-automatic mechanical fillers are available. Some are specifically designed for a particular product (for example, salmon and tuna fillers), whilst others are more flexible and can be used for a range of products.

The dosing principles in common use are as follows:

• Weight – the fill is controlled by weighing or by combining pre-weighed sub-portions.
• Volume – the fill is determined by filling a chamber of predetermined volume either by gravity or compression.

Figure 6.1 Packing line for sardines.

- Time – affecting a constant flow of product whilst cans pass beneath at a predetermined rate.

When selecting filling machines there are a number of important considerations to take into account. These include

(a) the capability to ensure a uniform and accurate fill;
(b) the degree of product damage incurred under normal operating conditions;
(c) the extent of any flange contamination, spillage or drip;
(d) the ease of maintaining good hygienic standards and suitability for cleaning in place;
(e) construction: strength and rigidity; the resistance of materials against corrosion; their susceptibility to form a potential source of product contamination; requirements for external connections;
(f) the adequacy of control systems, e.g. 'no can, no fill' devices, alarms, provision for statistical data monitoring; and
(g) capital costs, manning levels, availability of parts, local representation and service facilities.

Where appropriate, flexibility for different can sizes and fill rates (and the ease of change-over) and capability to handle a variety of products should be taken into account.

6.4 Meat filling

The type of mechanical filler employed for meat products is largely dependent on the physical properties, characteristics and nature of the product itself. Another consideration is the canning line speed required.

Certain products, such as canned luncheon meats, are submitted to a mechanically applied vacuum, prior to the filling operation. The fine particle size, in combination with the low temperature of the raw product, renders the removal of air difficult during a normal vacuum-seaming operation. This situation can result in the problems which are associated with occluded air within the can (see above).

For the filling of such products, a pump is usually used to meter the ingredients from the vacuum chamber into the cans. There are numerous fillers which employ this technique available.

Comminuted meat products which have larger particle sizes than luncheon meats, are able to be filled in a variety of ways. Canned corned beef falls into this category and will be used to demonstrate one of the more common methods of filling utilized. A piston-type, volumetric filling system is employed for this product. The mixed, formulated product is held in the feed hopper of the filler. The hopper, itself, is equipped with a conveyor screw system (single or dual screw) which feeds the product, via a valve into the cylinder of the filling head. (The valve is of the semi-rotary type.) When the cylinder is full of product, the valve rotates through 90° (the inlet and discharge ports maintaining their respective functions). The footplate lifter raises the empty can onto the filling mandrel, until the discharge outlet is in close proximity to the interior of the chuck panel of the can-maker's end of the can.

Located on the ventral surface or the plate of the footplate lifter which carries the can, are strong springs. The piston commences its forward (discharge) travel in the cylinder and for the initial movement, the footplate lifter maintains its position relative to the filling mandrel. This action ensures that the product is forced into the base of the interior of the can against the resistant pressure of the aforementioned springs. This allows for a good initial fill and facilitates the removal of air from the can. As the piston travel increases, the footplate lifter commences its downward movement whilst maintaining a good fill-out pressure on the product. The movement of the footplate lifter is cam activated. The subsequent movement of the semi-rotary valve performs a cut-off action which is completed by the rotary cut-off knife carried on the distal end of the filling mandrel. The semi-rotary valve reverses its 90° movement and the filling cycle recommences. A single-shot fill is used to fill 7 oz (198 g) and 12 oz (340 g) cans. The larger can sizes such as 6 lb (2.72 kg), require a multishot fill (Figure 6.2).

Figure 6.2 HEMA DM60CB filler.

Canned corned beef is produced from cooked ingredients and as such, exhibits a rather in-built natural 'elasticity'. In some cases, a crimper unit is utilised. This locates the canner's end onto the filled can and retains it in place by interlocking the flange of the can body, with the curl of the can end, over a short distance. Two diametrically opposed locations are employed. Sometimes the filler is supplied on a common base with the crimper unit.

Products which include a solid and a liquid portion, e.g. 'canned stewed steak with gravy', can be filled as a single-shot, or, the meat and the gravy portion may be filled separately.

A piston system is employed to fill meat products which have very large particle sizes. An example of such a product is 'pasteurised ham' contained in large sized cans (Pullman, Double Pullman, etc.) In this case, the cured ham muscle pieces are hand filled into the chamber of the cylinder which is in a horizontal attitude. A plastic bag is placed over the filling mandrel. The product is, therefore, contained in a bag within the can. This technique helps to minimise any reaction between the can and the product. A sacrificial anode is also located on the interior of the chuck panel of the can-maker's end.

6.5 Fish filling

Much of the fish-filling equipment has been specifically designed for individual species of pelagic fish.

More tuna is canned than any other fish, and most of the equipment used is highly specialised, particularly that used for solid or steak packs.

The Carruthers Pak-Shaper was introduced in 1948 (Figure 6.3). The design principle still remains largely unchanged today.

Solid loins are placed on a continuous conveyor-belt which carries the loins between vertical forming belts. These vertical forming belts mould the fish into a cylindrical mass. This cylinder of fish is then cut off in lengths to meet the target fill weight. The knife then ejects the cut portion into the can.

The can is positioned at the various stops by a Geneva mechanism. The filled can is then transferred to a conveyor for the packing media to be added.

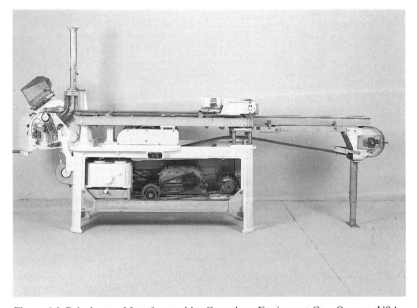

Figure 6.3 Pak-shaper. Manufactured by Carruthers Equipment Co., Oregon, USA.

The cut-off, ejection and Geneva are all automatically timed and are integral with all mechanisms of the machine.

Similar equipment is made by a variety of manufacturers, principally in the USA and Spain.

All such machines are robust and are simple enough to be maintained in less developed countries.

Flaked tuna is generally volumetrically filled. Many volumetric fillers are still semi-automatic, but more sophisticated volumetric fillers are increasingly used because of their filling accuracy and resultant yield savings.

The Carruthers Nu-Pak filler, introduced in 1980, is typical of such machines (Figure 6.4).

Product is transported to the filling basin (1) by a variable speed conveyor regulated by the control system. The controller uses a sensor in the filling basin which monitors the level of product. The conveyor speed is

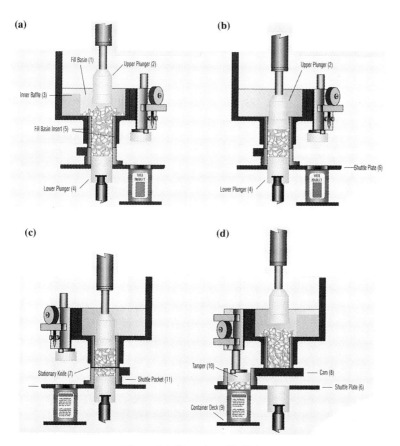

Figure 6.4 Carruthers Nu-Pak.

adjusted to maintain a constant product level in the filling basin. A series of baffles (3) channel the product into the openings (*bores*) in the filling basin, which are adjustable in diameter through use of a fill basin insert (5). Product in the filling basin bore is compressed between the upper plunger (2) and the lower plunger (4).

The adjustable cam (not shown) on which the lower plunger (4) rides determines the target fill weight. The lower plunger gains access to the product through holes in the inner section of the shuttle plate (6). Fill weight variations are eliminated through product compression provided by springs in the upper plunger (2). Product in the fill basin bore represents several container portions.

Product compressions occurs several times during the portioning process. Compression levels are adjustable over a wide range to allow for varying conditions and products.

The shuttle pocket (11) is located between the filling basin and shuttle plate (6) during the compression phase of the filling cycle. The filling basin, shuttle pocket and inner shuttle plate hole are stationary with respect to each other during this phase. As these parts rotate in unison, the shuttle pocket, now full of compressed product of normalised density, passes by a stationary knife (7) which slices the column of product level with the top of the shuttle pocket.

The lower plunger descends and a horizontal cam (8) moves the shuttle pocket and its portioned product outward to a position over an outer hole in the shuttle plate. Directly beneath this outer group of holes is the container deck (9) which supports the containers as they move around the machine in time with the shuttle plate (6). The portioned product is placed in the container with a downward stroke of a piston tamper (10). A tangentially located stationary cam returns the shuttle pockets to their previous position in preparation for a repeat of the cycle.

The equipment for filling Pacific salmon is also quite specific. Filling machines in the North American industry are leased from one of two can manufacturers, American Can (Ball Packaging) or Continental Can. (Now part of Crown Cork and Seal.)

These fillers were first introduced in the 1930s, and although many improvements have been subsequently made, the principle of operation of the early models (many of which are still in use) remains largely unchanged.

The American Can machines (Figure 6.5) allow the salmon to be placed flat on a spiked chain that advances intermittently through an elliptical cut-off knife that slices the fish into the proper length for the can size being filled. A spring-loaded fork then pushes the portion through a twister tunnel to place the cut in a vertical position. A six-pocket vertical rotary unit then receives both the fish and the can simultaneously, while a reciprocating chop knife (rotary cut-off knife on later models) slices off the measured portion which is deposited into the can by a plunger. The

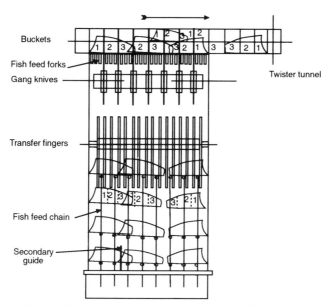

Figure 6.5 Schematic diagram of American Can Fish Feeder.

integrated cutting unit is regulated in speed by a cork slip clutch that is activated by a crude hydraulic cylinder. The slave cylinder senses pressure through the spring loaded pusher fork.

Around the same period, the Troyer-Fox filler was built by Continental Can Company. In their ½ lb size filler the cutter unit is attached to the filler and the fish are placed laterally on an advancing spiked chain and cut into can length portions by a rotating-oscillating cut-off knife. The cuts are then forwarded on a supply chain to a packing chamber located directly over a six-pocket, horizontal rotary filling unit. In the packing chamber an adjustable, spring-loaded pusher block raises in proper sequence to admit fish into the measuring box. As the pusher puts fish into the rotating unit, it advances and the entrance is blocked by a portion in that pocket.

At the same time, a can enters the opposite side of the respective pocket and as the rotary unit passes a dividing plate, a can-operated plunger pushes the contents into the can. The filled can is discharged through a twister chute that places it in an upright position.

The Continental tall (1 lb) filling machine is similar except the cutter unit uses a gang knife with multiple rotating cutters allowing two or more fish to be cut at once. The fish is then channelled to single file to supply the packing chamber. All the machines have a line speed of around 125 cans/ min.

Both American and Continental continued to make improvements in designs to achieve greater speeds. Fish has become more expensive and machines have to be not only high speed but relatively accurate in their fill without too much loss in the recovery of the fish. American Can designed an entirely new cutter and filler unit with a rotary unit using ball-bearings. These were part of the model 4 and 9 series. It eliminated bushings, sliding blocks and lubrication problems. The design smoothed the flow of fish through the cutting and transfer process by utilising ganged rotary knives, elliptical gears and tumbler forks. The integrated fish cutter was synchronised and automatically changed speed to keep the packing unit supplied with a constant flow of fish. This was accomplished by the use of an oil gear transmission unit.

Continental have also made improvements to their cutter drive by using an electronically sensed variable speed driving transmission on their tall machines. A hydraulic, adjustable drive was installed on their ½ lb cutter unit to keep it synchronised with the filling machine.

The speeds of more recently manufactured American and Continental fillers is approximately 240–300 cans/min. The basic difference between the Continental and the American fillers is simply vertical packing versus horizontal packing.

The uniformity of weight and the style and appearance of the filled can are largely dependent on how the fillers are adjusted and maintained to take a particular type of fish and how that fish is fed into the filling machine. Incorrect feeding or adjustment could result in any of the following:

- Overweight or underweight cans which can cause head space and vacuum problems as well as not meeting government or buyers' requirements.
- Cross-packs (fish not positioned vertically in the can, so skin lies across the top).
- Excessive 'gurrey' resulting in lower recoveries.
- Skin or bone over the flange which could result in droops when the end is engaged onto the can. This is usually due to soft fish and blunt knives.
- Under-salting or over-salting. Salters must be continually monitored as they are in a wet environment. If pellets are used, it must be checked that the pellets are not bouncing out of the can or that the broken pellets are not going into the can or jamming the dispenser.

For smaller pelagic fish, many mechanical fillers are in essence semi-automatic as there is an initial manual input, often placing the fish into pockets rather than into the cans themselves.

The Cabinplant Autopack line for mackerel fillets uses this principle (Figure 6.6).

A belt with pockets of fixed volume are filled with fish fillets by hand, individual fillets overlapping the next.

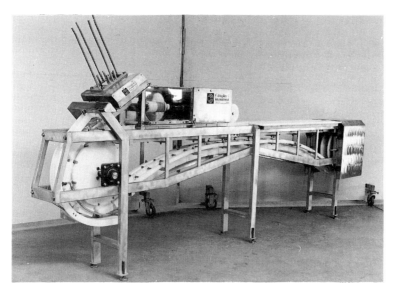

Figure 6.6 Cabinplant Autopack Line.

The belt travels past a circular saw which cuts these overlapping fillets to the exact length of the can. The cut fillets travel downwards onto the radius of a wheel where they are married with cans being fed upside-down from the wheel above.

Sardine packing machines which combine the nobbing and packing operations are now becoming widely available (Figure 6.7).

Fish are hand filled into pockets on a conveyor which passes through cutters to remove the heads, viscera and tails.

The headed and gutted fish in each pocket is then married up with an empty can and the fish pushed into the can with a piston.

Other products, such as dressed crab or pressed roe, may be filled with fillers using piston plungers, rotary screws or pumps such as those used for comminuted meats.

6.6 Liquid fillers

Almost all fish and some meat products will have a separate liquid fill.

Brine and oil are the most commonly used packing media, and many of the filler units are very simple.

Cans are often flood filled, and then inclined on the can conveyor to a constant angle to give a constant headspace (Figure 6.8).

Figure 6.7 Hermesa Sardine Packing Machine.

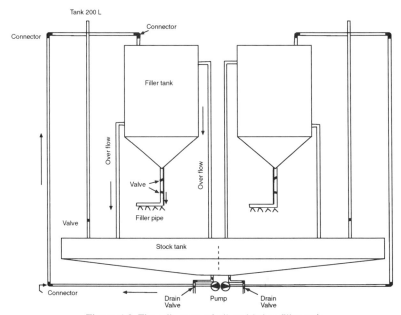

Figure 6.8 Flow diagram of oil and brine filler unit.

Rotary vacuum fillers are, however, becoming increasingly common. These fillers offer a number of benefits to the canner including the delivery of precise weights, automatic 'no can – no fill systems' and the elimination of the need for exhaust boxes for some product types (Figure 6.9).

The filling cycle consists of several distinct operations.

Immediately after the can is indexed, a vacuum is created in the container allowing air to escape, including air trapped in product cavities.

Upon completion of 'pre-vacuumising', liquid is added to the can, filling to an accurate predetermined headspace level. The vacuum that has been drawn in the can allows rapid liquid filling, and fast deep penetration of that liquid into the product cavities.

After filling a second vacuum is created, removing air bubbles. Then a small quantity of liquid is added, assuring a high degree of accuracy in headspace level.

Any liquid that comes out with the vacuum is reclaimed by a horizontal tank trap, easily removable and cleanable.

For more viscous sauces single or multihead fillers of the piston type are generally used.

The importance of controlling headspace in cans has been discussed above. The minimum headspace can be controlled in a variety of ways.

Where the meat or fish is packed in a mobile liquid medium which is

Figure 6.9 21-Valve vacuum oiler. Manufactured by Sud-Est Equipement.

flood filled, as described earlier, inclining the cans to a constant predetermined angle on the can track immediately after the filler will allow the unwanted surplus to spill from the can in a controlled way.

Alternatively, plungers can be used to displace the packing media. This is more effective for viscous sauces.

6.7 Fillers for fish and meat products in sauce

Pieces and cubes of meat and fish in sauces can be accurately filled by volumetric fillers.

The addition of the sauce actually bonds the particulates together, thereby eliminating potential air pockets which would result in excessive weight deviation. The sauce also acts as a carrying medium and lubricant for the particulates. It is possible to dispense meat or fish solids as large as 25 mm cubes.

The nature of a pneumatically operated volumetric depositor allows these products not only to be dispensed accurately but also with minimal product damage. For example, it is possible even to deposit soft fruits without noticeable breakdown in structure.

The maximum speed of a single unit depositor is typically 60 cycles/min, depending upon the deposit material. For applications which demand higher throughput rates, multiple machines can easily be linked together. For example, a typical can filling operation with a requirement of 200 cans/min would ideally need five depositing machines. These can be supplied either in a multi lane format or single lane format whereby the depositors address five cans simultaneously.

This would obviously simplify the transfer of materials to the depositors due to there being only one loading point. In addition, special hoppers or holding tanks can be manufactured to incorporate variable speed agitator paddles which are used to induce solids into suspension in instances where the sauce is of low viscosity or the ratio of sauce to solids is high.

Depositors can handle materials at temperatures between 5 and 90°C, and in instances where hot product fills are required the hoppers and holding tanks can be double-skinned and insulated.

A typical depositor manufactured by Apple Engineering is shown below (Figure 6.10).

6.8 Operational safety

Many filling machines have a lot of moving parts and the potential risk of something breaking off and falling in the can exists. This could be anything from chipped gang or cut-off knives to metal fragments from a can jam-up.

Figure 6.10 The Meterite single drop depositor. Designed and manufactured by Apple Engineering, Ltd.

To minimise the risk, procedures should be implemented. For example, after a jam-up the following should be done:

(1) Remove all cans, sound and damaged and all meat or fish from the filler.
(2) Inspect the contents of both sound and damaged cans for metal. Discard all damaged cans and product in those cans.
(3) Wash out the machine thoroughly, paying particular attention to the area where the jam-up occurred. Check for metal fragments.
(4) Run the machine empty for a short time, then re-wash.
(5) Start canning again; remove the first 18 cans through and examine the contents for metal.
(6) Record the number and location of jam-ups, the number of cans inspected and the number of metal fragments found.

Prior to operating the filler in the morning, the filler should be inspected for any damage to knives as well as a general inspection of the filler to look for loose parts, etc.

Checks should be done on a frequent basis and the results recorded. If a problem is found, the product affected would be limited to when the last satisfactory inspection took place and can thus be minimised.

6.9 Control of the filling operation

An effective weight control system is a key part of the filling operation.

The decision on what the average or target quantity per can should be, in relation to the declared quantity on the label (or a declared meat content or drained mass), is one of critical importance to canners of high-value products for sale in highly competitive markets.

Generally, most will set both the meat/fish target fill weights and total pack weights above the weight needed to fulfil any statutory requirement.

The sampling of product from the filling machines will generally result in a normal distribution with the peak at the target fill weight though for some solid packs the fixed volume cuts off the top end of a normal distribution (Figure 6.11).

To remain competitive, the canners ambition will be to keep the target weight as near to the declared weight (or minimum acceptable solids weight) as possible.

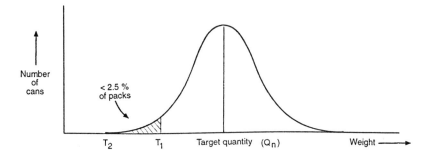

Figure 6.11 Frequency distribution which fulfils EU requirements with not more than 2.5% of packs below T_1 limit and none below T_2.

This may or may not be easy depending on the nature of the product to be filled. The use of automatic checkweighers after solids or paste fillers, to remove small numbers of part or short filled cans, can prove of great assistance in this objective.

In line control systems must be adequate, and at least 10 cans should be weighed both for solids fill (meat or fish) and net can contents every 30 min.

Filling performance is perhaps best recorded graphically in control charts (Figure 6.12) where each can weight is recorded and the median valve identified, or in mean and range charts (Figure 6.13). The former is less precise but easier to operate with unskilled personnel.

The weights at which action and warning limits are fixed will depend on the natural spread of weights from the filling machine, statutory requirements and the relative cost of overfilling.

For product for sale within the EU, no more than a certain percentage of cans (generally 2.5%) may be deficient by more than the permitted amount

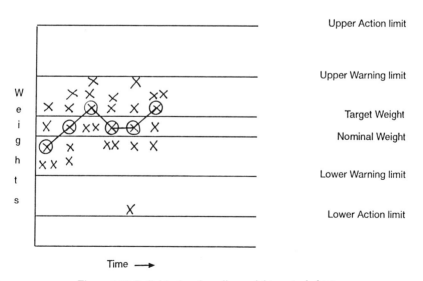

Figure 6.12 Individual and median weight control chart.

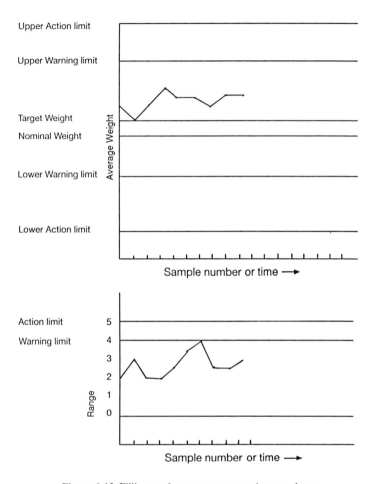

Figure 6.13 Filling performance range and mean charts.

Table 6.1 Tolerable negative errors

	Tolerable negative error	
Nominal weight (Qn) in grams	% of Qn	g
5–50	9.0	
50–100		4.5
100–200	4.5	
200–300		9.0
300–500	3.0	
500–1000		15.0
1000–10 000	1.5	
10 000–15 000		150.0
Over 15 000	1.0	

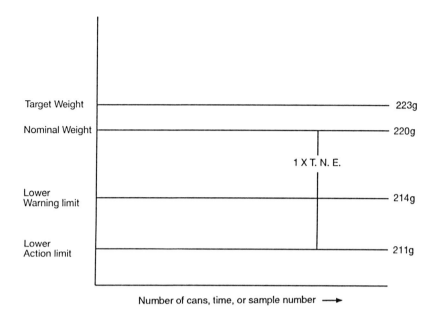

Figure 6.14 Control chart for product sold within the EU, illustrating tolerable negative error (TNE).

(known as the tolerable negative error (TNE) (Table 6.1). No pack shall be deficient by more than twice this amount. These limits are generally referred to as the T_1 and T_2 limits.

A canner selling within the EU may therefore consider it judicious to set the lower action limit at the T_1 limit.

A control chart for a can with a net content of 220 g is illustrated in Figure 6.14.

Acknowledgement

The help and assistance of Mr. Harold French is gratefully acknowledged.

Manufacturers of filling machines

Apple Engineering Limited,
Unit 23, Gothenburg Way,
Sutton Fields Industrial Estate,
Hull HU7 0YG,
UK

Tel 44–1482–824200
Fax 44–1482–824196

American National Can Co.,
8770 West Bryn Mahr Avenue,
Chicago,
Illinois 61331–3542
USA

Tel 1–312–399–3000
Fax 1–312–399–3391

Baynflax,
Welton Road,
Wedenock Estate,
Warwick CV34 5PZ,
UK

Tel 44–1926–498034
Fax 44–1926–410200

Cabinplant International,
Roesbjergvej 9,
DK 5683,
Haarby,
Denmark

Tel 45–9–732020
Fax 45–64–731253
Telex 50595 Cabin DK

Carruthers Equipment Co.,
1815 N.W. Warrenton Drive,
PO Box 40,
Warrenton,
Oregon 97146,
USA

Tel 1–503–861–2273
Fax 1–503–861–0352

Crown Cork & Seal,
9300 Ashton Road,
Philadelphia,
Pennsylvania 19163,
USA

Tel 1–215–698–5100
Fax 1–215–698–7050

Driver Southall Limited,
Maybrook Industrial Estate,
Maybrook Road,
Brownhills,
West Midlands WS8 7DG,
UK

Tel 44–1543–375566
Fax 44–1543–375979
Telex 338186

Daiwo Can Co. Ltd.,
Tokyo,
Japan

Fax 81–3–32135366
Tel 81–3–32135111

FMC Corporation,
57 Cooper Avenue,
Homer City,
Pennsylvania 15748,
USA

Tel 1–412–479–8011
Fax 1–412–479–3400

FMC Corporation (UK),
Holt Road,
Fakenham,
Norfolk NR21 8JH,
UK

Tel 44–1328–851111
Fax 44–1328–856833

Haustrups Fabriker A/S,
PO Box 178,
DK 5100,
Odense,
Denmark

Tel 45–9–133111
Fax 45–66114418
Telex 59862

Hema Technologies,
5 Rue Hervé Marchand,
29556 Quimper Cedex 9,
France

Tel 98–52–4000
Fax 98–52–4050
Telex 940879

Herfrega S.A.
Carballo (La Coruña),
Spain

Tel 34–81–70–0401
Fax 34–81–70–3356
Telex 86583 HEFR E

Hermesa,
PO Box 1207,
36200 Vigo,
Spain

Tel 34–86–45–0325
Fax 34–86–45–0351

Krones AG,
Bohmerwald Str. 5,
Neutraubling,
Germany

Tel 49–9401–700
Fax 49–9401–702488

Leider Maschinenbau GmbH,
1M Laab 3,
Postfach 40,
D–3033 Schwarmstedt,
Germany

Tel 49–5071–3055
Fax 49–5071–4140
Telex 925801 LIMAS D

Lubeca Maschinen Bund Anlagen GmbH,
Postfach 1229,
Glashuttenwee 34–42,
2400 Lubec 1,
Germany

Tel 49–451–31090
Fax 49–451–09145

Luthi Machinery & Engineering Ltd.,
1726 W 180th Street,
Gardena,
California 90248,
USA

Tel 1–213–324–3835
Fax 1–213–324–6915
Telex 316584

Manzini Comaco S.p.A.,
Tito, via Paradigma 88/A,
1–43100 Parma,
Italy

Tel 39–521–771231
Fax 39–521–774723
Telex 530238

Mather & Platt Engineering,   Tel 44–1706–364315
Bradshaw Street Works,   Fax 44–1706–3621362
Heywood,
Lancashire OL10 1PA,
UK

Solbern Corporation,   Tel 1–201–227–3030
8 Kulick Road,   Fax 1–201–227–3069
Fairfield,
New Jersey 07004,
USA

Sud Est. Equipment,   Tel 33–90–824383
Z.1. de Courtine,   Fax 33–90–850683
84000 Avignon,
France

Shin-I Machinery Works Co. Ltd.,   Tel 886–4–6224166
Ching-Shui,   Fax 886–4–6232129
Taiwan,   Telex 51240 Shini
ROC

Turbo Systems Limited,   Tel 44–1482–25651
Gillet Street,   Fax 44–1482–212650
Hessle Road,
Hull,
North Humberside HU3 4JA,
UK

Vemag Maschinenbau GmbH,   Tel 49–4231–7770
Postfach 1620,   Fax 49–4231–777241
27283 Verden,
Germany

7 Can seaming

P. MORAN

7.1 Introduction

The hermetic seal formed between the can body and the can end is referred to as the double seam. It is a metal-forming process consisting primarily of two operations although on difficult irregular closures this may be increased to three operations.

The double seam is formed with two seaming rolls, a first operation and a second operation. These seaming rolls are equipped with specific forming shapes known as seaming roll profiles which are varied in design relative to the can end seaming panel specification and material thickness being closed. As a general rule the larger the seaming panel and the thicker the material, the wider and deeper the seaming roll profile.

The optimum first operation seam is best described as one which is visually judged to have smooth even amplitude wrinkles which will easily compress during second operation seaming. The cross-section of the first operation seam will show a good overlap of body flange and end curl and the shape of the seam will not be distorted.

Specific details of first operation seam formation on irregular-shaped cans and ends will be referred to later in this chapter; however, the principles of acceptability apply equally to both round and irregular cans.

Having produced a well-formed first operation seam a second forming roller is used to compress the five thicknesses of metal (2 × body thickness, 3 × end thickness) to produce a hermetic seal (Figure 7.1).

Two identifiable seals are provided within the double seam. The primary seal is produced by embedding the body flange of the can (referred to as body hook) into the sealing compound or gasket within the end curl.

The secondary seal is created by the overlapping of the body hook and end hook within the double seam (Figure 7.2).

The principal aspects of seam formation which provide a leak-free double seam are referred to as the critical parameters of acceptability. These are:

- Body hook butting   (Primary seal formation)
- Actual overlap   (Secondary seal formation)
- Tightness rating   (Ensuring the seam is held under sufficient compression).

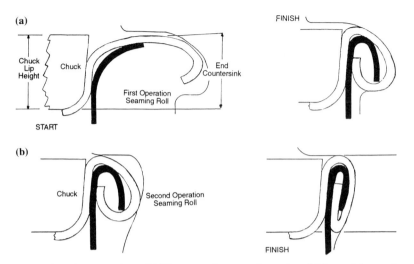

Figure 7.1 Seaming operations. (a) First operation seam formation. (b) Second, hermetic seal formation.

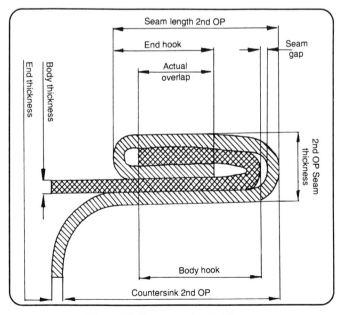

Figure 7.2 Structure of a double seam.

7.2 Can seaming

7.2.1 Double seamers

Meat and fish canning operations employ a considerable range of different double seamers. This range can be separated into two groups: irregular-shaped can seamers and round can seamers.

7.2.2 Irregular seamers

The word irregular describes all can shapes of a non-round variety. Seamers designed to close the oblong, square, pear and oval type shapes are usually slow speed but are of a complex design. Some of these seamers have also been designed to draw in-can vacuum which further complicates the mechanical operation of the machines.

The principle of operation is simple enough; cans filled with product are either mechanically fed or are hand fed onto the seaming table, commonly referred to by seamer manufacturers as the lower lifter table, prior to assembly with the can end.

Some irregular vacuum seamers of the hand fed variety have a two stage lift. This means that once the can is located onto the lifter table the mechanical motion of the machine raises the can to a point below the seaming chuck. At this position vacuum is drawn in the seaming chamber. A pre-set vacuum level triggers the second stage lift which raises the can to allow the seaming operation to commence. Higher speed irregular seamers normally operate with a pre-vacuum station prior to seaming.

Some forms of rotary valve allow the operation to be increased in speed but rarely above 100 cans/min output.

Where separation of the can and end cannot be accommodated within the seamer design during the time when the vacuum is being drawn prior to seaming, a specially designed end which provides a passage for air within the can to be exhausted is required.

Without this separation the flange of the can would embed itself into the lining compound of the end and would create a primary seal thus preventing in can vacuum being drawn. The type of end designed for this purpose is commonly referred to as a 'Swedish dimple' style.

The complexities of irregular seaming will be further described later in this chapter.

7.2.3 Round can seamers

By far the largest majority of cans are round. Higher manufacturing speeds and higher filling and seaming speeds are more easily achieved with this can design.

Within the meat and fish canning operations the need to maintain high levels of in-can vacuum restrict output speed unless the process allows hot fill and/or steam flow closure to be employed. Some developments by seamer manufacturers allow the use of sophisticated transfer valves to improve output speed when closing round cans; however, these machines are very expensive. Other machines are at the design and development stage but are not yet due to go into commercial operation. However, if successful, they will eliminate the need to build the seamer into an all-enclosing vacuum chamber with the necessary transfer ports for can entry and discharge together with a transfer port for auto-end-feeding which is currently all that is available for output speeds in excess of 300 cpm.

Because of the limitations in the speed of filling cans within the meat and fish canning operations, slower output speeds are the norm. Seamers operating in the speed output band of 5–150 cpm are designed as the stationary can closing type. In this principle of operations the can remains stationary whilst the seaming head of the machine rotates around the can. Higher speed seamers are of the rotating can design where the can spins during the formation of the double seam.

7.2.4 Irregular can seaming

Irregular-shaped cans have been traditionally used within meat and fish canning operations. However, the need to maintain high-quality double seams is far more difficult with any irregularly shaped can and end.

An appreciation of why this should be will best be gained by describing how the double seam is formed. Once the assembled can and end are located onto the seaming chuck the first operation seaming rolls (normally on irregular seamers there are two) move inwards and contact the cover curl. Once contact is made the metal-forming operation begins. The first operation rolls move progressively inwards as they traverse around the can. This forming operation creates a wave of metal in front of the seaming roll groove. On round cans this wave of material is evenly distributed during the first operation seaming cycle. On irregular cans this forming operation operates in the same way except that as the first operation roll traverses around each corner the wave of material before the seaming roll is deposited at the apex of the corner. This limited control of the metal in the area of each corner frequently leads to spurs or pleats forming on the end hook within the first operation seam.

When the second operation seaming rolls begin their cycle (again there are normally two on irregular seamers), the seam is compressed to produce a hermetic seal with the sealing compound or gasket held under sufficient compression to provide a leak-free double seam.

Understandably, the sharper the corner of the irregular-shaped can the greater the risk for a localised spur to form.

Many different methods are employed to reduce the risk of pleats and spurs at the corners.

End design can play a critical role in overcoming the problems described.

If the seaming panel of the end is waisted (reduced in length) at each corner, the wave of material which is deposited at this point during first operation seaming will make-up the reduction in seaming panel size. This produces an even end hook length on both the straight sides and corners of each irregular can. Clearly, critical design parameters are necessary in calculating the reduction in length of the seaming panel to anticipate the amount of material deposited at each corner during seaming.

Machine manufacturers have assisted with the design of seaming operations which produce a predictable increase in material at the corner. This revised forming operation is called 'plunge seaming'. The first operation seaming rolls travel inwards to the final first operation seam thickness within as short a distance as possible of each long straight of the irregular can. This produces a considerable wave of material to form in front of each first operation roll groove, however, the amount is more predictable than that produced with the progressive first operation seam formation previously described.

An additional benefit is that the first operation seam can be achieved within two revolutions around the can. This leaves additional time for a vacuum cycle ensuring maximum air removal prior to closure.

7.2.5 Round can seaming

Today's rotary can closing machines produce consistent, high-quality seams with few problems in terms of metal forming. Changes to end gauge thickness do, however, present seam formation problems which rely on end seaming panel design improvements to maintain high-quality double seams.

The introduction of drawn cans particularly for fish canning has significantly reduced the risk of poor-quality seams resulting in leaker spoilage. When soldered side seam three-piece cans were the norm, poor body hook and end hook overlap in the side seam region created localised areas of marginal seam quality.

Standards of seam acceptability were set to ensure that adequate integrity were maintained at the high-risk lap area.

With the advent of welded and drawn cans double seam levels of acceptability were maintained even though the lap area had been effectively eliminated. This, in turn, significantly improved seam quality because overlap values were maintained around the entire periphery of the can.

7.3 Double seam acceptability

Double seam integrity is of paramount importance and the minimum levels of acceptability are essentially the same for both round and irregular-shaped cans.

Within the double seam two aspects of the seam construction produce an effective hermetic seal. The primary area of seal is the amount by which the edge of the body hook of the can embeds itself into the sealing compound within the end curl. The secondary seal is the area of metal overlap of end hook and body hook within the double seam.

The critical parameters for double seam acceptability can therefore be listed as: actual overlap, body hook butting, end hook tightness rating and finally the seam must be free from visual defects.

Typical critical parameter dimensions for tinplate ends and bodies are 0.040" (1.0 mm) minimum for actual overlap, 70% minimum for body hook butting, and 75% minimum tightness rating. However, with aluminium cans the tightness rating should be 90% minimum.

Visual external seam assessment should be ongoing, with cans from each seaming station assessed once every 15 min. To assess cans for acceptable seams a full tear down of the double seam again from each seaming station must be carried out and the dimensions recorded. The frequency of evaluation should ideally be carried out and recorded hourly, however, cannery staffing levels may prevent this frequency of checks.

Statistical process control provides on-going confidence that the double seam remains in control providing that trend analysis is maintained. Assuming that the can and end specification are maintained by the supplier it is unlikely that double seam acceptability will rapidly decline. It is more usual to see a trend over a period of days where mechanical wear or aspects of adjustment within the seamer have an effect on seam quality. Trend analysis highlights seam dimensions going out of control before the minimum critical parameters for acceptability are reached.

7.3.1 Double seam appraisal

Double seam appraisal is the methodology by which seam acceptability is adjudged. Two principal methods of analysing seams are generally used. The first method is by seam teardown. This requires the seam to be disassembled, the component parts measured, and their dimensions or visual assessments recorded. The second method is seam sectioning. To carry out this form of assessment the seam is cut through and the resultant exposed cross section of the double seam projected onto a screen or through a microscope to allow accurate measurement of the body hook, end hook, actual overlap and with the aid of a nomograph, body hook butting.

The section method of seam assessment can be rapidly completed on round cans. However, the vulnerability of the corners on rectangular or irregular seams require each to be cross-sectioned to determine the overall quality of such seams. This becomes a lengthy task and is often considered to take longer than the teardown method of seam assessment.

One major drawback with assessment of seam quality by the section method alone is that the cross section does not reveal the tightness or wrinkle grading of the end hook (Figure 7.3).

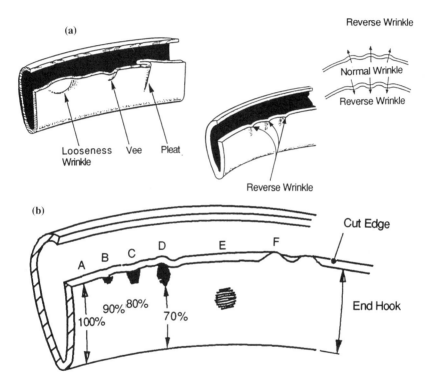

Figure 7.3 (a) End hook irregularities. (b) Assessment of wrinkle grade. The wrinkle free length of the end hook is an indication of the seam tightness. Tightness rating is the wrinkle free length of the end hook, expressed as a percentage of the total end hook. It cannot be measured. It must be visually estimated. Tightness rating is a critical parameter of seam quality. A minimum rating is 75%.

If the ends used come from the same supplier, then the seam tightness needs to be checked only once per shift. The seam must be opened or torn down for this check.

Example of illustration

A   Tightness Rating 100% – smooth end hook – even cut edge.

B–D   Tightness Rating 90–70% – end hook deformed by wrinkles – cut edge wavy.

E   Wrinkle caused by compound – end hook dented – cut edge is straight (normal seam check does not cover this fault).

F   Seam too tight – end hook smooth – cut edge over ironed.

7.3.2 Dimensional setting and control of double seamers

The quality of the double seam is a direct reflection of the ability of the seamer to perform successfully.

It is easy to see, particularly with irregular seams, that if for instance the seaming rolls do not track the shape of the seaming chuck precisely then no amount of roll adjustment will achieve ideal results.

Similarly, if the chuck to end fit is not correct or the seaming roll profiles are not the optimum shape to form and control the metal within the double seam, good dimensional performance will not be maintained.

Good seamer design enables the machine to produce quality double seams consistently with the minimum of downtime to repair mechanical defects or to make seam adjustments.

It is essential that first operation seam settings are checked on a regular basis and that both the first operation seam height and seam width are recorded. This provides the information necessary to determine when the seamer tooling requires replacement.

In recent years significant improvements in seamer tooling technology have seen the introduction of materials which are corrosion free together with surface coatings which, because of their hardness, provide longer periods of operation between replacements.

To a degree, however, these improvements are countered by the introduction of new or thinner materials for cans.

Certainly the change from tinplate to tin-free steel (TFS) ends resulted in a dramatic reduction in seamer tooling life due to the roll profile coming into contact with the chrome oxide coating on the end rather than the softer tin coating. The change to TFS still provides a cost-effective improvement, however, additional seamer tooling costs become part of the economics associated with the introduction of TFS.

If seamers are properly maintained and the seamer tooling, chucks and rolls are in a good condition, seam assessment merely provides the data to confirm that the seam is in control. To ensure that seamers are not the subject of frequent re-adjustment a process called target setting has been universally introduced into the cannery and can making industry to ensure the seamer is correctly set for the components being double seamed.

7.4 Target setting

To begin a target setting exercise it is first necessary to establish the mechanical condition of the seamer. For simplicity the assessment of a round can multispindle seamer will be described.

First and foremost the alignment of the chuck spindle to lifter assembly must be determined. To do this will require the removal of one lifter assembly from its support bush. By attaching a dial indicator to the chuck spindle the alignment can be accurately assessed and recorded. Ideally, the total indicator reading should be within 0.005″ (0.13 mm), however, rectification is only necessary when an excess of 0.012″ (0.30 mm) is measured. Each machine has its own system or design to re-address this condition. On some machines a simple jacking system is employed which allows easy rectification. On other machines the lifter carriage and seaming head are aligned with a key and keyway. Fitting stepped keys to re-establish accurate alignment is often a difficult task, however, to achieve quality double seams good alignment is essential.

Having established the alignment, the vertical lift and lateral play in the chuck spindle bearings should be measured and anything more than 0.002″ (0.05 mm) requires further investigation. Vertical lift in the complete seaming head assembly will require verification. Again, excessive lift, i.e. more than 0.005″ (0.13 mm), will require further investigation and repair where necessary. Following the chuck spindle assessment, the seaming shanks and bushes should be checked for vertical lift and lateral play. Again, anything measured in excess of 0.002″ (0.05 mm) on lateral play and 0.005″ (0.13 mm) on vertical lift should be investigated further.

Finally the lifters require assessment. Excessive lack of alignment or end play should be rectified to ensure that good quality double seams can be achieved.

Having established the mechanical performance of the key areas of the seamer which determine the seam quality, the target setting exercise can begin.

The first objective is to establish the seaming chuck to end fit (Figure 7.4). It is futile to target set a seamer accurately if the end is too loose or too tight on the chuck.

Assuming the chuck fit to be correct, the 'pin height' should now be set. The pin height is the description given to the distance or dimension between the top of the lifter plate and the underside of the seaming chuck. The formula to calculate this dimension is open can height minus the chuck lip height plus the constant of 0.043″ (1.09 mm). The constant of 0.043″

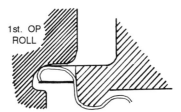

1st. OP ROLL

Figure 7.4 Seaming chuck. Non easy-open food can chucks are designed to be an interference fit in the end component to provide a positive drive.

(1.09 mm) represents the normal rise of the lifter during the first operation seaming cycle which is 0.022" (0.56 mm); added to which is the dimension by which the can shortens during the first operation seam which is 0.021" (0.53 mm). The pin height should be measured at the peak of the first operation seaming cam (Figure 7.5).

The next stage is to set the base plate load or lifter spring pressure. The base plate load is set relative to can body material thickness, i.e. the thicker the body material the higher the base load. For a typical 0.007" (0.18 mm) body thickness steel can the base load would be pre-set at 200 lbs load at 0.022" (0.56 mm) deflection (Figure 7.6).

A special gauge is necessary to set the lifters at this pre-set load. Most seamer manufacturers offer this equipment as part of the spares inventory.

The first operation seaming rolls are now fitted. Care must be taken at this stage to ensure that the roll adjusting screws are backed off to a maximum setting to avoid the inadvertent contact of the seaming roll profile with the chuck lip during this assembly exercise.

Once located onto their respective seaming roll arms the first operation seaming rolls are pre-set to the seamer manufacturers recommended wire gauge dimension at the peak of the first operation cam. Whilst at the peak of the first operation seaming cam, the height of the roll is set relative to the chuck lip. This dimension is normally 0.003–0.005"

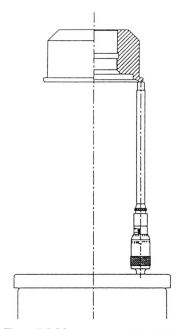

Figure 7.5 Measurement of pin height.

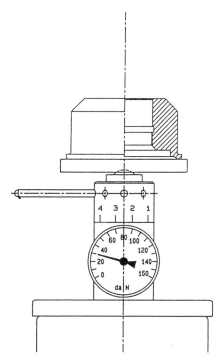

Figure 7.6 Setting the base plate load or lifter spring pressure.

(0.076 mm–0.13 mm) above the chuck lip face (Figure 7.7). Cans and ends are then run through the machine and first operation dimensions recorded and cut cross-sections analysed. Assuming the first operations to be correct, the procedure is now repeated for the second operation seaming rolls.

The double seam is now ready for assessment by either the tear down and/or the sectioning method previously described (Figure 7.8).

With a correctly set seamer any significant changes to the seam quality are more likely to result from varying incoming bodies and ends rather than specific seamer settings.

By carrying out trend analysis, facilitated by the plotting of double seam achievement on a day to day basis, the frequency of target setting exercises can be established relative to each seamer type. Well designed and engineered seamers may need a full target setting exercise as infrequently as 3-monthly where as other seamer types may need resetting on a weekly basis.

Target setting exercises on irregular seamers are in general not so precise due to the constraints within the seamer design. The principles, however, can still be applied.

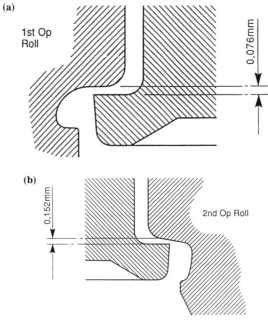

Figure 7.7 Recommended wire gauge dimensions at peak of first operation seaming cam.

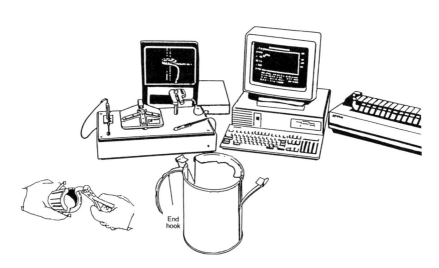

Figure 7.8 Computerised double seam analysis.

7.5 Seamer maintenance procedures

By far the most critical maintenance function is to carry out the correct lubrication procedures. The most vulnerable areas of any seamer are the higher velocity moving parts such as chuck spindles, lifter assemblies, seaming rolls and end feed magazines and, where fitted, mechanical end coding devices.

Seaming chuck spindles and lifter assemblies are particularly vulnerable to seizure, not only from lack of lubrication but from product contamination. Following each production run, planned maintenance time should be spent checking cleanliness of vulnerable areas where product build-up can create mechanical damage or localised generation of heat through frictional resistance. Once a thorough washdown procedure has been completed it is important to carry out a lubrication procedure to ensure entrapped water, and in particular cleaning fluids, are flushed out of vulnerable areas such as seaming roll bearings. It is pointless carrying out precision target setting exercises if corrosion of vulnerable parts and assemblies is going to occur when machines are lying idle. This is particularly true of seamers which are in production only when seasonal demand dictates.

Seamer manufacturers do their best to engineer machines in such a way as to reduce maintenance and lubrication frequencies. However, the recirculating oil systems and auto-lube facilities to seaming rolls only exist on modern seamers. Many of the older seamer types, which still perform perfectly adequately, need the care and attention necessary to keep them in a good order and capable of producing quality double seams.

7.6 Double seaming technology developments

The ever-increasing need to reduce the costs of the container results in technology changes to the manufacturing process of can and end making.

The significant advance made in round containers has been the introduction of two piece cans, i.e. a deep drawn body.

The obvious advantages this change has produced are the elimination of any form of side seam and the requirement of only one double seam at the canners end. Shallow drawn irregular cans have also benefited from this new can making technology.

The next major change is likely to be the significant material thickness reduction of the can end component. By adopting thinner and harder materials, financial savings can be made whilst at the same time retaining very similar processing performance through the use of double reduced steel stock.

The change will require the introduction of small seam or 'Mini Seam' technology to ensure the metal formation aspects are maintained with the use of the thinner and harder materials. The improved integrity of deep drawn cans or alternatively welded side seam three-piece cans lend themselves well to this change in double seaming. Inevitably a smaller seam means a reduction in the degree of latitude currently experienced with full-size double seams. However, to maintain the current minimum level for the critical parameters of tightness rating these changes will be necessary before the introduction of thinner and cheaper end components is achieved.

The canning industry has always adapted well to the introduction of new technology and the changes anticipated over the next 5 years will be no exception. With the correct re-training programmes for cannery employees the current high standards of integrity of canned foods will be maintained.

Glossary of terms and definitions

Actual overlap

The amount of overlap generated in the double seam by the body hook and end hook.

Base load

The force applied to the base of the can during the formation of the double seam.

Body flange

The flared projection at the top of the can body which is formed into the body hook during double seaming.

Body hook

The portion of the body flange which is turned down during double seam formation.

Body hook butting

The length of the body hook relative to the internal length of the seam expressed as a percentage to indicate the amount by which the body hook is embedded in the lining compound.

Can lifter assembly

The part of a seamer on which the can sits during double seam formation. This assembly is also known as seaming table, can holding chuck, lower lifter table.

Countersink depth

The measurement from the top of the double seam to the bottom of the countersink radius.

Double seam

That part of the can formed by joining the body and end components, the hooks of which interlock and form a strong mechanical structure.

Double seamer

A machine which double seams a can end onto a can body. This machine is also commonly referred to as a closing machine.

End seaming panel

The part of the end component which is reformed during the seaming operation.

End hook

The part of the end seaming panel curl which is formed during the double seam to interlock with body hook.

End hook wrinkle

The degree of waviness remaining in the end hook after second operation seam formation. This is also referred to as tightness rating.

Lining compound

A specially formulated compound based on rubber, for affecting a hermetic seal at the double seam. The lining compound is applied to the inside curl of the seaming panel on the end component.

Pin height

The dimension between the bottom radius of the seaming chuck and the top face of the can lifter assembly where the can sits. The pin height is measured at the peak of the first operation cam.

Puckers, pleats and spurs

This describes faults which can occur on the end hook of the double seam. Puckers, pleats and spurs are undesirable in that the hermetic seal is compromised if these faults are evident.

Seaming chuck

The part of the seamer which fits inside the end component during double seam formation. The seaming chuck provides the anvil against which the seam is formed.

Seaming chuck fit

The correct location and frictional drive of the seaming chuck into the end component.

Seaming roll

The part of the seamer which performs the metal forming operation of interlocking the body hook and end hook during the first operation and to then compress this formation during second operation seaming to achieve the required double seam integrity.

Seaming roll groove

The shape designed to achieve the correct metal forming capability for the specific can body and can end specification required. This is also referred to as seaming roll profile.

Side seam

The joint on a welded or soldered can body. The area where the side seam is formed into the body flange is referred to as the lap area.

Trouble-shooting chart

If you have a particular fault as on the trouble-shooting chart, follow the line down to each black dot and then across to see the possible causes to that fault. Diagrams and more details of these faults can be found in:

Carnaud metal box *Double Seam Manual*
Carnaud metal box *Double Seam Slide Programme from the Customer Training*
Visual Can defects Camden Food and Drinks.

Table 7.1 Trouble-shooting chart

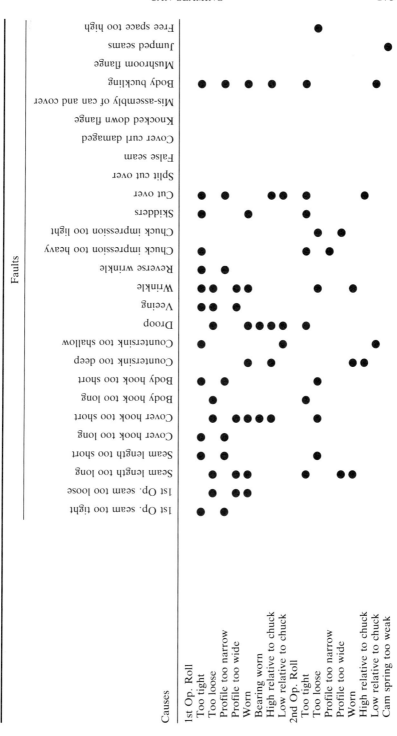

Faults

Causes	1st Op. seam too tight	1st Op. seam too loose	Seam length too long	Seam length too short	Cover hook too long	Cover hook too short	Body hook too long	Body hook too short	Countersink too deep	Countersink too shallow	Droop	Veeing	Wrinkle	Reverse wrinkle	Chuck impression too heavy	Chuck impression too light	Skidders	Cut over	Split cut over	False seam	Cover curl damaged	Knocked down flange	Mis-assembly of can and cover	Body buckling	Mushroom flange	Jumped seams	Free space too high
1st Op. Roll																											
Too tight	●							●		●		●	●	●	●		●	●						●			
Too loose		●		●	●	●		●			●	●	●					●									
Profile too narrow	●											●		●										●			
Profile too wide		●	●			●	●						●				●							●			
Worn			●			●			●		●		●					●						●			
Bearing worn						●					●							●									
High relative to chuck						●			●	●	●																
Low relative to chuck											●													●			
2nd Op. Roll																											
Too tight			●	●		●	●	●			●		●		●		●	●									●
Too loose																											
Profile too narrow															●	●											
Profile too wide													●			●											
Worn			●						●									●						●			
High relative to chuck			●						●																		
Low relative to chuck										●																	
Cam spring too weak																										●	

Table 7.1 *Continued*

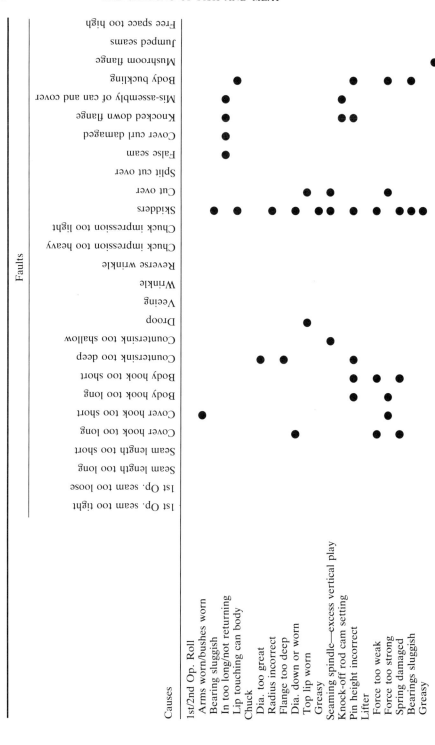

Faults (column headings):

- 1st Op. seam too tight
- 1st Op. seam too loose
- Seam length too long
- Seam length too short
- Cover hook too long
- Cover hook too short
- Body hook too long
- Body hook too short
- Countersink too deep
- Countersink too shallow
- Droop
- Veeing
- Wrinkle
- Reverse wrinkle
- Chuck impression too heavy
- Chuck impression too light
- Skidders
- Cut over
- Split cut over
- False seam
- Cover curl damaged
- Knocked down flange
- Mis-assembly of can and cover
- Body buckling
- Mushroom flange
- Jumped seams
- Free space too high

Causes (row headings):

- 1st/2nd Op. Roll
  - Arms worn/bushes worn
  - Bearing sluggish
  - In too long/not returning
  - Lip touching can body
- Chuck
  - Dia. too great
  - Radius incorrect
  - Flange too deep
  - Dia. down or worn
  - Top lip worn
  - Greasy
- Seaming spindle—excess vertical play
- Knock-off rod cam setting
- Pin height incorrect
- Lifter
  - Force too weak
  - Force too strong
  - Spring damaged
  - Bearings sluggish
  - Greasy

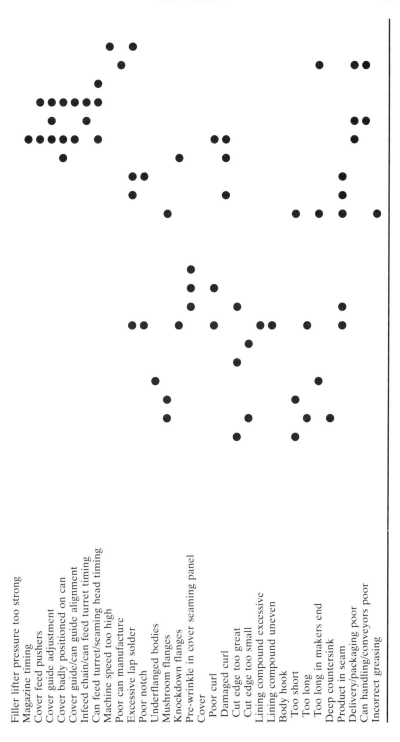

8 Heat treatment
L. BRATT

8.1 Introduction

Canning is the oldest and most important means of preparing ambient stable, long shelf-life foods. The technology allows food to be produced in countries around the world where supplies of natural raw materials are available for ultimate consumption in industrial societies many thousands of miles away. Canning is thus an important aspect of world trade and provides an income for many emerging nations. Canned fish, for instance, is supplied to the UK from countries as far distant as Peru, Thailand and Indonesia, and nearer home from North Africa and Europe.

The aims of the canner are in principle relatively simple: to place correctly prepared food into a container, to close the container by formation of a double seam, to effect a heat-sterilising operation, and to prevent recontamination of the can, particularly during initial post-process cooling. In practice, close attention to detail in the application of good manufacturing practice is vital if the health of the consumer is to be protected and expensive commercial spoilage avoided.

The introduction of the Food Safety Act (1991) within the UK has specified considerable responsibilities for the food trading companies, which effectively means that they must only conduct business with companies in which they are confident that good manufacturing practice is correctly applied. Central to the canning process is the retorting operation, in which cans of food are heat sterilised within some form of pressure vessel in order to achieve ambient stability.

8.2 Aims of the retorting process and commercial sterility

The aims of the retorting operation are three-fold:

(1) To cook the food so that it is in a form for consumption by the consumer with only a minimum of further preparation.
(2) To destroy chemical enzymes naturally present within the food which could lead to chemical deterioration of the food during storage.
(3) To destroy microorganisms within the food to give a condition of

commercial sterility. This implies the destruction of all pathogenic, i.e. food-poisoning, organisms, together with all spoilage organisms capable of metabolism under the anticipated conditions of storage. It is recognised that the spores of some thermophilic organisms are particularly heat resistant and to sterilise the food sufficiently for their complete destruction would lead to loss of product quality through overprocessing. As thermophiles will only grow at temperatures of about 55°C, the complete destruction of these organisms is not of consequence for cans of food stored in temperate climates.

8.3 The requirements for a retorting system

The size and complexity of a sterilising plant may vary considerably from simple batch retorts capable of holding just a few hundred cans to sophisticated continuous machines capable of processing in the order of 1000 cans/min. There are, however, a number of basic requirements which are common to many such systems. These may be listed as follows.

8.3.1 Pressure vessel

A pressure vessel capable of operation generally in the range of 0.8–4 bar. A batch retort would be securely closed by a hinged door or lid during processing, whereas a continuous cooker must have some means of controlled entry and exit of cans into and out of the vessel operating under pressure.

8.3.2 Can location

Means of locating the cans in a predictable and controlled manner inside the retort so that each can is reliably subjected to the heat transfer medium. It is recognised that irregular fish cans, for example, are often scramble packed within crates during processing, but even this method may be considered 'controlled' providing process definition studies have included the worst case condition for can orientation.

8.3.3 Heat transfer medium

A heat transfer medium, either steam or superheated water, able to impart its heat to the cans and hence to the food contained within. There are advantages for either medium. Steam, at a given temperature, has a high enthalpy content due to the latent heat of vaporisation of water. As steam condenses this heat is transferred directly onto the walls of the can. Steam is also a very fluid medium, inherently providing good temperature distribution. Superheated water, however, has the principal advantages that it may be pumped and distributed precisely where required and that the overpressure which is necessary to maintain water in the liquid phase may be independently adjusted in order to prevent container deformation during processing.

8.3.4 Control system

A control system capable of maintaining the principal controlled variables of temperature, pressure, time, and rotation speed, if applicable, within specified limits.

8.3.5 Venting and condensate removal

In the case of saturated steam systems in which temperature and pressure are dependently related, there is a requirement for initially venting the retort in order to remove any air, which might cause localised lowering of temperature. There is also a similar need for condensate removal which tends to build up in the base of the vessel.

8.3.6 Rotation

Means for providing rotation of the cans during processing. Most meat and fish products tend to be solid packs and heat solely by conduction; hence, they do not benefit from can rotation. For products which are semi-fluid, however, forced convection due to rotation may provide more rapid sterilisation, with the advantages of reduced product thermal degradation and increased productivity.

8.4 The classification and selection of sterilising systems

Sterilising systems may be classified in a number of ways, whether batch or continuous in operation, according to the heat transfer medium used to impart heat to the containers (steam, steam–air mixture, full immersion water (in which containers are completely submerged) or spray water), whether they are essentially horizontal or vertical vessels, and whether they have the facility for can rotation during processing.

There are many adequate systems available, but the deployment of a sterilising system represents a major capital investment and care is required in selection so that current and possibly future needs are catered for in the most suitable and economic manner.

Fundamental decisions relate to the need for continuous and/or rotary processing, and a list of factors under consideration might include:

8.4.1 Manufacturing output

Continuous sterilisers offer efficient means for manufacture at high line speeds provided only limited versatility is required in terms of numbers of product and container sizes. If relatively modest production rates or frequent changes of product/container combinations are part of the manufacturing pattern, batch retorts offer a more suitable alternative.

8.4.2 Available factory space

Sterilising equipment tends to be essentially vertical or horizontal in basic design. Vertical plant tends to require less floor space, but in the case of batch vertical retorts some form of overhead crane hoist is required for crate loading and unloading. Batch horizontal vessels in contrast are normally loaded by simply pushing in wheeled trolleys.

8.4.3 Requirement for rotation

If the product comprises a viscous fluid, such as a sauce, which may or may not contain chunks of food (for example, stewed steak in gravy), then rotation of the can will cause considerable movement of the food material within the can, and the principal mode of heat transfer will change from conduction to convection, which is considerably more rapid. Hence, product quality is generally improved due to reduction of thermal degradation, and production capacity effectively increased due to the shorter process time required. As containers become larger, the benefits greatly increase. It should also be noted, however, that the formulation of products to be rotary processed is important in that emulsions, for instance, may tend to be destabilised by the action of rotation.

8.4.4 Overpressure

In sterilising systems using saturated steam as the heat transfer medium, at any temperature of operation the pressure is effectively fixed and corresponds to the saturated water vapour pressure at the stated temperature.

In practice only one variable is controlled, which may be either temperature or pressure. With all other heat transfer systems, however, it is possible to apply overpressure. This is pressure in excess of the saturated steam pressure at the process temperature under consideration. Pressure and temperature must be independently controlled and this provides the means to continually modify the total system pressure during processing. The advantage of this is to prevent stresses and deformations of containers, including the loss of caps from glass containers.

It is noted that as more sophisticated control systems have become increasingly available, there has been increasing tendency to deploy these retort systems in which overpressure operation is used.

8.4.5 Factory location

The geographic situation of the factory may also have influence in the choice of sterilising system. Limited availability of water in desert countries may be offset by location immediately upon the coast. Certain types of retort, for instance, are able to use sea water as an indirect means of can cooling.

8.5 Batch retorts

8.5.1 Steam retorts

Steam retorts comprise the most numerous vessels used throughout the world for sterilising fish and meat products. They are of relatively simple construction, operate at modest pressures of perhaps 0.7–1.5 bar, and have only one controlled variable during operation. If temperature is controlled, then pressure is automatically fixed and vice versa. It is physically possible to successfully operate a steam retort under manual control, but great care is required and automatically controlled systems are greatly to be preferred.

The essential features comprise a vertical or horizontal pressure vessel into which crates filled with cans are loaded. Steam is introduced through some form of spreader pipe in the base of the retort and the introduction of steam will normally be metered through a control valve. In addition, there may be a bypass to the control valve to allow for rapid manual venting and bringing up of the retort to operating temperature.

The retort may be capable of in-retort cooling, in which case water will be supplied to the base and possibly the top of the vessel as well, and there will be an overflow outlet at the top of the retort to allow water circulation during cooling. Compressed air is normally introduced at the onset of cooling in order to counterbalance the internal pressure within the cans and thus prevent container deformation. It is vitally important, however, that air is not allowed to bleed past nor cooling water leak past a faulty inlet valve during sterilisation or localised lowering of temperature may occur, reducing the effectiveness of the thermal process (Figure 8.1).

Because the operation of a steam retort relies on a fixed relationship between steam temperature and pressure, venting to remove air, originally within the retort, is a crucial operation. As steam is vigorously introduced to the retort, air is purged outwards, often through the water overflow

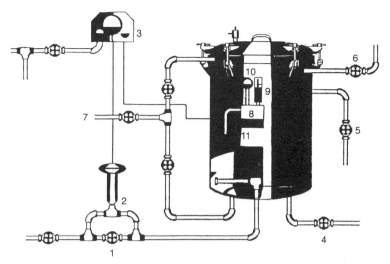

Figure 8.1 A vertical steam retort.

pipe. The volume of steam used for the venting operation is great, and the flow of steam, plus residual air, out from the retort, must be unrestricted. If vent/overflow pipes run into a common manifold, the size of the manifold must be sufficiently large to prevent the generation of any back pressure which might reduce the efficiency of venting. Guidance for venting operations is provided in Campden Food and Drink Research Association Technical Manual No. 2 or the NFPA Bulletin 26-L. Care is required, however, in interpreting these documents because steam supply practices to retorts vary both in legislation and use in different countries. It is essential that the venting procedure used is always confirmed by temperature distribution experiments to ensure that uniform temperatures exist within the retort during sterilisation.

As mentioned above, failure to remove pockets of air during venting may cause localised lowering of temperature and possible understerilisation. This may be demonstrated as follows.

If a retort is scheduled to operate at 121°C, steam tables indicate that this corresponds to a pressure of 15 psi (1 psi ≈ 6.9 kPa). The pressure throughout the retort is constant, and the total pressure will be equal to the partial pressure of all the gases. If in a particular location some residual air remains, then:

$$P_{Total} = P_{Steam} + P_{Air}$$

The retort will be controlled in response to the temperature of the controlling thermometer within the thermometer pocket. If the temperature in this pocket is 121°C, the overall pressure will be 15 psi, but if, for example, air was present at a localised partial pressure of 2 psi, then:

$$P_{Steam} = 15 - 2$$

$$P_{Steam} = 13 \text{ psi}$$

which corresponds not to 121°C but to the lower temperature of 117.5°C.

Other major fittings to the retort include the drain for emptying water from the vessel after cooling and also condensate water which forms during processing, and the instrument pocket. Master or controlling temperature sensors (mercury or platinum resistance thermometers) require protection and are consequently housed in a pocket on the side wall of the vessel. A flow of steam across the sensors and out through a permanent bleed is important in attaining accurate response from the instruments.

A small stopcock is also positioned on the lid of a vertical retort to act as a steam bleed during processing. This provides for a small amount of continual movement of steam within the retort, again as an aid to uniform temperature distribution.

The principal disadvantage of a simple steam retort is that is it impossible to independently control pressure and thus minimise the stresses experienced by the containers during processing. The sardine canning industry in Morocco historically used single-basket vertical steam retorts without facility for in-retort cooling (Figure 8.2). ¼ Club cans were typically sterilised for 60 min at 115°C. At the end of sterilisation the steam pressure within the retort was gently released until the retort could be safely opened. Containers, and particularly double seams, at this time were under considerable internal pressure, which may have been instrumental in relatively high recorded levels of leaker spoilage. Much of this industry has now changed to modern steam/air or showered water retorts with overpressure control and facility for in-retort cooling. The incidence of leaker spoilage has practically disappeared and the use of higher temperatures and shorter processing times has considerably increased productivity.

8.5.2 Steam–air retorts

These are horizontal pressure vessels which during sterilisation are loaded with crates of cans. The two key features are that temperature and pressure are independently controlled, and that a mechanical fan provides for continual mixing and circulation of the mixture of steam and air within the retort. In practice, there will be some form of programme control for the entire retort cycle. The input of steam is used to control temperature and the input of compressed air controls pressure. The action of the fan

Figure 8.2 Simple vertical retort used for processing sardines.

Sterilisation

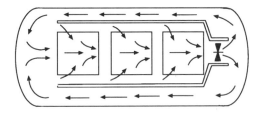

Cooling

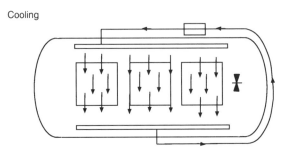

Figure 8.3 Mode of action of a Lagarde steam–air retort.

effectively draws the steam–air mixture through the crates of cans before re-circulation around the inner walls of the vessel. Cooling may be initiated by introducing water spray into this circulating steam–air mixture, which minimises heat shock when processing glass containers. Three- to six-basket versions are common and double-doored variants provide means for complete separation of processed and unprocessed containers. Efficient operation of the circulatory fan is vital in this type of retort to achieve uniform temperature distribution (Figure 8.3).

8.5.3 Full immersion water retorts

These are retort systems in which cans are completely submerged in superheated water during processing (Figure 8.4). There are normally two horizontal pressure vessels, one on top of the other and with a connecting pipe between. The top vessel comprises a pre-boiler in which water is initially heated to a temperature slightly in excess of the scheduled sterilising temperature. The lower vessel is loaded with crates of cans and, at the commencement of processing, water is allowed to flood down rapidly from the pre-boiler, totally filling the sterilising vessel. There will be means for independent programming of temperature and pressure throughout the retort cycle, together with all the other functions of the retort. In this type of system, pressure is controlled generally by the application of steam to the upper vessel. The lower vessel and the connecting pipe must be filled with water, and the upper vessel must have a residual cushion of water for this to be effective. Because of the relative volumes of the upper and lower vessels, special consideration may be required when processing part loads if these requirements are to be met (ballast load or two successive water additions). Water is continually circulated from the base of the steriliser through a heat exchanger, where live steam may be introduced for temperature control, and back into the top of the steriliser through a branched manifold. The continual circulation provides for good temperature distribution and facilitates contact between the container and the heat transfer medium. Cooling is achieved by introduction of cold water into the lower vessel, forcing the return of hot water to the pre-boiler. There is inevitably a degree of mixing, but nevertheless a significant amount of energy is conserved.

A considerable proportion of full immersion water retorts are capable of rotary operation. Cans are clamped within the crates and the crates rotate as a whole, generally at speeds of up to about 24 rpm.

Simple vertical retorts have also been modified for full water immersion operation. In this case pressure is independently controlled by the introduction of compressed air through the steam spreader in the base of the retort. Apart from pressure control, this also provides a degree of mixing of the water, but it would also be normal to provide for mechanical water circulation. Such retorts have found particular application in processing glass containers.

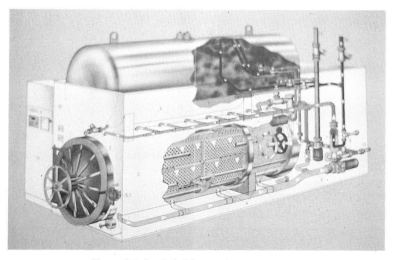

Figure 8.4 Stock full immersion water retort.

8.5.4 Showered water retorts

Superheated water is used as the heat transfer medium, but instead of completely filling the sterilising vessel, a small volume of water is rapidly circulated from the base of the vessel back into the top, where it cascades down through a perforated sheet as a shower onto the containers being processed. The significant feature of the most widely deployed type of showered water retort is that the circulation pipework passes through an external heat exchanger. The same water circulates through the retort during sterilisation and cooling, and temperature control is achieved by supplying steam or cooling water, as necessary, to the heat exchanger. An important advantage of this system is that the water in contact with the containers during cooling has itself been sterilised and chlorination is therefore unnecessary. A further advantage for fish canneries alongside the coast is that sea water may be used to provide cooling to the heat exchanger, provided that suitable metals have been used in the heat exchanger's construction.

Systems are also available in which the circulating water is sprayed onto the cans through nozzles situated along horizontal spray bars (see Figures 8.5–8.7).

8.6 Continuous sterilisers

8.6.1 Fundamental considerations

In a continuous processing system for sterilising canned foods, there is the practical problem of how to put cans into and take them out of a pressurised system without losing pressure. In the design of industrial

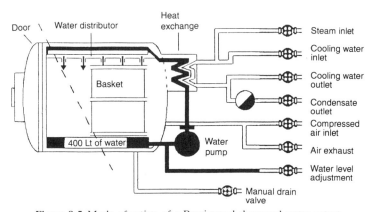

Figure 8.5 Mode of action of a Barriquand showered water retort.

Figure 8.6 Barriquand Steriflow retort showing action of raining water.

Figure 8.7 Deployment of Barriquand Steriflow retorts in canning factory.

equipment, two approaches have been particularly successful. In a hydrostatic machine, the pressure within the central sterilising chamber is balanced on either side by columns of water through which cans enter and leave the system held in specially designed carrier bars. Other systems use some form of mechanical means to control the entry and exit of cans. The most numerous type of continuous steriliser deployed throughout the world (the reel and spiral cooker/cooler) uses rotating segmented valves to allow infeed and outfeed of cans and also transfer from the cooker to the cooler. In other machines some form of double-door pressure lock arrangement is used to allow for entry of complete retort baskets rather than individual cans.

Continuous sterilisers represent a very significant capital investment, and inevitably deployment of such machinery leads to loss of flexibility in relation to products and container sizes which may be processed. Continuous sterilisers typically operate in the region of 1000 containers/ min and are best suited for extended productions of standard products.

As with batch retorts, these are essentially vertical or horizontal machines. A hydrostatic cooker, because of the height of the water towers, will be in the region of 30 m tall, but will occupy relatively little floor area, whereas a reel and spiral cooker is essentially a horizontal machine and requires considerably more floor space.

Reel and spiral cookers, by virtue of design, impart axial rotation to cans during processing, and this may be beneficial (depending upon the product) in significantly reducing process times. Hydrostatic cookers are also available in which cans receive end-over-end rotation, but stationary processing is more usual.

Continuous cookers are very large processing vessels. Steam is generally the heat transfer medium (although water versions are available for both reel and spiral and hydrostat machines) and therefore adequate venting is necessary during the bringing-up period in order to purge all residual air from the system. In fact, the bringing-up procedure may be relatively complex and manufacturers' instructions need to be carefully followed in order to avoid undue mechanical stresses to the machines themselves. Cans transit through the sterilisers and are subjected to a continually changing environment. Individual localised 'cold spots' do not represent the same sort of problem as would be the case for batch retorts where cans are in the same location throughout processing. However, every attempt must nevertheless be made to ensure uniformity of temperature throughout the processing system. Temperature control is often achieved indirectly by means of pressure sensing devices. Pressure will be constant throughout the sterilising vessel and arguably thus provides better means for ultimate control during processing.

8.6.2 Hydrostatic cookers

Hydrostatic cookers comprise a central vertical sterilising tower. The pressure within this tower is balanced on either side by columns of water. Cans are fed into horizontal carrier bars which are transported by a continuous chain in turn through the water filled preheating section, the sterilising section, the water filled cooling section and the final water spray cooling section. Sterilisation is normally accomplished in steam, but occasionally overpressure systems are used which utilise sprays of superheated water as the heat transfer medium and a number of hydrostatic legs to balance the system pressure.

The sterilising time is determined by the speed of the chain driving the carrier bars through the system. Control of this speed, therefore, is a critical factor and should be carefully monitored (see Figure 8.8).

8.6.3 Reel and spiral cooker/coolers

These comprise a modular arrangement of cylindrical horizontal pressure vessels. The number of cookers and coolers used will depend upon the product to be processed, the desired operating temperature, the process time and so on. A typical system might comprise a pre-heater, steriliser, pressure cooler and atmospheric cooler. Each vessel comprises a heavy rotating inner reel, and a spiral which is fixed to the inner surface of the vessel and which travels from the inlet to the outlet end (Figure 8.9). Cans enter the system through a rotary valve and are located in the spiral. As the reel rotates, projections upon the reel cause the cans to be pushed and to roll around the spiral.

Steam is the normal heat transfer medium, but water sterilising systems are also available and may be particularly used for processing products such as chopped ham and pork where relatively low process temperatures are used.

In the cooling sections, water flows counter-current to the cans being processed.

The process time is determined by the speed of rotation of the reel, and consequently monitoring and control of reel speed is a critical factor.

8.7 Instrumentation and control of sterilising systems

Process instrumentation and control may be defined as the equipment and techniques which are used to ensure that a process is kept within preset limits so that the desired standards of safety and quality are achieved.

In relation to the manufacture of canned foods, there are a number of critical parameters, variation in which could seriously affect the degree of

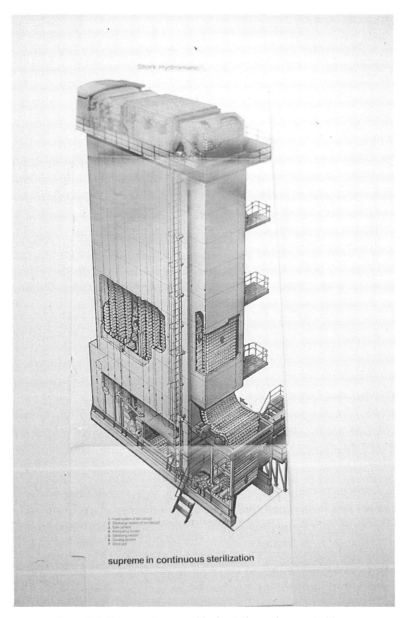

Figure 8.8 Cutaway diagram of hydrostatic continuous steriliser.

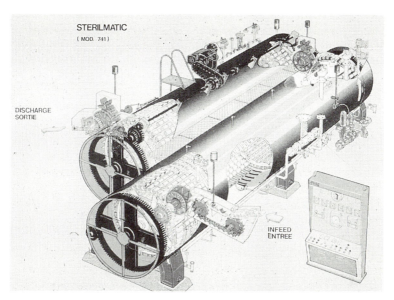

Figure 8.9 Cutaway diagram of FMC reel and spiral cooker/cooler.

sterilisation achieved and which therefore require to be monitored and controlled. They are listed below.

8.7.1 Temperature

The destruction of microorganisms is by exposure to heat, and the relationship between temperature and sterilising effect is logarithmic in nature. Thus, a relatively small change in temperature may have a very significant change in sterilisation achieved.

8.7.2 Time

Time is equally important with temperature in defining the sterilisation process. Because of the extended time taken for heat to travel to the centre of a can in conduction heating packs (which includes most meat and fish products), the great proportion of effective sterilisation occurs at the end of the process time. Any shortening of that time could therefore result in an apparently disproportionate reduction in the effective sterilisation.

8.7.3 Pressure

All sterilising equipment for low-acid foods operates at elevated pressures, and in most countries there are legal obligations for a pressure gauge to be fitted to the vessel. In addition, the application of pressure is used to maintain water in the aqueous phase in water processing systems and to prevent container deformation during processing and cooling. As cans have become progressively light-weighted and flexible, and semi-rigid plastics containers have been developed, the need for accurate measurement and control of pressure has necessarily increased.

8.7.4 Rotation speed/batch retorts

Rotation is used in batch retorts to provide a degree of product mixing and consequently convective heating. The speed of rotation will, within limits, have a significant effect on the rate of heat transfer within the can and thus the sterilisation achieved.

8.7.5 Continuous steriliser speeds

In continuous processing systems, the sterilisation time is determined solely by the rotation speed in a reel and spiral steriliser or by the chain conveyor speed in a hydrostatic cooker. Control of these operating speeds is therefore of vital importance in achieving the product safety required.

8.7.6 Water level

Control of water level is important in all water processing systems, and in steam systems also during the cooling phase of operations.

8.7.7 Water flow rate

The efficiency of water as a heat transfer medium is dependent upon the flow rate achieved across containers within the retort, as this will affect the surface heat transfer coefficient. The development of shower and spray-type water retorts has indicated a need for precise knowledge of water flow rate. In addition, water flow within a retort may be an important factor in maintaining adequate temperature distribution.

8.7.8 Instrumentation

Instrumentation deployed within the meat and fish canning industries varies considerably in sophistication, particularly as many processing units are in the developing countries of the world. What is important is that the limitations of the systems are fully understood so that the correct amount of supervision may be applied as necessary; that instruments are periodically calibrated; and that adequate facilities for maintenance are available, preferably on a local basis.

In the selection of instruments it is important to consider accuracy and resolution in measuring the desired parameter, durability for operation in the industrial environment, routine maintenance, the ease and frequency of calibration, and the location of the instrument, so that readings obtained truly reflect the value of the parameter to which the cans are exposed.

In operation there is effectively a minimum level for the instrumentation applied to a retort. This comprises:

- a master temperature indicator (MTI);
- a pressure gauge – usually a Bourdon tube type;
- a time/temperature recorder (this will normally also provide a control function to the steam supply).

Recording of time and temperature on a continuous basis during processing is of vital importance in being able to assess that sterilisation has been correctly undertaken, not only at the time of manufacture but during the shelf-life of the product. Importing and trading companies within the UK are bound by the Food Safety Act to show 'due diligence' in the acquisition of products which are safe for their consumers. The critical inspection of records plays a most important part in the ability to demonstrate that due diligence has been applied.

8.7.9 Temperature measurement – the master temperature indicator (MTI)

The MTI is the primary instrument for ensuring that sterilisation is achieved, and the instrument to which all other temperature measuring or recording devices on the retort are referenced. It provides the operator and quality assurance staff with means to monitor the true temperature achieved in the retort during the cook period. It is recommended that the MTI should indicate temperature with a measurement tolerance of no greater than 0.5°C and it must be regularly checked by comparing its measurements with a 'thermometer of known accuracy'. Great care must be taken to provide a realistic test environment when comparing readings.

Work at CFDRA has found that MTIs tested in small oil baths cannot be checked properly since their bulk conducts heat away from the oil at a rate greater than that at which heat is supplied by the bath's heaters. Therefore, MTIs should be tested either *in situ* on a retort or in a specially designed rig where steam is used as the heating medium. In both cases the 'thermometers of known accuracy' used to compare the MTI measurements must be located in the steam in a way which ensures their correct immersion depth, and in a way which minimises the effects of local outer environmental temperature on their outer exposed areas.

The choice of equipment for MTIs in practice falls between mercury-in-glass and platinum resistance thermometers of suitable specifications.

8.7.10 Mercury-in-glass thermometers

The traditional MTI for sterilising equipment is the mercury-in-glass thermometer. This generally comprises a brass case with a plexiglass front cover which houses the temperature scale and the mercury thread. The scale is about 25 cm in length and reads from 90 to 130°C in 1°C divisions. The mercury thread should be easily visible against a white or suitably coloured background and, with practice, the instrument should be readable to about 0.25°C. The whole instrument is mounted onto a retort instrument pocket in a ¾ in BSP threaded brass fitting. In the case of saturated steam retorts, care must be taken that the instrument pocket is fitted with a permanent bleed or petcock which allows fresh steam to continuously pass across the tailpiece of the thermometer. Failure to provide a bleed may lead to artificially low readings if a dead spot develops. In the case of water retorts, it is more customary to mount the thermometer on the water circulation line after the water leaves the retort and prior to the introduction of steam, if required, for temperature make-up.

8.7.11 Platinum resistance thermometers (PRT)

Platinum resistance thermometers which are sufficiently durable and accurate for use as MTI on sterilising equipment for canned food manufacturers have become available relatively recently. These instruments display a number of definite advantages over mercury-in-glass thermometers, which may be listed as follows:

- the display is digital and is therefore more easily read and less prone to reading error;
- temperature measurement may be made in remote sites and displayed centrally (particularly useful on large continuous sterilisers);
- temperature readings may be re-transmitted to a second display, recorder, controller or control computer;
- system components are interchangeable within overall measurable tolerances;
- mercury is not an inherently suitable material for use in a food processing environment;
- measurement resolution and overall measurement tolerances are improved.

8.7.12 Temperature-recorder controller

The scheduled process is essentially defined by a combination of time and temperature to which the cans are exposed during sterilisation. It is important, therefore, that a permanent record is made at the time of manufacture of the temperature within the sterilising vessel so that it is possible to check that the temperature is adequately controlled and the required scheduled process is achieved. It is, in addition, useful, and essential in the case of overpressure retort systems, to obtain a continuous record of pressure within the vessel. Deviations from scheduled pressures may indicate that undue stresses may have been placed upon the containers and their double seams.

Temperature and pressure recording instruments used in canneries making fish and meat products vary considerably in terms of sophistication. At the simplest level the output from a temperature probe provides a continuous record on a circular chart. More normally the chart recorder also functions as a temperature controller, so that differences in temperature between scheduled and actual values are used to regulate the introduction of steam into the retort.

Traditional instruments have been fitted with a range of sensors, including mercury/steel capillaries and PRTs. Early models of circular charts were driven by clockwork motors, but electrically driven instruments are now customary. Ink pens move along the radius of the chart continuously recording temperature, the resulting diagram being known as the retort temperature profile.

On these conventional instruments the control of the steam valve is usually implemented by a collection of pneumatic nozzles, flaps and levers which produce an air signal whose pressure is proportional to the difference between the retort temperature and its scheduled value. The air is piped to a pneumatic diaphragm actuator located on the steam valve. The air pressure acts on the diaphragm and against a valve return spring, and either increases the steam flow rate into the retort by further opening the valve or restricts the steam flow rate by allowing the return spring to move the valve towards its closed position. The valve and actuator assembly is designed to allow the steam flow to be controlled at any rate between full flow and zero flow.

There are a great number of traditional systems in current use and these have proved reliable and relatively accurate. However, there are inherent problems associated with mechanical/pneumatic instruments such as wear and tear on linkage or restricted air nozzles, and we are seeing the introduction of electronic instruments in which these deficiencies have been effectively eliminated.

Some modern recording systems have retained the circular chart form since it gives a continuous trace of retort temperature, but some employ printing techniques with moving charts to avoid the problems associated with pens on arms and linkages. Both types have been designed to offer improved recording accuracy and resolution.

A number of systems which incorporate both recorder and controller in a single unit are deployed; however, an increasing number of installations use separate controllers and recorders.

Digital printers are also sometimes used to record retort temperatures, but since temperature is printed at discrete intervals, some form of alarm system needs to be employed to cause an additional printout if the retort temperature varies outside prescribed limits relative to the temperature control setpoint.

8.7.13 Pressure measurement

Sterilisers are effectively pressure vessels operating in the region from 0.8 to 4 bar pressure. It is important to know that the safe working pressure of the vessel is not exceeded, but also that pressure fluctuations during processing and cooling do not place undue stresses on the containers. Too much external pressure causes panelling, in which the can walls are permanently deformed inwards; and too little pressure causes peaking, in which the can ends are buckled outwards.

It is generally a legal requirement that all sterilising vessels are fitted with a gauge indicating pressure, but continuous recording of pressure is also advisable, especially in the case of overpressure retort systems where pressure is an independently controlled variable.

The traditional pressure gauge constitutes a Bourdon tube with a scale of appropriate range divided into divisions of 0.05–0.1 bar. The gauge diameter is usually between 10 and 15 cm and is normally fitted onto the retort instrument pocket next to the MTI.

On modern systems where pressure is electronically controlled, it is necessary to use a pressure transducer to make the pressure measurements. A variety of transducer types is available. In the strain gauge type the application of pressure to the transducer causes a change in electrical resistance, and electronics, sensing the change, cause the new value to be displayed in terms of pressure. The Piezzo electric type, by contrast, generates a small voltage when pressure is applied, but again the signal is electronically converted to provide indication of pressure.

8.7.14 Control systems

Adequate control of process temperature and pressure is vital throughout the cycle of sterilising operations if the canned products are to be reliably and safely prepared for the consumer.

In saturated steam systems one variable control only is needed, although adequate venting is vital. Hence, there are still retorts deployed which are controlled entirely manually with reasonable success providing careful monitoring is maintained. However, it is far more normal to deploy a chart recorder/controller of the type described previously, temperature normally being the controlled variable, although in some systems pressure is used. Pressure measurement does have the advantage in that it is constant throughout the system, and for this reason is used to indirectly control temperature on large sterilisers such as hydrostats (Figure 8.10).

Overpressure systems with the need for independent temperature and pressure control, together with the whole sequencing of the retort cycle, have been programmed by a variety of optically read instruction cards or templates and by cam following devices, but these are generally being superseded by full microprocessor control. The microelectronic revolution and the development and widespread availability of microprocessors (individual chips) and microcomputers (systems which contain many microprocessors) have provided greatly improved means for the accurate control of sterilising systems.

8.8 Establishment of thermal process

It is important to be able to describe the relative effectiveness of the thermal process applied in order to achieve commercial sterility. Such effectiveness depends upon a number of factors, including the initial microbial population within the food, the time and temperature of the sterilising process, and a number of product related factors which effectively determine the heating processes which occur within the can.

In microbial terms foods may be readily classified into high acid foods, such as fruits, which have pH values of less than 4.5, and low-acid foods

Figure 8.10 Simple pressure controller in use on vertical retort processing sardines.

which have pH values of 4.5 or greater. Meat and fish products have pH values in the range from 5.5–6.5 and fall naturally into the low-acid category. Low-acid foods will support the growth of heat resistant, spore-forming, pathogenic organisms and therefore require a relatively severe thermal process to ensure microbial destruction. Process temperatures will be in the region of 115–130°C, whereas acid products may be simply pasteurised at temperatures of 100°C or even lower.

The most heat resistant of the pathogenic organisms is *Clostridium botulinum*, and by convention thermal processes are defined in terms relative to the destruction of this organism. When subjected to heat, microorganisms die in a logarithmic manner. The time taken at constant temperature to reduce a microbial population to 10% of its former value is itself constant and is known as the decimal reduction time or D value. When quoting D values, it is necessary to define the temperature and other factors affecting the rate of microbial death, such as the medium in which the microorganisms are situated.

The D value, as stated, varies with temperature. As temperatures increase, microorganisms die more quickly and the D value decreases. A further parameter, the z value, is used to describe the rate of change of D value with temperature. A rise in temperature of $z°$ will, by definition, cause a tenfold reduction in the D value.

The z value for *Clostridium botulinum* is generally recognised to be 10°C and the D value at 121.1°C (250°F), $D_{121.1}$, is 0.21 min.

As a means of defining the severity of a thermal process, a further parameter, the lethal rate L, is defined so that the killing power of exposure to different temperatures for a time of one minute may be mathematically described. The L value for 121.1°C is arbitrarily defined as unity, and the L value for all other temperatures may be simply calculated by reference to an appropriate z value. (If z value $= 10°C$, then L for 111.1°C would be 0.1.) Lethal rates are listed in Table 8.1.

During sterilisation the retort rapidly reaches its scheduled temperature, which is then maintained until cooling commences. The food within the container, however, behaves differently and normally only approaches the retort temperature after a considerable heating period. By integrating the lethal rates with time for all the temperatures experienced by the food, it is possible to provide a value describing the total relative effect of the thermal process. This is known as the F_0 value.

By convention between all the leading thermal process authorities in the world, it is customary to process all low-acid foods to an F_0 value equal to or greater than 3. Reference back to the $D_{121.1}$ value for *Clostridium botulinum* would indicate that this should be sufficient to cause a 14-fold decimal reduction in the *Clostridium botulinum* population. Assuming an initial population in a can of 100 spores, this would reduce the likelihood of spore survival to 1 in 10^{12} containers (effectively zero).

Table 8.1 Lethal rates based on minutes at 121.1°C (250°F) for z value $= 10°C^a$

Temperature (°C)	Lethal rate
100.0	0.008
100.5	0.009
101.0	0.010
101.5	0.011
102.0	0.012
102.5	0.014
103.0	0.015
103.5	0.017
104.0	0.019
104.5	0.022
105.0	0.024
105.5	0.027
106.0	0.031
106.5	0.035
107.0	0.039
107.5	0.044
108.0	0.049
108.5	0.055
109.0	0.062
109.5	0.069
110.0	0.077
110.5	0.087
111.0	0.097
111.5	0.109
112.0	0.123
112.5	0.138
113.0	0.154
113.5	0.173
114.0	0.194
114.5	0.218
115.0	0.245
115.5	0.275
116.0	0.308
116.5	0.346
117.0	0.388
117.5	0.435
118.0	0.489
118.5	0.548
119.0	0.615
119.5	0.690
120.0	0.774
120.5	0.869
121.0	0.975
121.5	1.094
122.0	1.227
122.5	1.377
123.0	1.545
123.5	1.733
124.0	1.945
124.5	2.182
125.0	2.448
125.5	2.747
126.0	3.082

Table 8.1 Lethal rates based on minutes at 121.1°C

126.5	3.459
127.0	3.881
127.5	4.354
128.0	4.885
128.5	5.481
129.0	6.150
129.5	6.901
130.0	7.743

a

$$L = 10^{\left\{ \dfrac{T - T_{ref}}{z} \right\}}$$

where T, temperature; T_{ref}, reference temperature = 121.1°C.

In practice, it is also not normal to process to this minimum $F_o = 3$ value. Firstly, it is necessary to make allowance for operational tolerances during processing which would reduce the F_o value attained below the desired minimum, and secondly, there may be non-pathogenic, but nevertheless spoilage, organisms present in the food which are relatively heat resistant and which need to be eliminated or reduced to a situation of commercial sterility. Depending upon the product and the climatic conditions of storage, typical F_o values used operationally for fish and meat products generally vary in the range 5–20.

8.8.1 The scheduled process

The scheduled process is minimally defined by the combination of temperature and time to which containers are subjected in order to effect sterilisation. In practice, however, there are a considerable number of equipment and product related critical factors which also require specification in order to ensure that safe sterilisation is consistently achieved. In the US, and for countries supplying the US, there is a legislative obligation for all such critical factors to be filed with the Food and Drug Administration on form FDA 2541a. Such critical factors include all those which affect the rate or mode of heat transfer within the containers. They include, but are not limited to, the following:

- product characteristics
    - particle size
    - pH
    - sauce viscosity
    - fill weight of components
    - presence of chemical preservatives

- container size and type
- headspace within container
- orientation of the container (stacking pattern during processing)
- minimum initial product temperature
- type of sterilising system (facility for can rotation during processing)
- venting schedule
- sterilisation temperature
- sterilisation time
- sterilisation pressure
- conveyor speed (in continuous processing systems)
- cooling method

In meat and fish products, piece sizes tend to be large relative to the dimensions of the container, or totally solid packed as in the case of chopped ham and pork. Consequently, the heat transfer mechanism within the can is by conduction. It is only where chunks of food are able to move within a sauce component, aided by can rotation, that convective heat transfer becomes significant and process times are reduced in consequence.

8.8.2 Special considerations for canned cured meats

Canned cured meats are different from the majority of low-acid foods in that heat and chemical inhibition (by the addition of sodium nitrite and salt) are used in combination to provide varying degrees of microbial stability to the product. In fact, three types of product may be identified:

- Products which, despite the presence of sodium nitrite, are fully sterilised to an F_o value $\geqslant 3$ and are, in consequence, ambient stable.
  Corned beef is an example of this category, where a relatively severe thermal process is necessary in order to provide the desired product texture.
- Products which rely on a combination of relatively mild heat treatment and the addition of a sufficient quantity of salt and sodium nitrite to achieve shelf stability under ambient conditions. Typically, the input level of sodium nitrite would be 150 ppm and the thermal process achieved would be in the region of F_o 0.5–1.0. The majority of canned cured meats packed in retail size cans fall into this category, and the reduced thermal process is beneficial in avoiding thermal degradation of, particularly, pork products.
- Products packed in very large, e.g. Pullman, cans, in which case a mild heat treatment is used to effectively kill the vegetative cells of microorganisms but which subsequently require refrigerated storage to maintain stability.

The specification of thermal process conditions must include all the relevant factors for the particular combination of product and can size under consideration. F_o values are often quoted but, in reality, the actual process temperature used may be just as significant. F_o values inherently assume a z value of 10°C, and this may be an inappropriate assumption in the processing of canned cured meats.

Primary factors affecting product safety are the levels of addition of salt and sodium nitrite, pH, the initial microbiological quality of the meat and other ingredients, and the heat process applied. Additional factors that may affect microbial stability are the available water, redox potential, and the addition of ascorbate/isoascorbate and polyphosphates.

The following typical combinations of brine concentrations and thermal processes, used in conjunction with an initial concentration of 150 ppm sodium nitrite in the meat mix, are offered as guidelines for products within the consultation paper prepared for the Codex Alimentarius Commission: ALINORM 86/16 Appendix VI:

- Luncheon meats
    - 3.0–4.0% brine F_o 1.0–1.5
    - 4.0–4.5% brine F_o 1.0
    - 5.0–5.5% brine F_o 0.5
- Ham and shoulder
    - 3.3% brine F_o 0.3–0.5
    - 4.0% brine F_o 0.1–0.2
- Sausages
    - 2.5% brine F_o 1.5

Care must be exercised, however, in implementing these recommendations in that the numbers of bacterial spores within the raw materials must be rigidly controlled.

8.8.3 Thermal process verification

It is important that any cannery processing meat or fish products is able to provide documentary evidence based on experimental trial, that the temperature distributions inside sterilising equipment are within specified tolerances, and that the thermal processes applied are adequate to provide the required degree of commercial sterility.

8.8.4 Temperature distribution tests

During the initial commissioning and after any significant change to a retort or sterilising system, it is necessary that experimental trials are made to ensure that during operation the temperatures throughout the system are effectively constant so that all containers are subjected to the same processing conditions. In practice, temperatures during steady operation should ideally be within ±0.5°C of the scheduled value.

Tests should be made using a fully laden retort and with a simulated worst case situation with respect to steam supply. The temperature distribution test is used to define the slowest heating location within the retort, so that this may be used in subsequent heat penetration tests, and also the venting process in the case of saturated steam retorts.

Temperature measurements are made using a number of temperature sensors, usually type-T thermocouples, distributed and positively located throughout the vessel under test. Temperatures are recorded at timed intervals on a multichannel recorder or data-logger, either as analogue signals or as digital readings. It would be normal in a temperature distribution test on a four-basket retort to use a minimum of 16 thermocouples during each experiment. The time taken to achieve uniformity of temperature within the operating specification is noted, together with an assessment of the ultimate temperature variation across the retort.

8.8.5 Thermal process evaluation

There are three principal methods available for the determination of the F_o (sterilisation values) of thermal processes:

- microbial spore reduction
- heat penetration
- calculation.

Microbial spore reduction methods involve processing cans containing initial numbers of microbial spores of known heat resistance. The spores may be distributed throughout the food, contained in small glass spheres which are positioned at the slowest heating location within the can, or otherwise encapsulated and similarly located.

The encapsulation method has the advantage over glass spheres in that the spores are in direct contact with the food material and, hence, growth medium effects constitute an experimental factor. After processing the number of spores remaining is counted. The number of decimal reductions experienced by the microbial population, together with knowledge of the D and z values of the organism, enables the F_o value to be calculated. In practice, the organisms normally used are strains of *Bacillus stearo-thermophilus* or *Clostridium sporogenes* PA3679, and for most applications the spores used have a $D_{121.1} > 1.0$ min and a z value of 10°C. The method is time consuming, however. The initial production of the spores and confirmation of the heat resistance in suitable buffer or the food itself take a considerable time and require the services of a microbiological laboratory. Incubation and counting after processing may also take several days or even weeks. In addition, because of the variation in results obtained from individual cans, relatively large numbers of cans are required for each experimental trial. In spore count reduction experiments, a minimum of ten cans should be used for each individual trial. The method does have an advantage, however, in that it provides a means for thermal process evaluation in continuous sterilisers where the use of thermocouple cables for in-can temperature measurement is not possible.

It should also be noted that in the case of inoculated pack studies where spores are distributed evenly throughout the can, the results provide the total lethal effect of the heat process on the whole can contents. This is termed the F_s value.

In the case of convection heating packs, the F_s value obtained will approximate closely to the F_o value. However, for packs with a significant element of conduction heating, the F_s value will be greater than the F_o value.

Heat penetration tests are the most widely used and most convenient means for the evaluation of thermal processes. Effectively, a temperature probe is located at the slowest heating point within the can and temperatures measured at timed intervals during the sterilisation cycle. Temperatures experienced by the food are converted to lethality values and integrated with respect to time to provide the F_o sterilisation value for the process. Type-T copper/constantan thermocouples are generally used as the temperature sensing devices, and commercial heat penetration equipment is readily available, including varieties of sensing probes, fittings for cans and retorts, and data-logging/computing equipment. It should be stated that although relatively sophisticated equipment is more normally used nowadays, in which F_o values are automatically calculated by means of a small computer, adequate results may still be obtained with simple temperature indicators and by reference to lethality tables.

Heat penetration tests may be undertaken either using factory production scale retorts or laboratory simulators. In the case of rotary processing equipment, some form of slipring assembly will be necessary to transmit temperature signals from inside the vessel to the indicator unit on the outside. Simulators are particularly useful for process evaluation studies if products are to be sterilised through continuous processing equipment. Specifically designed simulators are available for both the two major types of continuous processors: hydrostatic and reel and spiral sterilisers.

In order to obtain results which adequately validate an industrial thermal process, considerable care is required in the design and execution of the experimental work. The following summarise the major practical points to be noted:

- The temperature sensors should be of sufficient accuracy and be calibrated against a known standard (normal requirement ±0.5°C of standard).

- Temperature sensors must be located to record the temperature at the slowest heating point within the can. This may often be within a large particle and need not necessarily be at the geometric centre of the can.
- The test cans should be located at the slowest heating location within the retort (this should have been defined by temperature distribution studies).
- Fittings to the can, the temperature probes, and the orientation of the probes should be designed and installed in such a manner as to minimise conduction errors.
- The heat penetration test should be undertaken with respect to knowledge of the critical factors for the product and packed under the worst case conditions within the operating specification, for example:
  - lowest initial temperature,
  - longest delay before processing,
  - minimum headspace (particularly important for rotary processes),
  - highest fill weight, and
  - largest particle size.
- If cans are scramble packed during processing, there may be opportunity for two-piece cans, such as ¼ Club sardine cans, to nest tightly together. Under these conditions it is necessary that the heat penetration tests are undertaken with a nest of cans, the height of which is very significantly greater than the width of an individual can.
- In general, a minimum of three separate heat penetration runs should be carried out, with a minimum of three replicate cans in each run, to obtain nine results in close agreement before a thermal process may be scheduled for the manufacture of production batches.

A more recent development has been that of the Ball data-trace unit. This is a sufficiently small device (approximately 2.5 cm in diameter and 2.5 cm tall) able to fit inside most types of can during processing. It comprises a probe, memory storage unit, and battery. Time–temperature information is accumulated and subsequently obtained after sterilisation by interrogation through a PC computer. The device is particularly suitable for process evaluation work involving continuous sterilisers.

8.8.6 Calculation methods

The rate of heat transfer from the heat transfer medium (steam or superheated water) across the wall of the can and into the food may be described mathematically. Once certain initial data which define the heat transfer characteristics have been found experimentally (f_h and j values), it is possible to use mathematical means to calculate the sterilisation value for the thermal process. The advantage of calculation methods is that process conditions, such as initial temperature or sterilisation time, may be altered and the effect of change rapidly estimated. This may be particularly important in evaluating the effect of unscheduled process deviations.

A number of calculation methods have been developed. The widespread availability of personal computers, however, has greatly aided the application of such formulae, and packages such as the CTemp programme from the Campden Food and Drink Research Association have greatly increased the access to such methods for practical food technologists.

8.9 Procedures and records

The operation of sterilising equipment should be described within the good manufacturing practice documentation of every factory engaged in canning operations. The manner in which retorts are operated has a considerable effect on the ultimate safety of foods produced, and factory workers should be trained and supervised to work within clearly defined procedures.

During the canning operation a number of manual records should be made to augment those produced by items of automatic equipment such as temperature chart recorders. These records should be examined for compliance with operating standards as part of the routine quality function within the factory, and before the product may be approved for despatch.

Canned foods are long shelf-life products. It is normal to keep all relevant processing records for at least three years or longer if the product has a shelf-life in excess of three years.

Traceability is extremely important. If a food-poisoning or food-spoilage problem arises once food has been distributed from the factory, it is necessary to be able to identify the precise lot that is affected so that it may be recalled and an investigation into the cause undertaken. As under-sterilisation could be a cause of future problems, it is necessary to be able to identify canned product in relation to as small a period of sterilisation as practically possible. In the case of batch retorts, ideally this should be to the individual batch or at least to a relatively few number of batches. The availability of modern computer-controlled ink jet coding equipment has greatly facilitated the extent of container identification. It is now practically possible for each can to have its own unique serial number.

8.10 Retort operation

The operation of retorts and sterilisers will vary considerably with type and degree of sophistication. As a guide, however, the following checks and procedures relate to the operation of a semi-manual batch retort heated by saturated steam:

- Pre-loading checks:
    - retort empty,
    - product clearly identified,
    - scheduled process defined,
    - crates identified,
    - stacking pattern of cans within crates,
    - process status indicators attached to crate,
    - manually controlled valves correctly positioned, and
    - steam supply sufficient.
- Loading:
    - load crates centrally within the retort, and
    - close the door.
- Bring up to scheduled temperature:
    - fully open, drain, vent/overflow, steam bypass to controller, valves,
    - bring retort to 100°C, close drain valve,
    - vent retort for specified period, close vent valve,
    - bring retort to approximately 5°C below scheduled temperature, close steam bypass valve, and
    - allow retort to attain scheduled temperature using controlled steam supply.
- Sterilisation:
    - check time of commencement of sterilisation and calculate scheduled end of process,
    - check that the recorder chart is operating and that recorder temperature agrees with the MTI, and
    - periodically check that system is operating within specification.
- Cooling:
    - close steam supply to the retort,
    - introduce compressed air to prevent fall-off in pressure due to condensing steam, and
    - introduce cooling water, counterbalance pressure by adjustment to compressed air, allow water to overflow through overflow pipe until cans are sufficiently cooled.
- Unloading:
    - allow retort to drain,
    - open retort,
    - remove crates and tilt to remove water from headspace, and
    - check process status indicators have changed colour.

8.11 Process audit reconciliation

The process audit reconciliation should normally be conducted on the day following manufacture. Its purpose is to ensure that all cans have been correctly sterilised and that no cans have passed through the retort area without having been sterilised.

The retort operator's log should provide information detailing the number of crates loaded per batch, the vent time, process time, projected and actual let-down times, and scheduled and observed process temperatures.

An audit sheet should be produced in which the cans actually produced are compared with the cans sterilised through the retorting system. In particular, the following should agree:

- the number of crates loaded,
- the number of crates processed,
- the number of crates checked,
- the number of crate indicators,
- the number of processes (retort crates, including part crates), and
- the number of processes (operator's log).

If all details are correct, then the process audit sheet may be signed, dated and authorised. If the details disagree, then a full investigation must be undertaken and resolved in a satisfactory way.

Suggested further reading

There are a considerable number of publications which are helpful to the processor of heat sterilised foods. The following are suggested as further reading:

CFDRA (1968) *Canning Retorts and their Operation* (Technical Manual No. 2). Campden Food and Drink Research Association, Chipping Campden, Gloucestershire, UK.

CFDRA (1981) *Process Control in Hydrostatic Cookers, Part 1: Validification of Cooker Operating Conditions* (Technical Manual No. 5), Campden Food and Drink Research Association, Chipping Campden, Gloucestershire, UK.

CFDRA (1984a) *Process Control in Hydrostatic Cookers, Part 2: Factors Affecting Heat Penetration Rates* (Technical Manual No. 5). Campden Food and Drink Research Association, Chipping Campden, Gloucestershire, UK.

CFDRA (1984b) *Process Control in Hydrostatic Cookers, Part 3: Guidelines on Emergency Procedures* (Technical Manual No. 5). Campden Food and Drink Research Association, Chipping Campden, Gloucestershire, UK.

CFDRA (1984c) *The Heat Processing of Uncured Canned Meat Products* (Technical Manual No. 6). Campden Food and Drink Research Association, Chipping Campden, Gloucestershire, UK.

CFDRA (1990) *Process Control in Reel and Spiral Cooker/Coolers. Good Manufacturing Practice Guidelines, Part 1: The Operation of Continuous Cooker/Coolers* (Technical Manual No. 26). Campden Food and Drink Research Association, Chipping Campden, Gloucestershire, UK.

Eisner, M. (1988) *Introduction into the Technique and Technology of Rotary Sterilisation* (2nd edn). Private Authors Edition, Milwaukee, USA.

FDA (1983) Thermally processing low-acid foods packaged in hermetically sealed containers. *Food and Drug Administration Regulations*, **21**, Part 113.

FPI (1988) *Canned Foods, Principles of Thermal Process Control, Acidification and Container Closure Evaluation* (5th edn). Food Processors Institute.

Hersom, A.C. and Hulland, E.D. (1980) *Canned Foods: An Introduction to Their Microbiology* (7th edn). Churchill Livingstone, Edinburgh, UK.

Lopez, A. (1987) *A Complete Course in Canning* (12th edn). Canning Trade inc.

NFPA (1982) Thermal processes for low acid canned foods in metal containers. *National Food Processors Association Bulletin*, **26-L**, 12th edn.

Shapton, D.A. and Shapton, N.F. (eds.) (1991) *Principles and Practices for the Safe Processing of Foods*. Butterworth-Heineman, London, UK.

Stumbo, C.R. (1973) *Thermobacteriology in Food Processing* (2nd edn). Academic Press, London, UK.

Principal European suppliers of retorts and sterilisers

Atmos	Atmos-Lebensmitteltechnik GmbH, Box 80 01 29, D–2050 Hamburg 80, Germany
Barriquand	Barriquand SA, 32 rue De Cambrai, 75019 Paris, France
Carvallo	ATM Carvallo, 10 rue Rigollet, 93700 Drancy, France
Fishbam	Fishbam S. Coop. Ltda, Maquinaria Conserva, Poligono Industrial D–1, 48140 Igorre, Bizkaia, Spain
FMC	FMC Machinery Europe NV, Breedstraat 3, 2700 Sint-Niklaas, Belgium
Hermasa	Hermasa, Vigo, Spain
Hunister	Komplex Hungarian Trading Company, Nepkoztarsasag Utja 10, H–1807 Budapest VI, Hungary
Hydrolock	ACB-Ateliers et Chantiers de Bretange, Division Agro Alimentaire, Prairie au Ous, 44200 Nantes, France
Lagarde	J. Lagarde, 100 route de Valence, F–26200 Montelimar, France
Lubeca	Lubeca Maschinen und Anlagen GmbH, Glashutten 34–42, D–2400 Lubeck, Germany
Millwall	John Fraser & Son Ltd, SWS House, Stoddart Street, Newcastle upon Tyne, UK
Odenberg	Odenberg Engineering Ltd, Sandyford Industrial Estate, Dublin 18, Republic of Ireland
Phoenix	Denmark
Prominox	Prominox SA, 80 rue Capitaine Thiriat, Aïn Borja, Casablanca 05, Morocco
Steritech	European Container and Processing Systems SA, 5 rue des Paqerettes, 67115 Plobsheim, France
Stock	Hermann Stock GmbH, Rendsburger Strasse 93, PO Box 2611, 2350 Neumunster, Germany
Stork	Stork Amsterdam, PO Box 3007, 1003 AA Amsterdam, The Netherlands
Surdry	Surdry SL, Poligono Industrial Trana, 48220 Abadiano (Vizcayo), Spain

9 Warehousing and distribution

G. HAZLE and M.A. TERRY

9.1 Recent trends

The purpose of the warehouse operation is to hold the stocks of finished product in an enclosed, hygienic and climatically suitable environment in readiness for its orderly and timely onward distribution to the customer. It also includes the important task of stock control.

Although the number and type of functions can differ according to whether the company manufactures its own brands, processes brands on behalf of others, or markets, under its own brand name, products that have been processed by a co-packer, the basic requirement remains the same. This requirement includes the placing of the cans into cardboard cases or trays, packing them into conveniently transportable unit-loads, identifying them with a code that allows them to be drawn off in rotation and the stacking of the unit-loads so that they are accessible for despatch.

The warehouse operation can also include the holding of the product during incubation, the carrying out of further quality assurance checks and the labelling and packing of the cans. Some warehouse operations also include a facility for the re-packing of cans into customised merchandising packs specified by the customer.

Compared with other food sectors in the developed industrial world, the warehousing operations of the canned fish and meat industry are still relatively rudimentary. The industry has, after all, been established for many years and managers, understandably, have been reluctant to spend money on making drastic changes to what they believe are thoroughly well-proven practices. Furthermore, the product is not in itself inherently difficult to store.

Hence, products are commonly stacked on pallets and block stowed, although in lesser developed operations, stacking directly on the floor occasionally occurs. In some countries, notably the USA, a slipsheet is placed between the product and pallet in preparation for shipment. This slipsheet is a pallet-sized sheet of high-quality cardboard with tongues which allow it, together with the stock, to be moved off the pallet using special trucks.

For many companies a high degree of manual work is still involved in transferring the product to the warehouse, in handling it inside the facility and in carrying out the on-going stock control procedures. Because it is so labour-intensive, this type of warehouse operation can be costly to run and more liable to error.

Recent years, however, have witnessed the start of a gradual trend within the industry towards increased automation and computerisation of the warehouse management function. The trend has been driven largely by the giant retail grocery supermarket chains in Western Europe and the USA insisting that their suppliers match their own highly sophisticated logistics systems. In a bid to keep their operating costs down and remain more price-competitive, these grocery retailers are seeking to carry smaller and smaller inventories and are, as a result, demanding that their suppliers make smaller but more frequent deliveries.

This just-in-time approach, however, can make life very much more expensive and taxing for the supplier. But, because the concentration that has taken place within the grocery retail industry in both Europe and the USA has resulted in a high degree of purchasing power being passed into the hands of just a few retailers, their suppliers, understandably, are reluctant to resist these changes.

The trend, therefore is for the canned fish and meat companies to move away from using the traditional, labour-intensive, block-stacking arrangements. Some are already beginning to operate warehouses that are fitted with bays of metal racking, on which pallets can be stacked up to seven high. They are beginning to make greater use of mechanical systems for transferring product from the factory and onto or off lorries. Handling systems inside the warehouse are also making greater use of automatic equipment and are being used in combination with computer-driven warehouse management systems. Such systems enable the operations to be speeded up, allow the progress of individual items through the supply chain to be tracked and help reduce the risk of error and damage. They also help to increase the accuracy and efficiency of the stock control and customer order and delivery systems. Suppliers in Germany and the Benelux countries are currently taking the lead in these developments.

The computerised management systems use laser-driven, bar-coded EPOS (electronic-point-of-sale) technology and can theoretically form a direct information link between the cash-till at the supermarket check-out and the fork-lift truck operator selecting items for a delivery consignment at the picking face in the supplier's warehouse. Significantly too, such developments will inevitably have a knock-on effect for the canners with factories in the emerging nations since their customers will expect them to arrange for their own management information systems to be able to interface with such links.

Although such systems are making the replenishment cycle much shorter, down from 4 weeks to 1½ weeks or even less, in terms of cost per tonne the more frequent deliveries, if not managed correctly, can result in a big on-cost for the supplier.

Such facilities can be very expensive to set up. Managers deciding on whether or not to take this route need to balance the cost of the initially high capital investment required against the expected returns they hope to gain in terms of reduced operating costs and, equally importantly, in retaining a competitive edge in the market place in terms of the quality of customer service.

The fact that just-in-time deliveries can incur higher costs is forcing the suppliers to look to controlling their own storage and distribution costs. They are therefore cutting down on the inventory they themselves hold and the amount of space required to store it. This is resulting in a trend towards greater centralisation of the distribution function.

So, instead of having a number of separate warehouses spread across a country or region, each one carrying duplicate quantities of product, the policy now is to have just one central facility. Centralisation, it is argued, requires significantly lower levels of total investment in buildings and equipment, cuts down on administration costs, reduces manpower levels and lessens the risk of error.

One especially interesting development taking place in the UK is the trend for food suppliers, including some in the canned fish and meat sector, to move away from running the storage and distribution in-house and entrusting it to third-party contract specialists. Under the system the contractor manages the warehouse and the onward distribution of goods on behalf of the client. The contractor may also provide the warehouse itself. This might be leased from an institutional investor or property developer or, more likely, be owned by the contractor itself.

9.2 The storage problem

Compared to chilled and frozen foods the storage of canned fish and meat is relatively straightforward. The product's shelf-life is not critically short and it need only be kept at an ambient temperature. Cans are a dense product and are easy to stack. They make good use of space.

The warehouse building needs no special environmental controls but should be dry and in a sound condition. It should have doors which can be closed in the interests of security, as a protection against inclement weather, and unwanted intrusions by insects and stray birds and animals. The area and height of the warehouse will usually depend on the volume of product passing through as well as on decisions about whether to use block-stacking, or racking together with computerised warehouse management systems.

The requirement is to arrange the storage in a systematic and accountable way that allows cost- and time-efficient access to product for the making up and despatching of loads accurately and speedily.

In a manually operated warehouse, product is transferred from the factory to the warehouse, either by hand-driven trucks or by fork-lift trucks.

Warehouses in tropical climates are more susceptible to infestation than elsewhere. In the interests of hygiene, health and food safety any warehouses which are found to have such a problem must immediately be thoroughly fumigated, and a professionally designed pest-control system installed, within which the containers used for shipping product must be included.

Pallets should be treated with insecticide to prevent infestation. Pallets made from seasoned wood should be used in preference to those made from green wood.

9.3 Brightstacking

Generally, unlabelled cans (brightcans) are first moved in appropriate unit loads from the processing area into the warehouse and stored in stacks (brightstacks) to await call-up for labelling, packing and despatch.

Brightstacking involves a transfer to pallets of post-process cans either from a constant stream leaving a continuous cooker, or from the retort load containers (baskets, crates, busses).

In the latter case, manual, mechanical, pneumatic, or electromagnetic methods to present the cans for brightstacking may be used, but the potential for damaging cans in the process must be avoided as with all can handling.

Brightstacking can be a manual process, but usually uses semi-automated systems utilising electromagnetic transfer of cans, which have been accumulated in complete pallet area layers, to the brightstack, each layer being separated by a layer card.

Whole palletised brightstacks are shrink- or stretch-wrapped, and identified with pallet labels detailing product and batch information.

9.4 Block-stacking

Block-stacking on warehouse floors is an option where speedy access to product is not so important. This may be because through-put is slow, perhaps because of the seasonal nature of the product, or because outbound consignments consist of truck-loads of full pallets. The relationship between the input and output of the warehouse is key.

For block-stacking, unit-loads are configured on either wooden pallets or card slipsheets. Each unit-load consists of the specified number of cases on the pallet, stretch-wrapped for stability. A completed unit-load usually stands about a metre high. Pallet dimensions vary by country. In continental Europe the standard 1200 m × 1000 m pallet is giving way to the 1000 m × 800 m Euro-pallet which is reported to make better use of the cubic capacity available in containers and lorry trailers.

Pallets are constructed to be used with the forks of fork-lift trucks. For slipsheet loads, a special attachment is fixed to the forks to allow the load to be grabbed from underneath.

The unit-loads are stacked to a designated height which prevents damage to cases on the bottom pallet. Some operations use 18 mm-thick chipboard spacer between each unit-load to give added stability.

One method of stock control uses an identity ticket stuck to each unit-load and pallet, with the ticket's tear-off slip placed in a rack in the warehouse office that replicates the lay-out on the warehouse floor. This allows warehouse staff to readily locate the unit. The information on the ticket includes the production number, the date of production, batch number, the contents of the cans and their individual weights, the total weight and volume of the unit-load, the batch number and the best before date.

Other systems in use are designed to achieve the same control.

Because it is essential for the warehouse management to be able to trace cans in labelled or brightcan form in the event of problems, it is important that the stacking location index system employed is easy to understand and simple to operate.

Obviously, the warehouse management is dependent on the product identity system employed by its factory. But it should go without saying that the smaller the unit of identity the more flexible and economic will be the system for tracing cans.

Thus, systems where only a whole day's production can be identified at a time are far less effective than systems which allow cans to be identified on a specific, time-of-day basis. Ink jet printing of batch codes on individual cans allows a much greater degree of flexibility with tracing.

9.5 Semi-automated warehouse systems

A company which has very fast throughput and low storage requirements, or which despatches consignments which include part-loaded pallets, is more likely to select a semi-automated warehouse system, using a racking system.

In some semi-automated warehouse operations product is transferred on conveyor belts from the factory to the area where the loading and shrink-wrapping of trays, or loading of cases, automatic stacking on pallets and the fixing of bar-coded identity labels, takes place. From there it is conveyed into the warehouse.

In situations where the cans are processed at a different site from the warehouse, unit-loads of ready processed cans are brought into the warehouse by lorry. In this case the lorries are unloaded at the receiving dock, either by fork-lift truck or, occasionally, manually by hand-stowing.

A typical semi-automated warehouse would consist of lorry docking banks to receive goods inward as well as banks for despatch. It would have aisles of high racks which could be up to 45 ft high – about seven pallets high – and are narrow. These would be used for storing pallets until they are needed for either loading up full for despatch or for breaking down and repacking into smaller units.

In the narrow aisles the racks are accessed by a turret-truck, a very tall version of a fork-lift truck with a lift platform that lifts the truck operator up and down with the pallet. It allows the operator to see exactly where he is placing a pallet, thus reducing damage. Once in the aisle itself the trucks are guided automatically, avoiding the operator having to steer the truck so that he can concentrate on the work in hand. When the truck is driven out of one aisle to go to another it becomes free-steering.

The typical warehouse would also be likely to have an area of much lower racks for holding pallet loads that can be broken down to make smaller packages. This is called the picking area and it is served by reach-trucks whose operators supply product to the team of operatives that are carrying out the re-packaging.

Close to the despatch bank the warehouse would also have a marshalling area where full pallets and re-packaged goods are sorted and deployed into the appropriate outbound lorry loads ready for despatch.

When a pallet first arrives in the warehouse, the fork-lift operator scans its bar-coded label with a hand-held reader. This alerts the computerised warehouse management system which then allocates the pallet a space in the racking. The operator places the pallet in a special location at the end of the narrow aisle containing the designated stacking area. From here it is collected by the high-reach turret-truck operator for stacking. After the pallet has been stacked, the turret-truck operator scans the bar-code label again to confirm he has put it in the right place. Inventory details on the computerised warehouse management system are automatically updated. If the operator has made an error the system will alert him.

Each fork-lift truck and turret truck is equipped with a radio data terminal (RDT) on which the warehouse management control system displays instructions. The RDT will advise the turret-truck operator which full pallets need to be pulled out of the racking and taken to the marshalling area for despatch. It will also instruct to pick up pallets for transfer to the picking face for breaking down into smaller loads. Once again, by scanning the bar-coded labels with the hand-held reader he automatically updates the inventory on the warehouse management system.

The system will also alert the turret-truck operator of the need to replenish stocks on the picking face.

By using computerised warehouse management systems companies are able to reduce costs, increase the accuracy of stock control and thereby save costs and improve customer service. If a driver takes too long finding a suitable pallet space or collects an incorrect load it costs the company time and money. The computerised warehouse management system is programmed to eliminate errors.

9.6 Despatch

Customers' orders mainly come into the sales department via telephone, telex or fax. The details are passed onto the warehouse for assembly and loading into lorries for onward despatch.

The warehouses of companies processing customers' own brands are responsible for pulling out brightcans for labelling and assembly into consignments. If specified, they also create special merchandising packs.

Using special equipment, the pallet or slipsheet unit-loads have to be stretch- or shrink-wrapped to provide stability and protection during shipment.

9.7 Pallets versus hand stow versus slipsheets

Local factors will decide whether a warehouse chooses to load containers by loose stowing small unit-loads or using pallets or slipsheets in combination with fork-lift trucks.

Loose stowing is labour-intensive and time-consuming. In countries where labour is inexpensive or where political considerations favour greater use of manual labour this may not be a problem.

Loose stowage also makes better use of the container space than pallets. Although pallets make for a much quicker loading operation, the cubic capacity taken up by the pallets themselves means wasted container capacity.

For many companies the ideal compromise is the slipsheet method. It offers operators the speed of fork-lift loading without the disadvantage of wasted space. However, to avoid damage during transit and handling it is essential to ensure that the slipsheets themselves are made with card of very high specification.

9.8 Electronic data interchange

In a few exceptional cases in the UK, suppliers have been persuaded by their very large customers to establish electronic data interchange (EDI) links to provide paperless orders, delivery notes and confirmation of orders.

EDI is the exchange of structured business information by electronic means between computers. It can enable instant communication across vast geographic distances. It uses standardised protocols and message structures to allow paperless transactions between companies. Messages are simplified by the use of unambiguous identification numbers for goods, services and locations.

EDI is being actively promoted by the United Nations which is developing an EDI protocol entitled EDIFACT (Electronic Data Interchange for Administration, Commerce and Transport).

9.9 Stock control

Where companies use computerised warehouse management systems, stock control is carried out automatically throughout each and every day. Every time a pallet is removed and the fork-lift operator scans the bar-coded label with his hand-held reader, the system's inventory is automatically updated, using each product unique identity code.

In companies which use manual methods, stock records are amended as pack product is produced, received or despatched.

Over a period of time the number of amendments will run into thousands and this can result in anomalies. To ensure accuracy such companies usually arrange for a physical check of warehouse stock to be carried out at frequent intervals.

Companies which import product can use the warehouse stock control audit to calculate the value of Import duty which is owed to Customs & Excise.

9.10 Third-party contracts

The argument given for employing a third-party contractor is that it allows the client company to concentrate its efforts and resources on its core business while it leaves the specialists to get on with the specialist's activity.

The justification for third-party contract distribution is that it relieves the client company of the need to invest its capital in buildings and equipment, thereby permitting it to divert these funds into other, higher priority areas.

In some cases contractors will run a warehouse dedicated only to that client. In others, contractors run common-user warehouses, supplying warehouse management services to a number of clients, many of whom will deal in products other than canned food. The choice usually depends on the levels of volume throughput and how much the client is willing and able to afford.

In some instances the contractor will lease or even build a warehouse specially for a project. Because of the high cost involved and the potential risk, such contracts tend to be for a minimum of 5 years. Clauses protecting a contractor's financial and legal interests are therefore usually written into the contract to cover the eventuality of a client withdrawing from the agreement prematurely.

Some contractors charge for their services on a tariff basis, using an agreed cost per transaction. Transactions include activities such as moving a pallet, order picking, loading a lorry and configuring a pallet. A set level of transactions is agreed in advance. This system is common on mainland Europe.

The preferred charging system in the UK is referred to as 'cost plus'. Under it the contractor charges an agreed fee on top of the actual costs incurred in carrying out the contract. The system employs open-book accounting so that the contractor and the client can together control what is spent on the actual operation.

9.11 Performance measurement

To retain a competitive edge, companies look to their warehouse operations to ensure good customer service. To help them in their efforts, they need to measure whether or not they are being successful. They need to measure, for instance, the accuracy of deliveries and whether or not they are made consistently on time.

Computerised warehouse management systems can be used to carry out the measurements by comparing what was delivered against what was ordered.

Companies also need to measure the efficiency of their own warehouse operations as well as those that are put out to contract. One technique for measuring stock accuracy is called cycle counting and involves comparing blind checks of a random sample of items with the book stock.

One measurement to assess the cost-effectiveness of the warehouse operation involves adding up the total operating costs and dividing it by the throughput. It is usually done monthly.

Some computerised warehouse management systems can be programmed to measure the productivity of warehouse operatives.

9.12 Imports

Companies which market under their own brand name canned products processed by co-packers, need also to arrange the imports of goods supplied from overseas. It requires careful liaison between the buying, import and sales departments and the warehouse management to ensure customers' orders are not missed because supplies have run out as well as to avoid expensive log jams of inventory standing at the port of entry awaiting space in the warehouse.

The company's import department is first alerted to the departure of the consignment by the shipping line just prior to leaving port, and then constantly updates the progress of that shipment. The data is keyed into the company's computer system and downloaded to the warehouse. The warehouse management team arrange and update the schedule for receiving and storing the goods. The company arranges for a haulier to collect the container from the port of entry for delivery to the warehouse.

9.13 Distribution and shipping

9.13.1 Road haulage

Transport for the distribution of products to a supplier's customers is usually arranged by the warehouse management team. The predominant mode is by road. This is because few suppliers or customers have a railhead to load and unload direct from a train. More significantly, few, if any, loads are large enough to justify economic freight rates by rail, particularly when the additional costs of two lots of transhipment between lorry and train are also accounted for.

Most companies contract the deliveries out to road hauliers whose per-journey charges are related to distance, the number of drops and the amount of capacity used.

Hauliers are usually selected according to the number of vehicles they possess, the capacity they hold and the quality of their network for particular routes. Having a good network on a route is essential because the canned food supplier does not expect to pay for empty return journeys. The haulier must be able to arrange his own back hauls.

Lorry trailers do not need special environmental controls. However, they do need to be curtain sided so as to prevent the cans from external contamination.

Once the warehouse has been advised of an impending required delivery the management team updates its transport schedule. It arranges the time and date for the haulier to pick up the goods, advises him of the delivery address and date and leaves it to him to make the delivery arrangements.

Lorries are usually loaded by fork-lift truck. When the haulier has made his delivery he has to get proof of delivery and notify the client. To encourage hauliers to be prompt, some companies withhold the haulier's payment until he has produced the proof-of-delivery note. The customer is invoiced as soon as the goods are despatched.

The canned food suppliers try to arrange for full loads in order to benefit from the economies of scale.

9.13.2 Containers

Containers are used for export deliveries which have to go by sea. Fully loaded 40-ft-long trailers and containers can carry about 30 Euro-pallets. In the UK regulations on maximum gross lorry weights restricts this to about 22 standard pallets.

When taking delivery of an empty container the warehouse management at the cannery should inspect it thoroughly for physical damage and contamination by previous loads.

Damage and contamination of the container could result in damage to the load of cans. This could be very expensive. A damaged container should therefore be exchanged for one in good repair. A contaminated one should be thoroughly cleaned, or rejected if this would be ineffective.

Not all holes in containers can be detected visually. Many companies check for such holes by subjecting the container externally to a high-pressure spray of water and then examining it for internal leakage. Another check is to close the container doors and check for flecks of light inside the darkened chamber.

When fully stowed, the container may also be packed with a desiccant such as silica gel in order to protect the cans from the adverse effects of humidity. In some countries, fumigants are introduced into the container before closure, prior to shipping.

10 Laboratory services
M. HUTCHISON

10.1 Laboratory facilities

10.1.1 Location of laboratories

All canning operations require laboratory control of the products processed. The amount and type of control necessary will vary with the product, government and buyer requirements, and the management objectives.

The purpose of laboratory control of food processing operations is to ensure products are safe, nutritious and compositionally correct; to protect the end-consumer from foods which are contaminated, decomposed, adulterated, injurious of packaged or labelled in a false or misleading way. An increase in the demand and trade will be promoted when buyers and consumers have confidence in the quality and safety on the foods.

Laboratories analysing for pathogenic microorganisms should be well separated from food processing areas. Separation from the processing area will also minimise problems of contamination for other types of analyses. The structure should be free from vibrations.

10.1.2 Laboratory design

The design of the laboratory should be flexible to accommodate possible changes in the workload in the future.

A good laboratory design will have ceilings, walls and floors which are smooth and cleanable, and adequately supplied with utilities and safety features. There must be sufficient space for performing analyses, preparing media and reagents, sterilising, storage and clean-up, and space is necessary for offices and library.

A separate room for microbiological work is required to maintain a relatively sterile area and to reduce the possibility of cultures contaminating the processing area. Sample preparation should be done away from the work on microbiological and trace analysis and away from sensitive instruments. A separate sample preparation room may be necessary for some types of products. A pilot test retort and canning equipment is desirable for developing new products. The test retort should be suitable for conducting heat penetration studies and developing thermal processing schedules.

Laboratory bench tops should have surfaces that are impervious and level. Adequate safety features are necessary, and disposal of hazardous wastes must be accommodated. Fume hoods are required for performing analyses using toxic or corrosive agents. Flammable solvents and chemicals must be suitable stored. Adequate ventilation and air conditioning are essential to remove the build-up of fumes as well as to provide appropriate working conditions. The supply of electricity must be free of surges which may damage or affect the accuracy of sensitive electronic equipment; the installation of voltage conditioners may be needed.

10.1.3 Technicians and procedures

Selection of suitable laboratory technicians is very important. The technician will have knowledge of laboratory techniques and analysis and have shown an aptitude for producing reliable results. Initial training should be formal and structured to ensure initial consistency between technicians and to ensure the reliability of results. A continuing series of educational upgrading and training for the technicians will maintain and upgrade the performance and standards of the laboratory.

Laboratory procedures used should follow methods recognised by government or other local authorities to permit reliable interpretation and to avoid questions of technique should disputes arise. Management is responsible for maintaining records and for ensuring the accuracy of results.

10.1.4 Sampling plans

Representative samples from production are taken to assess the safety and quality of the product.

The sampling procedure must take into consideration the purpose of inspection, the nature of the lot, the nature of the test product, and the type of test procedures. Statistically valid sampling for destructive testing is usually not economically practical with food products. However, the sampling scheme used must attempt to represent the normal variation in the product and individual samples must be large enough for analysis. One should at least know the risk, or the statistical significance, or the level of confidence of the sample size used.

The reliability of the laboratory results depends upon the efforts spent minimising the sampling error and errors involved in analysis. There is little value performing expensive and time-consuming analyses on samples which do not adequately represent the lot.

Laboratory records must indicate that the samples were clearly identified and properly analysed. Samples must not be contaminated, and must be stored to avoid significant changes to the product before analysis. All samples to be submitted for bacteriological examination must be taken aseptically. Samples for bacteriological analysis which cannot be stored and other volatile samples must be tested soon after the sample is taken. Some samples require homogenising and blending before analysis.

The remainder of the sample is usually stored and reserved for re-analysis in the event of unusual results, to confirm the initial analysis. Samples are usually kept for several months to 1 year. When possible, reference standards and blanks should be used to confirm the accuracy of results.

10.2 Analytical testing

For all analyses the instrumentation must be routinely inspected and re-calibrated. Known standards should be analysed to confirm the accuracy and validity of results. The type of analyses required by the laboratory depends upon the type of products produced. The *AOAC Official Methods of Analysis* is a good reference for many commonly used chemical analyses, other standard methods are available from government agencies and other reference tests (Helrich, 1990).

The appended procedures are commonly used in canneries.

10.3 Microbiological testing

The bacteriological examination of food and food production facilities serves the purpose of protecting the health of the consumer and ensuring the quality of the food. Microbiological testing is a compliment to traditional sight, smell and touch inspection of facilities. To make use of limited resources, inspections are best directed at those points in production and processing that offer the maximum benefit in terms of protecting health and quality.

The cost to benefit ratio of microbiological testing can be measured against the consequences of a food-poisoning outbreak and quality loss, and the benefit of ensuring problems are discovered before they occur.

Microbiological indices for food products are used to provide a desirable margin of safety and quality. Local government standards for bacterio-logical quality are usually used for evaluating results. In many situations it is desirable or necessary for private companies to establish standards for their own products.

Many traditional culturing techniques require days or weeks before completion. The trends in food microbiological methodology are develop-ing towards methods that have higher sensitivity and specificity, are rapid, easy to perform and economical. When new methods are being considered, they must be reliable and should be recognised by authorities.

The bulk of microbiological work performed by laboratories in canneries is to analyse for indicator organisms of defective sanitation.

Tests for coliforms, faecal coliforms or *Escherichia coli* and aerobic plate counts are usually performed as measures of sanitation, in water and product samples. Swabs on equipment are analysed for aerobic plate counts to indicate the efficiency of the cannery sanitation programme.

There are several recognised techniques and media used for culturing coliforms, faecal coliforms, *E. coli* and aerobic plate counts. Aerobic plates are often cultured at 20°C for 3 days or 37°C for 2 days. Products, such as fish, with more psychrotrophic bacteria are best cultured at 20°C.

The laboratory also will often conduct incubation tests and product sterility tests. Microbiological issues such as product spoilage and consumer complaints are often dealt with by the laboratory.

10.4 Analyses recommended for cannery water and retort cooling water

Water samples are routinely taken and tested for chemistry and bacteriology. Specifications for the water quality used in the cannery must be established and there should be guidelines for action when samples do not comply with the specifications. Water samples may be taken from the flow or with a sterile pipette. When sampling from a tap or hose, allow the water to run for 10 minutes before sampling.

Water samples for microbiological analysis should be collected in sterile containers containing a 10% solution of sodium thiosulphate (2 ml of 10% sodium thiosulphate per litre of sample), to neutralise the free available chlorine in the sample. Test water samples immediately, if this is not possible refrigerate the sample and test within 1–2 h. Avoid freezing water samples for microbiological testing as this will affect the survival of bacteria in the sample.

The water supplied to the factory must be tested for the following:

- Colour, taste, odour, turbidity, pH, hardness, free residual chlorine, suspended solids, total aerobic plate counts and total coliforms.

The microbiological standards for water used in the factory are:

- Total aerobic plate counts 37°C/48 h   <10/ml
- Total aerobic plate counts 22°C/72 h   <100/ml
- Presumptive coliforms 37°C   0/100 ml (MPN broth method or membrane filtration method)

The can cooling water must be tested for free available chlorine. Samples of the cooling water must be tested pre-retort before the start of production and every 2 h during processing. Samples of the cooling water must be tested post-retort for every retort load during each day of production.

The post-retort can cooling water should also be tested at least weekly for total aerobic counts at 22°C for 96 h and at 37°C for 48 h and at least monthly for total coliforms.

The microbiological standards for water used for can cooling are:

- Total aerobic plate count 37°C/48 h <10/ml
- Total aerobic plate count 22°C/96 h <10/ml
- Coliforms 37°C   0/100ml (MPN broth method or membrane filtration method)

Any results outside these tolerances necessitates holding of the production involved and further investigation to determine if reprocessing of the product is required. Samples of the production in question must be incubated and tested for sterility as described elsewhere in this chapter.

10.5 Swab testing

Equipment surfaces with which the product comes in contact are routinely tested with bacteriological swabbing techniques, to confirm that the surfaces are adequately cleaned and sanitised. The surfaces tested should be representative of all contact surfaces.

Swabbing is an imprecise technique and results will vary from technician to technician, efforts should be taken to minimise this type of error. The type of surface tested will also affect the recovery of colonies, whether the surface is smooth, rough, porous, or irregular.

Swabs should be taken after the clean-up has been completed. Swabs may be taken during production for comparison purposes, it would be expected that the bacterial counts on the same surfaces would be lower after the clean up, and that they would not have reached unacceptable levels by the end of production and before clean up.

The number and frequency of swabs taken will depend upon the size of the operation and desired application of the information. This information may also be used to determine the frequency that equipment should be sanitised to maintain low levels of bacterial growth in critical processing areas.

Procedure: An acceptable technique for taking bacteriological swabs is to roll the stick of the swab between thumb and finger while wiping the surface to be evaluated. If a dry surface is to be swabbed, dampen the swab in the diluent before swabbing. Repeatedly swab the area crossing in two or three directions. Break the tip of the swab into the dilution bottle, so that the portion of the swab touched by the fingers does not contaminate the sample. Swab samples are normally only tested for aerobic plate count. Before plating, shake the dilution bottle 30–50 times to disperse the threads of the swab in the diluent. Direct contact plates may be used on flat surfaces.

The area for swabbing is governed partially by the type of equipment to be swabbed. Swab a minimum of 2 in^2 and preferably 10 in^2. Record the area swabbed in order to calculate the results. All bacterial counts should be calculated per 1 in^2 or per 4 in^2. On a large flat surface, eg. conveyor belts, it is more representative to swab 5 areas of 2 in^2 on different parts of the surface using the same swab. Note on the report when and where the swabs were taken.

Individual canneries must develop their own guidelines for acceptable aerobic plate counts from swab tests. The type of products and other processing and environmental factors will influence what is considered a desirable bacterial load on food contact surfaces. Usually the main concern is that clean-up and sanitation should have a significant effect on bacterial load and will minimise conditions which will promote bacterial growth on product. In canneries which mechanically handle wet and warm cans all post-retort can conveying surfaces must be routinely swabbed to confirm adequate sanitation for all production days.

On some raw product contact surfaces a total aerobic plate count of 50 000 per 4 in^2 may be satisfactory. In other areas, such as on can run ways in the post-retorting area, counts of less than 500 per 4 in^2 are recommended.

10.6 Incubation tests

Incubation is defined as the holding of a sample at a specified temperature for a period of time for the purpose of permitting, or stimulating the growth of microorganisms which may be present.

Incubation tests are performed on flat, normal appearing containers and in some operations samples of regular production cans are taken routinely and incubated. Routine incubation is recommended by some buyers and canners as a test of the overall quality and sterility of aseptic products. In some jurisdictions incubation testing is mandatory and exact programmes are established.

The sample size per production day will vary from operation to operation, depending upon the production capacity of the factory and the level of confidence desired for the test. A recommended sampling scheme is two cans from each retort load or 2 cans/h from continuous sterilisers. However, because of the small sample size, the results should be treated with great caution and must not be used by themselves as evidence of safely produced product.

If the cannery does not conduct incubation tests, it is recommended to hold all products for 1–2 weeks or longer.

In either case, whether incubation tests are performed or if the production is held the production must be statistically sampled and inspected for swells, leakers and other defects before shipment to market.

The methodology of conducting incubation tests on low acid product involves incubating the intact sample cans at 30°C for 14 days, 37°C for 10 days, or 55°C for 5 days, depending upon the optimum growth conditions for the expected flora in the product. It is sometimes useful to incubate samples at all three temperatures, if there are sufficient samples; 55°C is used for most products for the culturing of thermophiles.

At the end of the incubation period the samples are examined for swells. The contents are examined for:

- pH,
- direct microbiological smear and staining,
- smell and appearance, and
- nitrite level if appropriate.

Suspect samples should be cultured following the sterility test procedures outlined in the following section.

10.7 Sterility testing

Sterility testing of aseptic containers may be necessary when investigating spoilage outbreaks, suspect product, or may be performed routinely.

The normal characteristics of the product and package should be known before investigation. Examine the container(s) for defects. Review the production records of the suspect lot, if available. With experience and knowledge it may be possible at this stage to make an early diagnosis of the problem. The line of investigation can be shortened to tests necessary to confirm the diagnosis, without the need for lengthy analysis and investigation.

Safe working practices should be followed, particularly when dealing with suspect samples. Pathogenic microorganisms and toxins can be present in apparently sound containers.

For a full description of this procedure refer to the *Campden Technical Manual Number 18*. An outline of the procedure for the sterility testing is as follows:

10.7.1 Examination of containers

Record the can code and identify the can with a sample number. Examine each container for defects with the label on. Remove the label and re-examine. Record any defects which may be correlated to bacteriological results later.

Weigh the cans. Overfilling may cause the ends to bulge slightly, and the container will have low or no vacuum.

Samples should be incubated before cultures are made, except in the case of swollen cans. Perform sterility tests on swollen cans immediately. Flat cans should be incubated at 37°C for 10 days or 55°C for 5 days. Sets of flat cans may be incubated at both temperatures if there are sufficient samples.

The number of organisms which survive heat processing may be extremely few. Preliminary incubation will stimulate the growth of survivors and increase the chance of culturing them from the inoculum.

10.7.2 Cleaning the container

Immerse the sample cans in 100–300 ppm chlorinated water for 10–15 min. Dry the cans with disposable paper towels to avoid corrosion. If cans are dirty, wash them in warm soapy water before sanitising in chlorinated water.

10.7.3 Opening the container

Contamination of the sample or the media is the major concern when performing sterility tests. Measures must be taken to avoid contamination of the test media to obtain dependable results. Laboratories not properly equipped or without properly trained technicians will have poor or meaningless interpretation of the results because of contamination problems.

Open cans to be tested in a sterile safety cabinet (Class I or II). Place the cleaned cans in the cabinet with the non-coded end of the can facing up. Flood the surface of the end with alcohol (70%) and flame, or otherwise sterilise the end to be opened.

Use a sterilised stainless-steel spike to pierce the cans. Dip the spike in alcohol and flame to sterilise. Gently pierce the sterilised end, release the pressure of the can gradually. Protect the opening with a sterile half Petri dish. If there is insufficient fluid in the can, use sterilised metal cutters to further open solid pack cans to obtain samples of the product.

A face shield should be worn when opening swollen cans. Do not flame swollen cans, wipe the end to be opened with alcohol or other sanitiser and allow to evaporate about 20 min. Swollen cans may be opened in a bag to reduce spray, or punctured through an inverted funnel.

Remove liquid with a sterile pipette and inoculate media directly. Remove solid material with a sterile cork borer or other sterile tool. Place solid material into sterile diluent and homogenise before inoculating media.

If a portion of the sample or the balance of the can is aseptically stored, this can be used as a reference for reconfirming test results. Do not freeze the sample, this will destroy some of the thermophiles.

10.7.4 Inoculation

Inoculate the media with 5–10 ml samples in triplicate for each test and temperature.

A variety of culturing methods and media are available. Choice of procedure will depend upon the product and expected spoilage organisms. Samples should be tested for aerobes, facultative anaerobes and anaerobes.

Incubate all sets of cultures at 55°C for 5 days for thermophiles, and another set at 37°C for 10 days or 30°C for 14 days (or two other sets at both temperatures) for mesophiles. The incubation times required may be longer for some organisms. When culturing anaerobes and facultative anaerobes place media in anaerobic jars and incubate. When culturing for thermophiles preheat the media before use.

Examine the samples for direct microscopic smear, and pH. Remove the contents of the cans, note any unusual odours and examine the product and the inside of the can. Record the results. Autoclave suspect product and containers before discarding. The container may be retained to obtain the container weight, to perform leak tests and/or to assess the integrity of the seam.

Examine the broth cultures daily and the plates after 48 h. Examine any growth under the microscope and identify the characteristics of the organisms. Growth in broth media may be indicated by change in the pH, apparent change in colour, odour or cloudiness of the media, or change in the viscosity of the media. Only discard cultures when it is certain that the samples are negative.

10.7.5 Interpretation of results

Table 10.1 can be used for interpretation of the tests results for low-acid canned foods. Any interpretation of results must be made by experienced, knowledgeable personnel.

Care must be taken not to misinterpret bacteriological results due to contamination causing false positives, or false negative results.

Table 10.1 Aids to the most probable interpretation of bacteriological results from conventionally canned low-acid packs[a,b]

Condition of can	Odour	Characteristics of pack				Key points from cultures[d]	Possible indications
		Appearance of liquid packs	pH[c]	Smear			
Swell	Sour	Frothy, possibly ropy brine	Below normal	Cocci and/or rods and/or yeasts		Positive aerobe and/or anaerobe at 30°C and 37°C	Post process leakage
Swell	Slightly off (sometimes ammoniacal)	Normal to frothy	Slightly to definitely abnormal – may be higher	Rods, spores sometimes seen		Positive aerobe and/or anaerobe at 30°C and/or 37°C. Often pellicle formation in aerobic broths	Post process leakage or gross under process
Swell	Sour	Frothy; possibly ropy brine; food firm and uncooked	Below normal	Mixed population often spores		Positive aerobe and/or anaerobe at 30°C, 37°C and often 55°C	No thermal process given
Swell	Normal to sour to cheesy	Pale colour or distinct colour change; frothy	Slightly to definitely below normal	Medium to long rods, often granular, spores seldom seen		Positive anaerobe at 55°C; no growth at 30°C; possibly growth at 37°C	Thermophilic anaerobes; inadequate cooling or storage at elevated temperature; *Clostridium* spp.
Swell	Normal to cheesy to putrid	Usually frothy with disintegration of solid particles	Slightly to definitely below normal	Rods; spores may be seen		Growth and gas in anaerobic culture at 37°C and/or 30°C but no growth in aerobic cultures	Under-processing; mesophilic anaerobes; high risk: consider survival of *Clostridium botulinum* and presence of toxin

	Odour	Brine	pH	Microscopy	Culture	Diagnosis
Swell	Normal	Normal	Normal	Normal	Negative	Insufficient exhaustion of can before seaming, low filling temperature, overfill or hydrogen swell
Swell	Little or no gas on opening sometimes 'fruity' odour	Normal	Normal to below normal	Large number of evenly stained cocci and/or rods	Negative	Pre-process spoilage
Swell	Sour to cheesy	Frothy	Often below normal	Poorly stained cocci and/or rods	Negative	Leaker spoilage followed by auto-sterilisation
Apparently sound	Sulphurous	Contents blackened	Normal to below normal	Rods	Anaerobic growth without gas at 55°C only	Thermophilic sulphur stinker. Under-processing. Inadequate cooling
Apparently sound	Normal to sour	Normal to cloudy brine	Normal to below normal	Cocci and/or rods	Positive aerobe and/or anaerobe at 30°C and usually 37°C	Post process leakage
Apparently sound	Normal to sour	Normal to cloudy brine	Below normal	Rods (often granular)	No growth below 37°C; aerobic growth without gas at 55°C; may get no growth if samples old or incubated for a long period	Thermophilic aerobes (flat sour); *Bacillus* spp.; inadequate cooling or storage at elevated temperatures
Apparently sound	Normal to sour	Normal to cloudy	Below normal	Rods, spores may be seen	Positive aerobe at 37°C and 30°C	Underprocess or leakage, mesophilic aerobic spore formers; *Bacillus* spp.

Table 10.1 *Continued*

Condition of can	Odour	Appearance of liquid packs	pH[c]	Smear	Key points from cultures[d]	Possible indications
		Characteristics of pack				
Apparently sound	Normal to sour	Normal to cloudy brine	Below normal	Granular rods	Negative	Underprocessing with auto-sterilisation of thermophilic aerobes
Apparently sound	Normal to sour	Normal	Normal to below normal	Large number of evenly stained cocci and/or rods per field	Negative	Pre-process spoilage
Apparently sound	Normal	Normal	Normal	Negative to occasional rods and/or cocci, i.e. normal	Negative	No microbiological problem

[a]Adapted from *Examination of Suspect Spoiled Cans and Aseptically Filled Containers* (Technical Manual No. 18). ed. K. L. Brown. The Campden Food Preservation Research Association, Gloucestershire, UK.

[b]Any evidence of mesophilic microorganisms and underprocessing could indicate the survival of *Clostridium botulinum* and should be treated with the required urgency and seriousness. These diagnoses must be considered as tentative. Substantial experience is required to make correct judgments. The characteristics in the tables must be considered with the overall pattern of the particular spoilage incident being investigated and the product history.

[c]The pH may rise particularly with microbial growth in meat or protein-rich food.

[d]There may be difficulty in isolating *Flavobacterium* spp. from milk or milk-based products at 25°C as they may not grow in aerobic broths.

10.8 Types of spoilage

The purpose of canning is to produce a safe and nutritious product which is also shelf stable, and which may not be used by the end consumer for several years after production. Canned food spoilage may be caused by improper processing or damage during handling and storage.

The usual defects or causes of spoilage for canned meats or fish are listed below:

- Microbiological
    - Underprocessing
    - Inadequate cooling
    - Infection resulting from leakage through seams
    - Pre-process spoilage
- Physical
    - Faulty technique in retort operation
    - Under-exhausting
    - Overfilling
    - Panelling
    - Metal plate faults
    - Seam defects
    - Contamination
- Handling
    - Corrosion
    - Denting and other damage

When spoilage occurs, review of production records and/or examination of the product and/or auditing processing procedures must be done by personnel knowledgeable in food processing science.

The cause of the spoilage must be identified and steps taken to prevent future occurrences.

10.9 Consumer illness complaints

All cases of illness complaints must be thoroughly investigated. When investigating a consumer complaint, obtain the actual can from the complainant and examine. If samples of the can contents are available have the sample analysed for suspect toxins and/or bacteria, depending upon the practicality of analysis and the suspected cause of illness.

Examine the production records for the suspect product. Obtain intact samples of the same can code as the illness complaint. Conduct a sterility test on the product and examine the product quality. When dealing with product from countries with uncertain sanitary standards the exterior of the container should also be swabbed and tested for pathogenic bacteria. Incidents have occurred where product from countries with uncertain sanitary standards have pathogenic bacteria on the exterior of the can or in the glue used for the label. The list below provides a brief summary of questions for the initial investigation of illness complaints.

Frequently, consumers will make illness complaints when they have flu-like symptoms after eating a canned product. Many food-poisoning bacteria create symptoms similar to flu illnesses. However true food poisoning from canned foods is extremely rare. Most of these illness complaints are unfounded, however the food may be blamed by association, even by medical practitioners.

Table 10.2 provides a list of common microbiological causes of food poisoning for comparative purposes.

Table 10.2 Selected list of illnesses from food poisoning of microbiological origin

Disease	Incubation period	Symptoms
Botulism	2 h to 8 days mean: 18–36 h	Vertigo, double/blurred vision, dryness of mouth, difficulty in swallowing, difficulty speaking and breathing, muscular weakness, constipation, pupils dilated/fixed, respiratory paralysis, gastrointestinal symptoms may precede neurological symptoms.
Staphylococcal intoxication	1–8 h mean: 2–4 h	Rapid onset of illness is characteristic, nausea, vomiting, abdominal pains, diarrhoea.
Clostridium perfringens	8–24 h mean: 10 h (abates within 12–24 h)	Gastroenteritis, abdominal pain, diarrhoea (chills and headache rare), without vomiting.
Salmonellosis	6–72 h mean: 18–36 h (abates after 2–5 days)	Abdominal pain accompanies diarrhoea (possibly bloody), chills, fever, nausea, vomiting.
Shigiellosis	1–7 days mean: <4 days	Abdominal pain, diarrhoea, bloody and mucoid stools, fever, vomiting.
Pathogenic E. coli gastroenteritis	5–48 h mean: 10–24 h	Abdominal pain, diarrhoea, nausea, vomiting, fever, chills, headache, muscular pain.
Vibrio parahaemolyticus	2–48 h mean: 12–18 h	Abdominal pain, diarrhoea, nausea, vomiting, fever, chills, headache, (usually from raw shellfish), symptoms similar to Salmonella but with mild fever and headache.
Typhoid fever	7–28 days mean: 14 days	Malaise, confusion, headache, cough, nausea, vomiting, chills, constipation, abdominal pain, bloody stools.
Paralytic shellfish poisoning	Within 30 mins (abates after 3–4 days)	Tingling sensation of lips and tongue, progressive feeling of numbness in arms, legs and neck, respiratory paralysis, vomiting, diarrhoea and abdominal cramps may occur.

Questionnaire for suspected food-poisoning complaints

- Name of complainant(s)?
- Number of people involved?
- The number of people who became ill?
- The number of people at the same meal who did not become ill?
- Suspect product and can code?
- Where purchased?
- List of other foods consumed at the meal and which individuals ate what? (Analyses of these foods should be performed.)
- Are there remains of the food(s)? Are they kept frozen or refrigerated?
- Symptoms and degree of illness? e.g. nausea, vomiting, abdominal pains, diarrhoea (bloody), chills, fever, headache, neurological symptoms?
- Time of onset of illness of symptoms: date and hour
- Time of eating suspected food or meal: date and hour
- Duration of illness?
- How was the suspected food prepared/stored before eating?
  - Failure to refrigerate or allowing the foods to remain warm for hours or days.
  - Preparing foods several hours or days before use or leftover foods.
  - Infected food preparer.
- Was a physician or hospital consulted? (Obtain the address and phone number. Obtain their opinion on the cause.)
- Was a stool sample taken for analysis?
- Were medications taken for treatment?
- Any medications taken by, or allergies of the complainant that may have contributed to the illness?
- If the onset of symptoms is very rapid, or if there was a wide range of times for a group, check meals from previous 24 h or longer.

10.10 Botulism

Botulism is caused by ingesting a neurotoxin produced by *Clostridium botulinum.*

Thermal processing schedules, for products heat treated to ensure commercial canning sterility, have been developed to destroy the spores of *C. botulinum* under normal processing conditions. *C. botulinum* may survive and grow in canned foods if the product has been underprocessed, or may infect the product after processing if the seam is defective or if the product is contaminated while the seams are still weak during cooling or shortly after. Pre-process spoilage, such as from excessive time delays from when the can is filled and seamed to the time that the product is processed, may also be a factor leading to the survival of *C. botulinum*.

Needless to say, instances of botulism from commercial products are extremely rare due to high industry standards.

10.11 Staphylococcal poisoning

Staphylococcal poisoning is a very rare occurrence in canned foods. In incidents of gross abuse of the product prior to canning and heat processing Staphylococcal growth may occur. The toxin produced by coagulase positive *Staphylococcus* is heat stable and will survive normal heat processing.

Samples of suspect product should be tested for the toxin; this is the only way to confirm the presence or absence of the toxin in the suspect product. The product itself may appear normal.

Examination of the processing conditions would determine if there has been a failure in good manufacturing practice. *Staphylococcus* is not a very competitive bacteria and prefers to grow in partially sterilised product. The product may also be held at elevated temperatures or otherwise abused, promoting conditions suitable for growth and the production of toxin.

Any failure of good manufacturing practice must be corrected immediately. The possibility of actually isolating *Staphylococcus* from samples drawn from processing will depend upon the sample size and the frequency of this incident occurring.

Bibliography

Brown, K.L. (ed.) (1987) *Examination of Suspect Spoiled Cans and Aseptically Filled Containers* (Technical manual no. 18). Campden Food Preservation Research Association, Gloucestershire, UK.

Franson, M.A.H. (ed.) (1987) *Standard Methods: For The Examination of Water and Waste Water* (16th edn). American Public Health Association, Washington, DC, USA.

Helrich, K.(ed.) (1990) *Official Methods of Analysis* (15th edn). Association of Official Analytical Chemists, Washington, DC, USA.

Hersom, A.C. and Hulland, E.D., 5th edition, (1964) *Canned Food: An Introduction to their Microbiology* (5th edn). Chemical Publishing Company Inc.

Martin, P.G. and Weatherwax, J. (1986) FOA *Manual of Food Quality Control: The Food Control Laboratory*.

The Food Processing Institute (1988) *Canned Food: Principles of Thermal Process Control, Acidification and Container Closure Evaluation* (5th edn). The Food Processing Institute, Washington, DC, USA.

Thorpe, R.H. and Barker, P.M. (1986) *Hygiene Design of Food Processing Equipment* (Technical Manual No. 8). Campden Food Preservation Research Association, Gloucestershire, UK.

Thorpe, R.H. and Everton, J.R. (1986) *Post-process Sanitation in Canneries* (Technical Manual No. 1). Campden Food Preservation Research Association, Gloucestershire, UK.

WHO (1976) *Microbiological Aspects of Food Hygiene* (Technical Report Services No. 598). World Health Organization, Geneva, Switzerland.

Laboratory in-house quality assurance and accreditation

Quality assurance

All laboratories should have a quality assurance programme to guarantee the validity of the test results. A quality assurance programme will validate the organisation of the laboratory programme, reduce costly errors, prevent erroneous results, improve efficiency, and control costs.

An outline of the programmes which should be in place is as follows:

Organisation
- Prepare an organisational chart
- Prepare job descriptions for all employees
- List fields of testing
- List types of clients

Human resources
- Keep on file resumes of personnel
- List training
- List memberships and professional societies

Physical resources
- Maintain equipment inventory, listing serial number, manufacturer, and model
- Establish calibration and maintenance programme of equipment
- Outline safety features and programmes
- Outline procedures for sub-contracting

Quality control procedures
- Describe sample control, storage and disposition procedures
- Outline sample receiving, identification, sample/test tracking, storage control and sample disposition

Test data, reports and records
- Accurate data recording
- Accurate checking of computations
- Use a recognised and approved testing procedure, have available copies of the original source of the testing procedure and outline reasons for any modifications
- Accurate reporting of test results
- Outline how errors of reporting are corrected

- Maintain records of test data, and reports for a minimum of 3 years or product shelf life if longer
- Describe confidentiality and security procedures

Measurement accuracy
- Maintain inventory control
- Describe how the equipment is calibrated
- Describe maintenance programme
- Ensure the use of defective equipment is prevented
- Obtain and file standard certificates for chemicals and reagents
- Properly store standards
- Maintain records for the above list

Quality control documents
- Describe internal quality control procedures
- Document all reviews of procedures, and individuals responsible
- Document how changes are made and when changes are made

Monitoring of testing
- Run samples in duplicate
- Run check samples of a known value
- Run reagent blanks
- Monitor the shelf-life of reagents and standards and prepare as required
- Maintain instruments following the recommended maintenance frequency
- Run samples spiked with a known quantity to check recovery of testing procedure

Technical documents
- List how and who controls the technical library
- Determine if the resources are adequate
- Maintain and update library as necessary
- Document how employees are updated on current developments

Complaints
- Outline how a disagreement with a test result is handled

Accreditation

To have accreditation of a laboratory, the overall programme of the laboratory is 'officially' recognised by a government agency responsible or some other independent organisation. The programmes in place in the laboratory are reviewed and periodically audited to confirm compliance with the rules and standards established by the auditing agency.

Accreditation would be based upon competence of the management responsibility, document control, process control, inspection and testing, corrective action, maintenance of records, internal quality audits, the physical resources of the laboratory, the skills and knowledge of the technicians, training programmes, and the freedom of conflict of interest.

Accreditation should assure both customers and laboratory management of the following benefits:

- validity of test results:
- promotes good testing practices:
- improves testing methods by providing feedback on the adequacy of test methods:
- promotes the acceptance of test results produced by one laboratory by another laboratory without further testing:
- facilitates international trade through the acceptance of test data.

ISO 9000

The ISO 9000 series of international standards have been adopted by the EU to provide a framework for quality assurance. These standards can be applied to quality assurance in the laboratory. In countries where it is available, a laboratory can obtain ISO 9000 certification. A laboratory which is a part of a food processing factory will play an important role in obtaining ISO 9000 certification for the factory; the same type of programme must be in place through the entire operation to guarantee the quality of the final product.

To obtain ISO 9000 certification the normal steps are as follows:

- Commitment of management to obtaining certification.
- Training of management and staff in the ISO programme.
- Document the quality management system, keep records to prove the quality management system is effective and develop a corrective action programme, following the ISO standards.
- Start internal audits to determine the effectiveness of the quality management system.
- Select a registrar, have the registrar or a consultant review the programmes in place to identify major deficiencies before the official assessment procedures.
- Make the identified improvements.
- The formal assessment is conducted by a audit team or registrar: they will determine if the quality manual conforms to the ISO

standard, then they will review procedures and work instructions to ensure these conform to the quality manual, and then will ensure the employees follow procedures and work instructions.

- Any deficiencies identified by the registrar will be corrected, then another audit will follow.
- Registration follows when the company is approved by the registrar.
- Internal audits must be conducted to maintain registration as outlined by the quality manual, and twice per year the registrar will conduct surveillance audits.

Acknowledgement

Dr K. Mussar of the Diversified Research Laboratories Ltd, Toronto, Canada is gratefully acknowledged.

Reference

Surak, J.G. (1992) The ISO 9000 Standards, establishing a foundation for quality. *Food Technol.* **46** (11), 75–80.

Introduction to quality indicators

Analytical methods to quantify fish spoilage have been worked upon for many years because of perishable nature of the product.

There has been limited success due to the variety of chemical pathways through which spoilage may occur. Each individual species has its own characteristics of spoilage, the chemistry of the product will vary depending upon the handling conditions of the raw product and the processing treatments and methods for the finished product, and storage time and temperature variables.

The following procedures include methods frequently used for quantifying spoilage. These methods can be useful for routine quality control inspections in specific applications under controlled processing conditions.

Quality indicators: Ammonia

Application: Fresh and frozen fish.

DISCUSSION
Ammonia is the major component of the volatile amines formed by

the decomposition in many species of fish, and is recovered in the estimation of total volatile bases (TVB).

There are commercially available tests kits for ammonia from Sigma (St Louis, MO, USA), Boehringer Mannheim (Mannheim, Germany) and Merck (Darmstadt, Germany).

Quality indicators: Total volatile bases (TVB)

Application: Estimation of enzymic and baterial spoilage in fresh marine fish. Not recommended for salmon.

REAGENTS

(a) Magnesium sulphate solution (dissolve 600.0 g of $MgSO_4.7H_2O$ in distilled water, add 3.5 ml concentrated H_2SO_4, transfer to a 1000 ml volumetric flask and make up to volume with distilled water).
(b) 20% sodium hydroxide (dissolve 20 g NaOH in 100 ml distilled water).
(c) 0.10 N sodium hydroxide standardised solution.
(d) 1.0 N sodium hydroxide standardised solution.
(e) Potassium acid phthalate, analytical grade (dry 3 g in a drying oven at 103°C overnight).
(f) Phenolphthalein indicator (dissolve 1 g phenolphthalein in 100 ml of 95% ethanol).
(g) 0.10 N hydrochloric acid standardised solution.
(h) Methyl red indicator (to 100 ml ethanol add 0.05 g methyl red and 0.075 g bromocresol green).
(i) 2% boric acid solution (dissolve 20.0 g boric acid in 1 litre distilled water)
(j) 1 N sulphuric acid solution.

PROCEDURE

(1) Sample must be held on ice to retard further spoilage. If held longer than 2 h the sample should be frozen. Blend or commute 30.0 g of the product with 70 ml distilled water.
(2) Add 100 ml magnesium sulphate solution, blend for 1 min.
(3) Add an additional 100 ml magnesium sulphate solution, then blend again for 1 min. Permit the mixture to stand a few minutes to allow the foam and liquid to separate. Filter liquid through a Buchner funnel under vacuum, using Whatman no.1 filter paper (or equivalent).
(4) Adjust filtrate to pH 2 using the 1.0 N sulphuric acid or 1.0 M sodium hydroxide.

(5) Set up a distillation assembly, use a Kjeldahl apparatus or assemble a similar distillation and condensing unit.

(6) Place a receiving flask containing 20 ml of 2% boric acid solution at the collection end of the unit. Make sure the outlet of the still is below the level of the boric acid.

(7) Place 25 ml of sample extract into a distillation flask using a volumetric pipette (a larger or smaller volume can be used as necessary). Place 200 ml distilled water in flask (use a smaller volume if a micro-Kjeldahl unit is used), then add 5 ml 20% sodium hydroxide, rinse neck of flask with distilled water.

(8) Attach the sample flask to the distillation unit. Mix and begin heating. Collect 100 ml of distillate (collect 50 ml of distillate if using a micro-Kjeldahl).

(9) Add 5 drops of methyl red indicator to the distillate.

(10) Titrate with standardised 0.10 N HCl (alternatively 0.010 N HCl may be used).

(11) A blank with 100 ml distilled water should also be prepared. Continue starting at step (2) above.

CALCULATION

$$TVB = \frac{(\text{Volume sample} - \text{Volume blank}) (\text{Normality HCl}) (1400) (f)}{\text{weight of sample (g)}}$$

where f is the dilution factor (if the directions are followed $f = 300/25$).

REFERENCE

Botta, J.R., Lauder, J.T. and Jewer, M.A. (1984) Effect of methodology on total volatile basic nitrogen (TVB-N) determination as an index of quality of fresh Atlantic cod. *J. Food Sci.*, **49**, 734.

Quality indicators: K-*value analysis*

Application: Fresh or frozen fish.

DISCUSSION

The K value is an index of enzymic decomposition of nucleotides. A decrease in ATP levels triggers the onset of rigor mortis and the degradation of nucleotides. This index correlates well with sensory evaluation for some fish species.

The biochemical sequence of decomposition can be represented as:

$$ATP \rightarrow ADP \rightarrow AMP \rightarrow IMP \rightarrow INO \rightarrow Hx \rightarrow X \rightarrow U$$

where ATP is adenosine-5'-triphosphate; ADP is adenosine-5'-diphosphate; AMP is adenosine-5'-monophosphate; IMP is inosine-5'-monophosphate; INO is inosine; Hx is hypoxanthine; X is xanthine; and U is uric acid.

The formula for the K-value is

$$K = \frac{([INO] + [Hx]) \, (100\%)}{[ATP] + [ADP] + [AMP] + [IMP] + [INO] + [Hx]}$$

A simplification of the K-value formula is

$$K_i = \frac{([INO] + [Hx]) \, (100\%)}{[IMP] + [INO] + [Hx]}$$

This alternative calculation of the K-value permits the concentration of each compound to be measured enzymically by an enzyme sensor which is coupled to an oxygen electrode. The correlation between the K-value and K_i-value is usually good. Commercially available instruments to measure the 'K-value' are available, such as the Freshness Meter Model KV-101, supplied by Oriental Electric Company (9–7, Nobidome, 3-Chome, Niiza Saitama 352, Japan). HPLC methods for calculating the K-value components are also used.

REFERENCES

Burt, J.R. *et al.* (1976). Comparison of methods of freshness assessment of wet fish. II. Instrumental and chemical assessments of boxed experimental fish. *J. Food Technol.*, **11**, 73.

Hughes, R.B. and Jones, N.R. (1966) Measurement of hypoxanthine concentration in canned herring as an index of the freshness of the raw material with a comment on flavour relations. *J. Sci. Food Agric.*, **17**, 434.

Jones, N.R. and Murray, J. (1962) Degradation of adenine and hypoxanthine – nucleotide in the muscle of chill-stored trawled cod (*Gadus callarias*), *J. Sci. Food Agric.*, **13**, 475.

Karube, I., *et al.* (1984) Determination of fish freshness with an enzyme sensor system. *J. Agric. Food Chem.*, **32**, 314.

Kramer, D.E., *et al.* (1985) Postmortem reaction rates for nucleotide changes in Pacific salmon muscle during partial freezing storage, Paper No. 99. International Congress on the Engineering of Food, Edmonton, Alberta, 7–9 July.

Watanabe, E. *et al.* (1983) Determination of hypoxanthine in fish meat with an enzyme sensor. *J. Food Sci.*, **48**, 496.

Quality indicators: Ethanol

Application: Fresh, frozen or canned fish.

DISCUSSION

The advantage of ethanol as an indicator of quality is that it is not altered by thermal processing of hermetically-sealed containers. The main interest in the use of ethanol is as a quality indicator in canned salmon.

Ethanol is a common metabolite of bacteria derived from anaerobic glycolysis, and the deamination and decarboxyllation of amino acids.

Commercially available tests kits for ethanol have been used to correlate to sensory evaluations of fish product, such as is available from Boehringer Mannheim (Germany). AOAC describes a GC method.

REFERENCES

AOAC (1990) *Official Methods of Analysis* (15th edn). Association of Official Analytical Chemists, Washington, DC, USA, method 986.12.

Hollingworth Jr, T.A. and Throm, H.R. (1983) A headspace gas chromatographic method for the rapid analysis of ethanol in canned salmon. *J. Food Sci.*, **48**, 290.

Kelleher, S. and Zall, R.R. (1983) Ethanol accumulations in muscle tissue as a chemical indicator of fish spoilage, *J. Food Biochem.*, **7**, 87.

Quality indicators: The Torry meter

Application: Fresh fish, whole, whole gutted, and headed and gutted. Not recommended for fillets or previously frozen product.

DISCUSSION

The Torry meter is an electrical device used to correlate readings to quality. The meter measures dielectric properties of the fresh fish and displays the reading. The range of the reading is from 0 to 16. A reading of 0 represents badly spoiled fish and a reading of 16 represents very fresh fish. All displayed readings are corrected to 0°C.

The dielectric properties of the fish changes with the quality and age of the fish. Fish of different species, of the same quality, will display different meter readings. The oil content will also affect the reading. The Torry meter has a constant consistent reading over time.

Correlations of meter reading to quality for fillets is not as good, and then only with the skin-on side.

A commercial modification of the Torry meter is the RT Fish Freshness Grader manufactured by Pafagnataekni Electronics (Reykjavik, Iceland) with a throughput of 100 tons per 8 h for 3 kg fish.

Total crude protein

Application: Meat products, fish products, meals.

REAGENTS

(a) Concentrated sulphuric acid (H_2SO_4, CIL, CP, sp.gr. 1.84).
(b) Red mercuric oxide (HgO).
(c) Anhydrous sodium sulphate (Na_2SO_4).
(d) Sodium thiosulphate solution (80 g $NaS_2O_3 \cdot 5H_2O$ in 1.0 litre distilled water).
(e) Concentrated sodium hydroxide solution (180 g NaOH dissolved in 260 ml distilled water).
(f) Boric acid solution (40 g H_3BO_3 in 1.0 litre distilled water).

(g) 0.500 N hydrochloric acid standardised solution (HCl).

(h) Bromocresol green indicator solution (0.04% solution).

PROCEDURE

(1) Mix or blend the product if necessary to obtain a homogenous sample.

(2) Accurately weigh 3.0–5.0 g of meat or fish products, or 1.0 g for meal samples, weigh and record the sample weight to the nearest 0.0001 g.

(3) Analytically transfer the sample to a 500 ml Kjeldhal flask.

(4) Add 0.7 g red mercuric oxide and 15 g of anhydrous sodium sulphate (or 1 Kel-Pak unit #5). Add three glass boiling beads.

(5) Add 35 ml concentrated sulphuric acid. Swirl to mix well. Place the Kjeldhal flask in the digestion rack and boil for 2 h.

(6) Allow to cool at the end of the digestion time. Then add 200 ml distilled water and allow to cool again. Then add 25 ml of sodium thiosulphate solution to precipitate the mercury.

(7) Into a 250 ml Erlenmeyer flask add 75 ml boric acid solution. Place this flask at the collection end of the condenser unit.

(8) Cautiously add 90 ml concentrated sodium hydroxide solution. Tilt the Kjeldhal flask and slowly pour in the solution to form a layer on the bottom of the flask. Place flask on the distillation rack and connect to the condenser unit.

(9) Swirl the Kjeldhal flask to mix and distill into the boric acid solution. End the distillation when approximately 75 ml is collected or until 'bumping' starts.

(10) Add approximately 1 ml indicator solution to the boric acid condensate. Accurately titrate with 0.500 N hydrochloric acid standard solution to the first clear golden yellow end-point.

CALCULATION

$$\% \text{ Protein} \quad \frac{(\text{ml of 0.5 N HCl}) \times (4.3775)}{\text{Weight of sample in (g)}}$$

REFERENCE

AOAC (1990) *Official Methods of Analysis* (15th edn). Association of Official Analytical Chemists, Washington, DC, USA, method 981.10.

ALTERNATIVE METHODS

There are many commercially available units for performing crude protein analyses. Many have advantages of reducing analysis time, or increasing number of samples, or permitting smaller sample size. Selection of alternative methods can be tailored to the individual requirements of the laboratory.

Estimation of moisture

Application: Meats, fish and meals.

PROCEDURE
(1) Dry a moisture dish in a drying oven at 105°C for 20–30 min and cool in a desiccator.
(2) Blend or mix the sample if necessary.
(3) Tare the predried moisture dish and accurately weigh 10.000 g of meat or fish sample into the dish, or 2.000 g of meal, weigh and record the sample weight to the nearest 0.0001 g). 0.0001 g).
(4) Place the sample in a drying oven at 105°C for 3 h.
(5) Allow to cool to room temperature in a desiccator, then re-weigh.

CALCULATION

$$\% \text{ Moisture} = \frac{(\text{Initial weight} - \text{dried weight}) \times 100\%}{\text{Initial sample weight in (g)}}$$

ALTERNATIVE METHODS
AOAC methods 950.46 and 985.14. Cited in AOAC (1990) *Official Methods of Analysis* (15th edn). Association of Analytical Chemists, Washington, DC, USA.

Total ash

Application: Meat products, fish products, meals.

PROCEDURE
(1) Preheat the muffle furnace to 500°C.
(2) Accurately weigh and record the weight of a crucible and to the nearest 0.0001 g.
(3) In the weighed crucible accurately weigh and record the weight of the sample to the nearest 0.0001 g. Use sample weights of 3.000–5.000 g for meat and fish products and 1.000 g for meals.
(4) Place the crucible with the sample in the 500°C muffle furnace for 1.5 h. Do not cover the crucible.
(5) Remove the crucible, place in a desiccator to cool for 30 min.
(6) Weigh and record the total weight of the crucible and ash.

CALCULATION

$$\% \text{ Ash} = \frac{((\text{Weight of crucible and ash}) - (\text{weight of crucible})) \times 100\%}{((\text{Weight of crucible and sample}) - (\text{weight of crucible}))}$$

REFERENCE
AOAC (1990) *Official Methods of Analysis* (15th edn). Association of Official Analytical Chemists, Washington, DC, USA, method 900.02A/B.

Crude fat: Goldfisch method

Application: Meat products, fish products, meals.

REAGENTS:

(a) Ether.

PROCEDURE

(1) Mix or blend the product if necessary to obtain a homogenous sample.
(2) Dry a Goldfisch sample thimble in an oven at 105°C.
(3) Accurately weigh 10.00–20.00 g of meat or fish products, or 4.00 g meal, weigh and record the sample weight to the nearest 0.01 g.
(4) Quantitatively transfer the sample to the predried sample thimble. Dry the thimble and sample in an oven at 105°C for 25 min.
(5) Accurately weigh an extraction beaker and record the weight to the nearest 0.001 g.
(6) Fill beaker with 60 ml ether. Secure in place on the Goldfisch apparatus the dried sample and thimble and beaker with ether. Turn water on condensing unit and heat.
(7) Reflux for 2 h. Allow to cool a few minutes. Lower beaker and replace sample tube with solvent reclaiming tube. Secure unit and heat.
(8) Turn the unit off when only a few ml of ether/oil remain in the bottom of the beaker. Remove the beaker. In a fume hood place the beaker on a hot plate at low heat to evaporate the remaining ether. Do not overheat, do not permit the fat to 'splatter'.
(9) Place beaker in a desiccator to cool for 30 min to 1 h until a constant weight is attained. Weigh beaker.

CALCULATION

$$\% \text{ Fat} = \frac{(\text{Weight of beaker and oil} - \text{weight of beaker}) \times 100\%}{\text{Weight of sample (g)}}$$

ALTERNATIVE METHODS

AOAC methods 972.21, 985.15, 948.15, 964.12, 948.16 and 969.24. Cited in AOAC (1990) *Official Methods of Analysis* (15th edn). Association of Official Analytical Chemists, Washington, DC, USA.

There are other commercially available units for performing crude fat. Selection of alternative methods can be tailored to the individual requirements of the laboratory.

Salt analysis

Application: Meat products, fish products, meals.

REAGENTS

(a) 0.100 N silver nitrate standardised solution ($AgNO_3$).
(b) 0.100 N ammonium thiocyanate standardised solution (NH_4SCN).
(c) Ferric ammonium sulphate indicator (saturated solution of $FeNH_4(SO)_4)_2.12H_2O$).
(d) Concentrated nitric acid (HNO_3).
   (All reagents must be chloride free.)

PROCEDURE
(1) Mix or blend the product if necessary to obtain a homogeneous sample.
(2) Accurately weigh 3.000–5.000 g of meat or fish products, or 1.000 g for meal products, weigh and record the sample weight to the nearest 0.0001 g.
(3) Analytically transfer the sample to a 500 ml Erlenmeyer flask.
(4) Add 25.0 ml 0.100 N silver nitrate from a burette or volumetric pipette.
(5) Add 25 ml concentrated nitric acid.
(6) Boil gently on a hot plate in a fume hood until the liquid is clear, usually 10–30 min. Allow to cool to room temperature.
(7) Add 50 ml distilled water and 5 ml ferric ammonium sulphate indicator.
(8) Titrate with 0.100 N ammonium thiocyanate until the solution turns a permanent light brown.

CALCULATION

$$\% \text{ NaCl} = \frac{(\text{Volume silver nitrate} - \text{volume } NH_4SCN) \times 0.5845}{\text{Weight of sample (g)}}$$

$$= \frac{(25 - \text{ml } NH_4SCN) \times 0.5845}{\text{weight of sample in (g)}}$$

REFERENCE
AOAC (1990) *Official Methods of Analysis* (15th edn). Association of Official Analytical Chemists, Washington, DC, USA, method 937.09.

ALTERNATIVE METHODS
AOAC methods 971.19, 935.47. Cited in *Official Methods of Analysis* (15th edn). Association of Official Analytical Chemists, Washington, DC, USA.

Salt determination in solutions

Application: For solutions free of organic material.

REAGENTS

(a) 0.100 N silver nitrate standardised solution ($AgNO_3$).
(b) 5% potassium chromate solution (K_2CrO_4).

PROCEDURE
(1) Using a volumetric pipette place 2.0 ml of sample into a 250 ml flask (sample size may be varied depending upon the salt content). Add 50 ml distilled water.
(2) Add 1 ml of 5% potassium chromate solution.
(3) Titrate with 0.1 N silver nitrate to the first permanent colour change.

CALCULATION

$$\% \; NaCl = \frac{\text{Volume silver nitrate} \times 0.5845}{\text{Volume of sample}}$$

ALTERNATIVE METHODS
Sodium chloride refractometers and hydrometers are available, sodium chloride and chloride electrodes may also be used depending upon the application required by the laboratory.

Total carbohydrates calculated as dextrose

Application: Meat products and fish products containing filler, binder or other ingredients including flour, cereal meals, starch and sugars.

REAGENTS

(a) Copper sulphate solution (dissolve 40.0 g $CuSO_4 \cdot 5H_2O$) in distilled water and dilute to 1.0 litre in a volumetric flask).
(b) Rochelle salt solution (dissolve 200 g sodium potassium tartrate crystals in approximately 600 ml distilled water, allow to cool then add 150 g NaOH, mix and dilute to 1.0 litre in a volumetric flask).
(c) 1.5 N hydrochloric acid.
(d) 1+2 hydrochloric acid solution (mix concentrated HCl 1 to 2 with distilled water).
(e) 0.025 N sodium thiosulphate standardised solution.
(f) 10% potassium iodide solution (dissolve 100 g KI in 1.0 litre distilled water).

(g) 20% sodium hydroxide solution (dissolve 200 g NaOH in 1.0 litre distilled water).

(h) 1+3 sulphuric acid solution (mix concentrated H_2SO_4 1 to 3 with distilled water).

(i) Starch indicator solution (mix 1 g soluble powdered starch in 20 ml distilled water and pour mixture into 500 ml boiling distilled water. Boil 10 min to dissolve starch, then cool. Store in a glass-stoppered bottle, add 0.625 g salicylic acid as a preservative).

(j) 20% phosphotungstic acid ($P_2O_5.24WO_3 \cdot xH_2O$).

(k) Standard dextrose solution (dissolve 0.200 g dextrose in 100 ml distilled water in a volumetric flask).

(l) Ammonium thiocyanate.

PROCEDURE

(1) Mix or blend the product if necessary to obtain a homogenous sample.

(2) Accurately weigh 10.00 g of sample into a 200 ml phosphoric acid flask. Add 90 ml of 1.5 N HCl, heat for 90 min in a boiling water bath, then cool to room temperature. Use 20% NaOH to make the solution just alkaline, testing with pH paper (approx. 25 ml 20% NaOH will be used). Add 10 ml of 1+2 HCl solution, allow to cool.

(3) Add 20 ml of 20% phosphotungstic acid solution, make to volume with distilled water, mix. Allow to stand 15–30 min, then filter (use Whatman no. 41 or 42 or equivalent).

(4) Using a volumetric pipette, place 5.0 ml of filtrate into a 125 ml Erlenmeyer flask. (If the sample contains over 8% reducing sugars use 2.0 ml filtrate and 3.0 ml distilled water and adjust the calculations accordingly.) Add 5.0 ml copper sulphate solution by volumetric pipette and 5.0 ml of the Rochelle salt solution by volumetric pipette. Heat on a hot plate with glass boiling beads, boil for 1 min, allow to cool.

(5) Add 20 ml of 10% potassium iodide solution, then add 4 ml of 1+3 H_2SO_4. Titrate with standardised sodium thiosulphate solution until the yellow iodine colour has almost disappeared. Then add 4 ml of starch indicator and 1 g of sodium ammonium thiocyanate. One drop of sodium thiosulphate should change the colour from blue to white or a faint lilac colour.

(6) Prepare a blank determination using 5 ml of distilled water instead of the filtrate starting at step (4). Also run a standard determination using 5 ml of the standard dextrose solution instead of the filtrate starting as step (4). The blank and standard determination must be tested daily.

CALCULATION

$$\% \text{ Dextrose} = \frac{((\text{ml of blank titration}) - (\text{ml of sample titration})) \times 4}{(\text{ml of blank titration}) - (\text{ml of standard titration})}$$

Report results as dextrose.

REFERENCE

AOAC (1990) *Official Methods of Analysis* (15th edn). Association of Official Analytical Chemists, Washington, DC, USA, method 958.06.

Qualitative determination for starch

Application: Meat products, fish products containing filler, binder or other ingredients including flour, cereal meals, starch and some hydrolysed vegetable proteins or broth preparations which contain starch.

REAGENTS

Iodine – potassium iodine solution (dissolve 20 g I_2 and 60 g KI in 1000 ml distilled water, store in a brown glass bottle).

PROCEDURE
(1) Obtain 1–10 ml of liquid from sample. If the product does not have any free liquid, blend or commute sample with a small quantity of nitrite-free distilled water.
(2) Pour 1–10 ml of sample liquid into a beaker. Add 1–5 ml of the iodine–potassium iodine solution.
(3) The mixture will turn a blue – black colour if starch is present. This method may also be used to indicate the presence of some forms of hydrolysed vegetable protein or broth which are commonly used in canned tunas.

REFERENCE

AOAC (1990) *Official Methods of Analysis* (15th edn). Association of Official Analytical Chemists, Washington, DC, USA, method 935.49.

Histamine determination: Fluorometric method

Application: Canned tuna, fresh and other scombroid fish.

REAGENTS

(a) Histamine dihydrochloride solutions
　　(i) 1 mg/mL stock solution (weigh exactly 0.1691 g histamine·2HCl, transfer into a 100 ml volumetric flask, dissolve

and dilute to volume with 0.10 M HCl). Prepare fresh weekly, store in a refrigerator.

(ii) 10 mg/ml intermediate solution (pipette 1 ml from stock solution into a 100 ml volumetric flask, dilute to volume with 0.10 M HCl). Prepare fresh weekly, store in a refrigerator.

(iii) 0.5, 1.0 and 1.25 μg/5 ml working solutions (pipette 1, 2 and 2.5 ml from intermediate solution each into 100 ml volumetric flasks, dilute to volume with 0.10 M HCl). Prepare fresh daily.

(b) 0.2% o-Phthalicdicarboxaldehyde (OPT) solution (weigh exactly 0.100 g OPT, transfer into a 100 ml volumetric flask, dissolve and dilute to volume with methanol, store in an amber bottle and refrigerate, prepare fresh weekly).

(c) 3.57 N phosphoric acid (dilute 121.8 ml of 85% H_3PO_4 to 1 litre with distilled water. Standardise with 1.00 N NaOH, titrate 5.0 ml acid to phenolphthalein end-point, adjust concentration as necessary).

(d) Bio-Rad AG (or Dowex) 1–X8, 50–100 mesh ion exchange resin (approximately 30 g resin will be adequate for six ion exchange columns, convert resin to OH- form by adding 15 ml of 2N NaOH per gram of resin in a beaker, swirl and let stand 20–30 min, decant the liquid and repeat with additional base, decant the liquid and add distilled water to the beaker to wash the resin, continue decanting and washing with distilled water four to five times). Prepare fresh weekly.

PROCEDURE

(1) Prepare ion exchange columns: Use 7 mm i.d. glass columns with Teflon stopcocks. Fill glass columns with distilled water. Soak glass wool and place a small plug in the base of each column. Pour the previously prepared resin into the columns, adjusting the height of the resin to form a 8 cm bed. Do not allow the resin to become dry. Do not regenerate resin in the packed columns. Cover the tops of columns when not in use. Prepare new columns weekly, discarding old resin.

(2) Prepare standard curve:
    (i) Pipette 5.0 ml of each working standard solution into separate 50 ml glass test tubes. Prepare a blank using 5 ml 0.10 N HCl. To the blank and each standard make the following additions.
    (ii) Pipette 10.0 ml 0.10 N HCl to each tube, mix on a vortex mixer.
    (iii) Pipette 3.0 ml 1.0 N NaOH to each tube; mix immediately.

     (iv) Within 5 min, pipette 1.0 ml OPT, mix immediately.

     (v) After exactly 4 min, pipette 3.0 ml 3.57 N phosphoric acid, mix immediately. (The blank and standards or samples are usually run in series, timing 10–15 s between additions to the standards or samples. In this fashion, additions to 6–12 samples may conducted at one time.)

     (vi) Within 1.5 h read and record the fluorescence.

(3) Sample preparation and analysis:

     (i)   Mix or blend the product if necessary to obtain a homogenous sample.

     (ii)   Weigh 10 g of the samples into a 250 ml beakers and add 50 ml methanol. Homogenise with a polytron blender for 2 min. Rinse blender with methanol into the beaker. Quantitatively transfer the methanol/sample to a 100 ml volumetric flask, rinsing the beaker with several portions of methanol. Make up to volume with methanol and mix well. Filter through folded filter paper. The filtrate may be stored in the refrigerator several weeks.

     (iii) Pass approximately 5 ml distilled water through the ion exchange columns and discard eluate. Lower the water level in the columns to the top of the column resin. Place a 50 ml volumetric flask containing 5 ml 1.0 N HCl under each column to collect the eluate. Pipette 1.0 ml sample extract onto the column head, allow the column to flow to move the extract into the resin head. Add 4–5 ml distilled water, continue column flow. When the liquid level in the column is 2 mm above the resin head add more distilled water. Follow with larger portions of distilled water. When approximately 35 ml is collected in the 50 ml volumetric flask close the flow, make up the sample eluate to volume with distilled water and mix. Continue with other samples. Refrigerate eluted samples if not used within one hour, eluted samples should be used the same day. (An experienced technician can run 6–12 ion exchange columns at the same time.)

     (iv) Pipette 5.0 ml aliquots from the eluate of the each sample into separate 50 ml glass tubes. To each sample make the following additions.

     (v) Pipette 10.0 ml 0.10 N HCl to each tube, mix on a vortex mixer.

     (vi) Pipette 3.0 ml 1.0 N NaOH to each tube, mix immediately.

     (vii) Within 5 min, pipette 1.0 ml OPT, mix immediately.

     (viii) After exactly 4 min, pipette 3.0 ml 3.57 N phosphoric acid, mix immediately. (The samples are usually run in series, timing 10–15 s between additions to the individual samples. In this fashion additions to 6–12 samples may conducted at one time.)

(ix) Within 1.5 h read and record the fluorescence. If the fluorescence is over scale, dilute the sample 1:1 or 1:2 with the blank-OPT mixture and read the fluorescence.

CALCULATION

(1) Calculate the slope of the standard curve:

$$m = ((I_a/1.25) + (I_b) + (I_c) (2))/3$$

where I_a, I_b and I_c = the fluorescence of the 1.25, 1.0 and 0.5 μg histamine standards.

(2) Calculate histamine concentration in samples:

mg Histamine/100 g fish = (10) (F) ($1/m$) (I_s)

where F is the dilution factor if the sample was diluted, if undiluted $F = 1$; m is the slope of standard curve (assume slope is linear); and I_s is the fluorescence of sample.

REFERENCE

AOAC (1990) *Official Methods of Analysis* (15th edn). Association of Official Analytical Chemists, Washington, DC, USA, method 977.13.

REFERENCE ALTERNATIVE METHODS

J. Food Sci., **42**, (6) (1977), 1584 – 1586.
AOAC methods 954.04, 957.07. Cited in *Official Methods of Analysis* (15th edn). Association of Analytical Chemists, Washington, DC, USA.

Quantitative determination of nitrite by the Griess–Ilosvay reaction

Application: Meat products, fish product.

REAGENTS

(a) Modified Griess–Ilosvay reagent. (Weigh 0.500 g sulphanilic acid and 0.100 g N-1-naphthylethylenediamine dihydrochloride and quantitatively transfer to a 500 ml Florence flask containing 300 ml 15% v/v acetic acid. Mix on a magnetic stirrer to dissolve. Store in a brown-coloured glass bottle.)

(b) Saturated mercuric chloride. (Weigh 6.9 g $HgCl_2$ in a 250 ml beaker, dissolve in 100 ml distilled water mixing on a magnetic stirrer for 1 h. Add more $HgCl_2$ if necessary to ensure saturation.

(c) Standardised sodium nitrite stock solution (Dry AR $NaNO_2$ in a drying oven at 100°C for 1 h and cool in a desiccator for 20–30 min. Weigh 0.500 g dried $NaNO_2$ and quantitatively transfer to a

1000 ml volumetric flask. Dissolve and make up to volume with distilled water, mix. 1 ml = 500 µg $NaNO_2$.)

(d) Standardised sodium nitrite working solution. (Transfer 10 ml of stock $NaNO_2$ stock solution with a volumetric pipette to a 1000 ml volumetric flask. Dissolve and make up to volume with distilled water, mix. 1 ml = 5 µg $NaNO_2$.)

(e) Filter paper (ensure filter paper is nitrite free).

PROCEDURE

(1) Prepare standard curve:

(i) Prepare working standards from the dilute standard solution of $NaNO_2$ following the table below to seven 50 ml volumetric flasks, use volumetric pipettes to transfer aliquots:

Flask	Volume dilute standard (ml)	Final concentration (µg $NaNO_2$/ml)
1	0	0
2	2	0.20
3	3	0.30
4	4	0.40
5	5	0.50
6	10	1.00
7	20	2.00

(ii) Fill each flask to 3/4 full with distilled water and mix. Then add 2 ml Griess–Ilosvay reagent to each flask. Dilute to volume with distilled water, mix.

(iii) Allow the standards to stand 1 h to allow maximum colour development. Measure and record the absorbance on a spectrophotometer at 540 nm against the reagent blank.

(2) Sample preparation and analysis:

(i) Weigh 10.00 g of meat or fish products into a 150 ml beaker. Add approximately 50 ml distilled water. Heat on a hot plate, boil for 1–2 min, stirring with a glass rod to break up the sample.

(ii) Quantitatively transfer sample and liquid to a 250 ml volumetric flask. Add 5 ml saturated $HgCl_2$ to clarify the extract. Dilute to volume with distilled water, mix. Filter through nitrite free filter paper, the filtrate must be free of turbidity.

(iii) With a volumetric pipette transfer a 25 ml aliquot of the filtrate to a 50 ml volumetric flask. Fill the volumetric flask to 3/4 full with distilled water, mix. Add 2 ml Griess–Ilosvay reagent. Dilute to volume with distilled water and mix. (The sample should provide a mid-range absorbance in step (5) below. If the 25 ml aliquot of the filtrate is not appropriate, adjust the volume of this dilution step as necessary.)

(iv) Allow the sample to stand 1 h to allow maximum colour development. Measure and record the absorbance on a spectrophotometer at 540 nm against a reagent blank.

CALCULATION

(1) Calculate the slope of the standard curve:

$$m = ((A2/0.20) + (A3/0.30) + (A4/0.40) + (A5/0.50) + (A6) + (A7/2.0))/6$$

where $A2$, $A3$, $A4$, $A5$, $A6$, $A7$ = the absorbance of the working standards at 540 nm

(2) Calculate $NaNO_2$ concentration in samples:

$$\mu g\ NaNO_2/g = \frac{(A_s)\ (1/m)\ (50)\ (250)}{(\text{Volume aliquot})\ (\text{sample weight})}$$

where A_s is sample absorbance; m is slope of standard curve (assume slope is linear); 50 is volume of volumetric flask, step 2 (iii); 250 is volume of meat extract, step 2 (ii); volume aliquot is volume of filtrate, step 2 (ii).

REFERENCE

AOAC (1990) *Official Methods of Analysis* (15th edn). Association of Official Analytical Chemists, Washington, DC, USA, method 973.31.

Qualitative determination of nitrite

Application: Meat products, fish products.

REAGENTS

(a) Potassium iodide solution (dissolve 5 g KI in 100 ml distilled water).
(b) Diluted sulphuric acid (mix concentrated H_2SO_4 1 to 4 with distilled water).
(c) Saturated starch solution.

PROCEDURE

(1) Obtain 1–10 ml of liquid from sample. If the product does not have any free liquid, blend or commute sample with a small quantity of nitrite-free distilled water.
(2) In a fume hood, pour 1–10 ml of sample liquid into a beaker. Add a few drops of potassium iodide solution, then a few drops of dilute sulphuric acid, then a few drops of saturated starch solution.

(3) The mixture will turn a blue – black colour if nitrite is present.

REFERENCE

Food Chemicals Codex (3rd edn). National Academy Press, 1981, p. 517.

Quantitative determination of hydroxyproline

Application: Meat and meat products.

REAGENTS

All reagents should be of analytical quality. Distilled or deionised water should be used.

(a) Hydrochloric acid solution containing tin (II) chloride. Dissolve 15.0 g tin (II) chloride dihydrate in water and dilute to 1 litre. Add 100 ml hydrochloric acid (1.19 g/ml).

(b) Hydrochloric acid, approx. 6M solution. Mix equal volumes of hydrochloric acid and water.

(c) Sodium hydroxide, approx. 10M solution. Dissolve 40 g NaOH in water. Cool and dilute to 100 ml.

(d) Sodium hydroxide, approx. 1M solution. Dissolve 4 g NaOH in water. Cool and dilute to 100 ml.

(e) Buffer solution. Dissolve in water: 50 g citric acid monohydrate, 26.3 g NaOH, and 146.1 g sodium acetate trihydrate. Dilute to 1000 ml with water. Mix this solution with 200 ml water and 300 ml propan-1-ol. This solution is stable for 4 weeks at 4°C.

(f) Chloramine-T reagent: dissolve 1.41 g of *N*-chloro-*p*-toluenesulphanamide, sodium salt trihydrate (chloramine-T) in 10 ml water and successively add 10 ml propan-1-ol and 80 ml of the buffer solution. Prepare this solution immediately before use.

(g) Colour reagent: dissolve 10.0 g *p*-dimethylaminebenzaldehyde (AR) in 35 ml perchloric solution (60%(m/m)) and then slowly add 65 ml propan-2-ol. Prepare this solution on the day of use.

(h) L(-)-Hydroxyproline standard solutions: prepare a stock solution by dissolving 50 mg 4-hydroxyproline-α-carbonic acid in water. Add 1 drop of the hydrochloric solution and dilute to 100 ml with water. Make up a fresh stock standard each time. On the day of use, dilute 5 ml of the stock solution to 500 ml with water in a volumetric flask. Then prepare four standard solutions by diluting 10, 20, 30 and 40 ml of this solution to 100 ml with water to obtain L(-)-hydroxyproline concentrations of 0.5, 1, 1.5 and 2 μg/ml, respectively.

APPARATUS

Ordinary laboratory apparatus, and the following in particular:

(1) Mechanical meat mincer, laboratory size, fitted with a plate with holes not exceeding 4 mm in diameter.

(2) Round or flat bottomed hydrolysis flask, capacity about 200 ml, wide necked, equipped with an air-cooler or water-cooled condenser.

(3) Electric heating device (e.g. heating mantle, hot-plate or electrically heated sand bath).

(4) Filter paper, diameter 12.5 Whatman GF/A are suitable.

(5) pH meter.

(6) Aluminium or plastic foil.

(7) Water bath, capable of being thermostatically controlled at $60 \pm 0.5°C$.

(8) Spectrophotometer, capable of being used at a wavelength of $558 \pm 2nm$ or a photoelectric colorimeter with an interference filter with absorption maximum at $558 \pm 2nm$.

(9) Glass cells of 10 mm optical path length.

(10) Analytical balance.

PROCEDURE

(1) Preparation of test sample

(i) Raw meat and raw meat products. Reduce intact meat to small cubes (approx. 0.5 cm^3, i.e. length of side approx. 8 mm by cutting it with a knife while it is cold (just below 0°C), using a sharp knife. Either place the sample in a container and seal the latter hermetically, or vacuum pack the sample in heat-resistant plastic film; then heat so as to maintain a temperature of at least 70°C for at least 30 min; cool and proceed as in (ii). During the remaining stages of preparation of the test sample and the weighing out of the test portions, ensure that the sample is kept well mixed and, in particular, that any fat or fluid is kept evenly distributed.

(ii) Cooked meat and cooked meat products. Make the sample homogeneous by passing it at least twice through the meat mince and mixing. Keep the homogenised sample in a completely filled, air-tight, closed container and store it in such a way that deterioration and change in composition are prevented. Analyse the test sample as soon as possible, but always within 24 h.

(2) Test portion. Weigh, to the nearest 0.001 g, about 4 g of the test sample into the hydrolysis flask. Ensure that none of the sample adheres to the side wall of the flask.

(3) Hydrolysis. Place some silicon carbide boiling chips in the flask and add 100 ± 1 ml of the hydrochloric acid solution containing tin (II) chloride. Heat to gentle boiling using the heating device

and maintain for 16 h under reflux (conveniently overnight). Filter the hot hydrolysate through a filter paper into a 200 ml volumetric flask. Wash the flask and filter paper three times with 10 ml portions of hot hydrochloric acid solution and add the washings to the hydrolysate. Make up to the mark the water and mix. Continue the determination as soon as possible, but at the latest on the day after hydrolysis.

(d) Colour development and measurement of absorbance. Using a pipette, transfer into a beaker a volume, V, of the hydrolysate so that, after dilution to 250 ml, the L(-)-hydroxyproline conc. will be within the range 0.5–2 µg/ml. With the aid of the pH meter adjust the pH to 8 ± 0.2 by the addition, drop by drop, first with the 10M sodium hydroxide solution and then, when approaching the required pH, with the 1M NaOH solution. Filter the contents of the beaker into a 250ml volumetric flask. Wash the beaker and the tin hydroxide precipitate on the filter paper at least three times with 30 ml portions of water, collecting the washings in the volumetric flask. Make up to the mark with water and mix. Transfer 4.00 ml of this solution into a test tube and add 2.00 ml of the chloramine-T reagent. Mix and leave at room temperature for 20 ± 1 min. Add 2.00 ml of the colour reagent, mix thoroughly and cap the tube with aluminium or plastic foil.

Transfer the tube quickly into the water bath controlled at 60°C and heat for exactly 20 min. Cool under running tap water for at least 3 min. Measure the absorbance at 558 ± 2nm in a glass cell against water, using the spectrophotometer or the photoelectric colorimeter equipped with an interference filter. Subtract the absorbance measured for the blank solution (see below) and read L(-)-hydroxyproline conc. of the diluted hydrolysate from the calibration graph obtained as described below.

BLANK TEST

Carry out in duplicate the procedure described above (from 'Transfer 4.00 ml . . . etc.) substituting water for the diluted hydrolysate. Note: If the absorbance of the blank exceeds 0.040 a fresh colour reagent should be prepared and, if necessary, the p-dimethylaminebenzaldehyde should be purified. This is done as follows: Prepare a saturated solution of the p-dimethylaminebenzaldehyde in hot 70%(v/v) ethanol. Cool, first at room temperature and finally in fridge. After about 12 h, filter on a Buchner funnel. Wash with a little 70% ethanol. Again dissolve in hot 70% ethanol. Add cold water and agitate thoroughly. Repeat this procedure until a sufficient quantity of milk-white crystals has been formed. Place in a fridge overnight. Filter on a Buchner funnel, wash with 50% ethanol and vacuum dry over phosphorus (V) oxide.

CALIBRATION GRAPH

Carry out the procedure described above (i.e. from 'Transfer 4.00 ml ... etc.) substituting in turn 4.00 ml of each of the four diluted standard L(-))hydroxyproline solutions for the diluted hydrolysate.

Plot the measured absorbance values, corrected for the blank value, against the concentrations of the standard L(-)-hydroxyproline solutions, and construct the best-fitting straight line through the plotted points and the origin.

EXPRESSION OF RESULTS

For each of the two test portions, calculate the L(-)-hydroxyproline content, a percentage by mass, from the formula

$$\frac{5c}{m \times V}$$

where c is the L(-)-hydroxyproline concentration, in µg/ml, of the diluted hydrolysate as read from the calibration graph; m is the mass (g) of the test portion; (V) is the volume (ml) of the aliquot portion of the hydrolysate taken for dilution to 250 ml.

Take as the result the arithmetic mean of the two calculated values, provided that the requirement below is satisfied. Report the result to the nearest 0.01%.

AGREEMENT BETWEEN DUPLICATES

The difference between the two calculated values obtained simultaneously in rapid succession from the duplicate test portions by the same analyst shall not exceed 5% of the arithmetic mean value.

NOTE   % Collagen = % Hydroxyproline $\times \dfrac{100}{14}$

Hydroxyproline nitrogen = % Hydroxyproline $\times \dfrac{14}{131.13}$

REFERENCE

BSI (1979) British Standard Methods, BS4401: Part II. British Standards Institute, HMSO, London, UK.

Phosphate determination

Application: Meats and fish products.

REAGENTS

(a) Dilute nitric acid. (1 volume concentrated nitric acid mixed with 4 volumes of distilled water.)

(b) Quimociac acid reagent. (dissolve 70 g sodium molybdate di-hydrate ($Na_2Mo_4.2H_2O$) in 150 ml distilled water. Dissolve 60 g citric acid monohydrate in a mixture of 85 ml concentrated nitric acid and 150 ml distilled water, then cool. Gradually add the molybdate solution to the citric–nitric acid solution while stirring. Dissolve 5 ml synthetic quinoline in a mixture of 35 ml concentrated nitric acid and 100 ml distilled water. Gradually add the quinoline solution to the molybdate solution, mix well and let stand for 24 h. Filter and add 280 ml acetone. Dilute to 1 litre with distilled water and mix. Store in a dark-brown glass bottle.)

PROCEDURE

(1) Prepare one Gooch crucible for each sample and one for the reagent blank, pass 100 ml distilled water through each Gooch crucible with a glass filter, dry at 110°C for 2 h, cool in a desiccator, weigh and record the weight to the nearest 0.0001 g.

(2) Mix or blend the product if necessary to obtain a homogenous sample. Remove bones before mincing.

(3) Accurately weigh 2.5 g $\pm$ 0.0001 g of sample into an ashing dish. (The sample should contain less than 25 mg of phosphate.) Dry the sample in a drying oven at 110°C for 30 min. Ash the sample in a muffle furnace at 550°C for several hours until white ash is produced.

(4) Allow the sample to cool. In a fume hood, add 25 ml of dilute nitric acid and heat on a hot plate for 30 min, or until the digestion is complete. Add 50 ml distilled water and allow to cool. Refrigerate for 30 min to solidify the fat. Warning: wet ashing with nitric acid may cause an explosive mixture with fatty products containing glycerol.

(5) Quantitatively filter the liquid into a 250 ml beaker. Rinse the beaker and filter paper three to four times with distilled water. Make the volume to approximately 100 ml.

(6) Slowly add 50 ml quimociac reagent, cover with a watch glass. Heat and boil for one minute. Remove from heat, rinse the residue on the watch glass into the beaker. Allow to cool to room temperature while swirling carefully.

(7) Quantitatively filter the precipitate through the prepared Gooch crucible under suction, washing the beaker with five 25-ml portions of distilled water and filtering through the Gooch crucible. Allow each portion to drain thoroughly before adding the next portion.

(8) Dry the crucible and contents in an oven at 250°C for 30 min, do not heat above 250°C. Cool in a desiccator and weigh.

CALCULATION

$$\% \text{ Phosphorus} = ((100) \, (A-B) \, (0.014)/C) - 0.0106$$

where A is weight of precipitate; B is weight of blank; C is weight of sample; 0.014 is the gravimetric factor = atomic weight phosphorus (30.91) divided by molecular weight QPM $((C_9H_7N_3)_3H_3PO_4.12MoO_3$: 2212.71); and 0.0106 is the correction factor for phosphorus of meat proteins.

$$\% \text{ Phosphate} = (\% \text{ phosphorus}) \, (F)$$

where F is the correction factor for the form of the phosphate

$$= \frac{\text{Anhydrous molecular weight of phosphate}}{(\text{Number of atoms phosphorus in phosphate}) \, (\text{atomic wt phosphorus})}$$

The following table lists factors for phosphates, if the phosphate is unknown calculate as sodium tripolyphosphate ($Na_5P_3O_{10}$):

Phosphate	Factor (F)
Na_2PHO_4	4.58
$(NaPO_3)_6$	3.29
$Na_5P_3O_{10}$	3.96
$Na_4P_2O_7$	4.29
NaH_2PO_4	3.87
$Na_2H_2P_2O_7$	3.58

REFERENCE

AOAC (1990) *Official Methods of Analysis* (15th edn). Association of Official Analytical Chemists, Washington, DC, USA, method 969.31.

Free fatty acids in oils

Application: Crude animal and vegetable oils.

REAGENTS

(a) Neutralised alcohol (for every 50 ml reagent grade ethanol add 2 ml phenolphthalein solution and add enough 0.1 N NaOH to produce a faint permanent pink.)
(b) 0.50 N standardised sodium hydroxide solution (NaOH).

PROCEDURE
(1) Weigh 20.0 g of the oil sample into a wide mouth Erlenmeyer flask.
(2) Add 50 ml of neutralised alcohol reagent.
(3) Heat gently to boiling with constant mixing.
(4) Titrate while hot with 0.50 N sodium hydroxide to the first permanent pink end-point.

CALCULATION
(Estimated as oleic acid)

$$\% \text{ Free fatty acid} = \frac{(\text{ml of 0.5 N NaOH}) \times (14.1225)}{\text{Weight of sample in (g)}}$$

REFERENCE
AOAC (1990) *Official Methods of Analysis* (15th edn). Association of Official Analytical Chemists, Washington, DC, USA, method 940.28.

Estimation of moisture and volatiles in oils

Application: Animal and vegetable oils.

PROCEDURE
(1) Dry a beaker in a drying oven at 105°C for 20–30 min and cool in a desiccator.
(2) Tare the predried beaker and accurately weigh 20.000 g of well mixed sample into the beaker, weigh and record the sample weight to the nearest 0.0001 g.
(3) Heat the sample on a hot plate, rotating the beaker gently by hand to avoid splattering. Do not exceed 130°C.
(4) The approach of the end point can be judged by the cessation of rising bubbles and the absence of foam. Alternatively, place a clean, dry watch glass on the beaker to observe condensation on the glass.
(5) When the apparent end-point is reached, heat momentarily to the point of incipient smoking. Do not overheat.
(6) Allow to cool to room temperature in a desiccator, then re-weigh.

CALCULATION

$$\% \text{ Moisture and volatiles} = \frac{(\text{Initial weight} - \text{dried weight}) \times 100\%}{\text{Initial sample weight in (g)}}$$

ALTERNATIVE METHODS
AOAC methods 926.12 and 984.20. Cited in *Official Methods of Analysis* (15th edn). Association of Official Analytical Chemists, Washington, DC, USA.

Peroxide value

Application: Animal and vegetable oils.

REAGENTS

(a) Acetic acid – chloroform solution (mix three parts by volume of glacial acetic acid with two parts chloroform).
(b) Potassium iodide solution (freshly prepared saturated solution of KI, approximately 20 g KI in 15 ml distilled water).
(c) 0.10 N sodium thiosulphate standard solution ($Na_2S_2O_3.5H_2O$).
(d) 0.010 N sodium thiosulphate standard solution ($Na_2S_2O_3.5H_2O$).
(e) Starch indicator solution (boil the starch to dissolve to make a 1% solution in distilled water).

PROCEDURE

(1) Weigh 2.00 g of oil sample into a 250 ml Erlenmeyer flask, weigh and record the sample weight to the nearest 0.01 g. Prepare a blank following the methods below, the blank titration must not exceed 0.1 ml of the 0.10 N sodium thiosulphate solution.
(2) Add 30 ml of the acetic acid – chloroform solution and swirl until the sample is dissolved.
(3) Add 0.5 ml of the KI solution by pipette.
(4) Allow the solution to stand for 1 min with occasional agitation, then add 30 ml distilled water.
(5) Titrate with 0.10 N sodium thiosulphate, agitating constantly, until the yellow colour has almost disappeared. Add 0.5 ml starch indicator and continue titrating until the blue colour disappears. (If the titration is less than 0.5 ml, repeat the determination using 0.010 M sodium thiosulphate solution.)

CALCULATION

$$\text{Peroxide Value} = \frac{(\text{ml sample} - \text{ml blank}) \, (\text{Normality } Na_2S_2O_3) \, (1000)}{\text{Weight of sample in (g)}}$$

Express peroxide value in milli-equivalents of peroxide per 1000 g of sample.

REFERENCE

AOAC (1990) *Official Methods of Analysis* (15th edn). Association of Official Analytical Chemists, Washington, DC, USA, method 965.33.

Determination of Iodine number: Rosemund Kuhnenn method

Application: All fats and oil not containing conjugated systems.

REAGENTS

(a) Potassium iodide solution (7.5 g KI dissolved in 50 ml distilled water. Cover with a watch glass.) Note: This solution must be prepared just prior to use.

(b) Rosemund Kuhnenn reagents. (Into three 250-ml Erlenmeyer flasks add to each 40 ml of glacial acetic acid. To the first flask slowly add 28.4 g $\pm$ 0.2 g pyridine, then allow to cool. To the second flask slowly add 35.5 g $\pm$ 0.2 g concentrated H_2SO_4, then allow to cool. When cool, add the contents of the second flask to the first flask, and allow to cool. To the third flask add 28.35 g bromine, and add this solution to the first two mixtures. Make up the mixture to 1 litre with glacial acetic acid, then mix thoroughly. Transfer to a 4-litre amber bottle with a screw cap, add 2.5 litres of glacial acetic acid, making a total 3,500 ml of reagent.)

(c) Mercuric acetate solution. (2.5% mercuric acetate in glacial acetic acid.)

(d) Starch indicator. (2.5 g potato starch boiled in 500 ml distilled water with 5 ml glacial acetic acid.)

(e) 0.10 N sodium thiosulphate standardised solution.

(f) Chloroform.

PROCEDURE

(1) Warm the oil in a 250 ml beaker on a hot plate until clear.

(2) Filter the warm oil into a 100 ml beaker. While this is filtering make up the KI solution.

(3) With a dropper weigh 0.200 g of the warm oil into a clean iodine vial and place it in an iodine flask, weigh and record the sample weight to the nearest 0.0001 g.

(4) Add 5 ml chloroform by pipette to each sample and to a clean empty iodine flask for the blank. Shake.

(5) From a burette, add 50.0 ml Rosemund Kuhnenn solution to each flask.

(6) Pipette 10 ml mercuric acetate solution to each flask. Shake well and place flasks in a dark cupboard for at least 1 min.

(7) Into a 50 ml beaker pour 10 ml KI solution and 20 ml distilled water. Add this mixture to each sample flask and the blank, shake and return to the dark cupboard for at least 1 min.

(8) Titrate the blank with 0.10 N sodium thiosulphate standardised solution. When the colour changes to orange, add 5.0 ml starch solution by pipette. Continue the titration to the point when the blue colour first disappears completely. Record the volume.

(9) Repeat the titration for each sample.

CALCULATION

$$\text{Iodine number} = \frac{(\text{ml blank} - \text{ml sample})\,(\text{Normality Na}_2\text{S}_2\text{O}_3) \times 12.69}{\text{Weight of sample in (g)}}$$

ALTERNATIVE METHODS

AOAC methods 920.158 and 920.159. Cited in *Official Methods of Analysis* (15th edn). Association of Official Analytical Chemists, Washington, DC, USA.

Method for testing cans for potential rusting:

These tests are usually done on empty cans and ends to determine if there is exposed metal which is likely to rust during processing or routine handling of the finished product.

(1) Potassium Ferric Cyanide Test

Reagent: potassium ferricyanide	5 g
sodium chloride	2.5 g
distilled water	500 ml

PROCEDURE

Dip the sample in the solution. After 2 minutes gently rinse the sample in cold water to remove the excess solution and to halt the reaction. Do not wipe dry. A blue colour on exposed metal indicates areas that may potentially rust on the outside of the can or end, or areas that may potentially sulphide on the inside of the can or end. This test is best suited for tin plate.

(2) Copper Sulphate Test

Reagent: copper sulphate	40 g
concentrated hydrochloric acid	100 ml
distilled water	700 ml

PROCEDURE

Dip the sample in the solution. After 1 minute gently rinse the sample in cold water to remove the excess solution and to halt the reaction. Do not wipe dry. A reddish colour on exposed metal indicates areas that may potentially rust on the outside of the can or end, or areas that may potentially sulphide on the inside of the can or end. This test is best suited for tin free steel plate.

For either test the time that the sample is in the solution may be extended. The longer the sample is in the solution, the more the metal will react and may simulate more severe abuse of the finished cans during storage and handling. When comparing different lots of cans with these tests the test conditions must be the same for exposure time, temperature of solution and solution concentration.

Method for testing available free chlorine in water samples

REAGENT

Free available chlorine can easily be measured using DPD colorimetric test kits (N,N:Diethyl-para-phenylene diamine) which are available from commercial suppliers.

PROCEDURE

(1) Allow water from taps to run for several minutes before sampling and testing. Water for can cooling in retorts should be tested before the start of production and every two hours throughout production.

(2) Test retort cooling water after contact with cans from the retort overflow, cooling canal, or other suitable location. Retort cooling water must be tested for every retort load, or every two hours throughout production.

This test is an immediate indication of the likely bacteriological quality of the water. Water without traces of free available chlorine must be suspected to contain significant bacterial loads.

11 Cleaning

K. BARBER and P. BIRD

11.1 Introduction to cleaning in the fish canning industry

There is a bewildering array of information in the literature and from chemical suppliers on cleaning and sanitation requirements for food processing plants. However, there is little information specific to the needs of the fish canning industry and even less on developing a cleaning programme using the 'Hazard Analysis Critical Control Point' (HACCP) approach. The purpose of this chapter is to address these issues; to present information on general principles of cleaning and the HACCP system as they relate to fish canneries to enable the development of an effective, comprehensive cleaning programme.

Successful development and implementation of a cleaning programme requires the commitment of all plant employees and all levels of management. Good cleaning and sanitation practices are an attitude or way of thinking rather than merely a set of procedures to be followed. This attitude must be woven into the corporate culture by extensive education and training, consultation and ownership.

Before designing a cleaning programme be familiar with all applicable regulations. These are often in the form of broad guidelines such as 'Good Manufacturing Practices' (GMP) but some countries may require that specific microbiological tolerances be met or that certain procedures be followed.

The GMP may be broadly based on international 'Codes of Practice' such as those published by the Codex Alimentarius Commission. Of pertinence to the fish canning industry are: *General Principles of Food Hygiene*, *Low Acid and Acidified Low Acid Canned Foods* and *Canned Fish and Meat Codes of Practice*. While these documents are general in nature, they are the framework into which a cleaning programme must fit.

Particulars of plant design have been well covered in the above documents and therefore will not be dealt with here. Few fish canneries are 'state of the art' to facilitate the ultimate in cleaning; most canneries will have to design the best cleaning programme given their current plant facilities.

Seriously contaminated foods can be produced in modern, well-constructed plants while clean safe foods can be produced in basically poor plants. It is therefore the quality of operations to maintain cleanliness rather than the quality of the physical plant that determines the quality and safety of the products.

The material in this chapter will be presented as follows:

(1) Cleaners and sanitisers
(2) Methods and equipment
(3) Applying HACCP principles to cleaning

11.1.1 Cleaners and sanitisers

An effective cleaning programme involves the use of two classes of chemicals; cleaning agents which remove soils and sanitising agents which kill microorganisms. All chemicals used must be 'approved' for use in food processing plants by the appropriate regulatory agency.

Cleaners and sanitisers must be treated with respect; it is imperative that the safety, use, mixing, storage, transportation and incompatibility instructions be followed to protect the health of employees. All employees involved in the cleaning operation must wear protective clothing of rubber or plastic and protective eyewear. Safety equipment should include easy access to eyewash and shower stations.

To ensure complete control over chemicals used in the plant, it is recommended that they be purchased through a single department within the organisation and preferably a single individual.

All chemicals should be stored in a secured area away from processing areas, and which is kept neat and tidy at all times. Strict inventory control should be exercised.

11.1.1.1 Cleaning compounds. The primary function of cleaning compounds is to loosen deposits so that they can be lifted and flushed away. Cleaning agents are not meant to kill bacteria but to remove the soils which harbour and protect them. Effective cleaning contributes up to 90% of the removal of microorganisms whereas sanitisers contribute the remaining 10%. The most common commercial cleaners are blended products which are formulated from a variety of ingredients to perform specific functions. Selecting a suitable product for a particular operation may not be simple – there are hundreds of detergent manufacturers and each may have many formulations. What works for one application may be totally ineffective for another.

A basic understanding of the types of cleaning compounds and common ingredients used to formulate them will make the job of selecting an appropriate compound much easier:

11.1.1.1.1 Types of cleaners.

(a) *Alkaline-based cleaners (pH 7–14)*

Primarily effective against organic soils such as fat and protein. The higher the pH of the compound, the stronger and more corrosive. This is the class of cleaner used for routine cleaning of fish canneries – mild to moderate strength for daily clean-ups. A heavy-duty alkaline cleaner may be occasionally necessary on certain surfaces to remove difficult organic deposits.

Because most fish canneries have a variety of surfaces to be cleaned, certain precautions must be taken:

Aluminium:	All alkaline cleaners are corrosive to aluminum. However, this can be minimised by using a mild to moderate alkali and reducing the contact time. If soft water is used, an appropriate ingredient would be one of the silicates because they are slower to cause corrosion than caustics. However, silicates produce a white film if used in conjunction with hard water.
Brick/concrete:	Requires a detergent not based on caustic but on silicates, phosphates and carbonates.
Galvanised metal:	If damaged, alkalis may attack the zinc.
Glass:	Use of glass is not recommended in canneries; may be etched if a strong alkali is used.
Steel/copper:	Use low alkali cleaners with silicates, phosphates and carbonates with the equivalent of 2.5 g/litre anhydrous sodium sulphite in the solution.
Vitreous enamel:	Use is not recommended in canneries; use mild alkali cleaners with high silicate content.
Wood:	Use of wood is not recommended in canneries, avoid strong alkalis.
Mild steel, nickel alloys, rubber, stainless steel:	Any alkali may be used.

(b) *Acid-based cleaners (pH < 7)*

Primarily effective against inorganic or mineral soil deposits formed as a result of hard water used during processing or the use of alkali cleaners. They can be formulated with a surfactant to remove organic soils also. The lower the pH, the stronger and more corrosive the compound. A very strong acid cleaner is also effective in removing encrusted protein and fish scales. Acid cleaners are not considered daily all-purpose cleaners for fish canneries; they are most suited for the control of tough accumulated mineral or scale deposits. Most are corrosive to many surfaces and should therefore be used with caution.

Aluminium:	All acid cleaners are corrosive to aluminium. They remove a layer of aluminium oxide resulting in a brightening effect; over time the aluminium is stripped away. Minimise this effect by using a mild acid cleaner and reducing contact time.
Brick/concrete:	Avoid strong acids.
Galvanised metal:	If damaged, acids may attack zinc.
Mild steel:	If acids are used, ensure they are inhibited against corrosion. Check with the chemical supplier.
Stainless steel:	Use acids with care, check with the chemical supplier.
Vitreous enamel:	Use is not recommended in canneries; use acids with care, check with the chemical supplier.
Wood:	Use of wood is not recommended in canneries; avoid strong acids.

(c) *Solvent-based cleaners*
These are primarily alcohol- or ether-based products and are very effective against petroleum deposits such as lubricating oils and greases. Solvent cleaners are generally appropriate for the end of season clean-up where machines are dismantled and/or repaired.

Rubber and Plastics:	Avoid use of solvent cleaners.

11.1.1.1.2 Functions of cleaners.

- Dispersion: ability to break up clumps into individual particles.
- Emulsification: ability to break fat and oil into tiny globules.
- Saponification: action of alkali on fats resulting in the formation of soap.
- Rinsability: ability to be removed easily without leaving a residue.
- Suspension: ability to lift and hold particles in suspension.
- Water softening (chelation or sequestration): binds minerals present in hard water.
- Wetting: ability to lower surface tension to allow penetration of soils.
- Penetration: ability to enter porous materials and get to soils.
- Suds formation: ability to foam.
- Peptisation: physical formation of collodial solutions from partially soluble materials.
- Non-corrosive.
- Synergism: a chemical used as a builder with a detergent which results in an effect which is greater than if both were used separately.

11.1.1.1.3 Common ingredients of cleaners.
(a) Sodium hydroxide (caustic soda): powerful and very corrosive detergent. Major function is as a saponifer in alkali-based cleaners.
(b) Silicates (sodium *meta, ortho* and sesqui silicates): not as corrosive as caustic soda, main function is emulsification and saponification in alkali cleaners.
(c) Phosphates (sodium tetra, tripoly, hexameta phosphates, sodium pyrophosphate): excellent emulsifying, dispersion, suspension and peptising agents. Also easily rinsed, non-corrosive and soften water. However, environmental impact may be negative. Check with appropriate authorities.
(d) Organic acids (citric, tartaric, sulphamic, gluconic); used as the base for acid cleaners. They soften water, control mineral deposits and rinse well.
(e) Inorganic acids (phosphoric is most common): similar abilities to organic acids but can be extremely corrosive. None are effective saponifiers or emulsifiers.
(f) Surfactants (wetting agents): these may be separated into three categories; all are good penetrants, are rinsable, non-corrosive and are responsible for suds formation:

  ● Cationic: release positively charged ions in water
    – these are the poorest of the wetting agents but have strong bacteriostatic properties
    – quaternary ammonium compounds fall into this category
    – not compatible in acid solutions
  ● Anionic: release negatively charged ions in water
    – compatible in acid solutions
  ● Non-ionic: no charge associated
    – may produce excess foam and are affected by water hardness

(g) Enzymes: useful in removing tough protein build-ups. Not commonly used in the fish canning industry; enzymes can cause polyethylene conveyor-belts to bubble and crack and they are very expensive.

11.1.1.2 Sanitisers. The definition of sanitise is to reduce the numbers of vegetative cells (and spores and viruses depending on the sanitiser) to levels judged to be safe by public health authorities. Therefore, sanitising controls but not necessarily eliminates microorganisms from the environment. Sanitising must not be confused with sterilisation (killing of all forms of life) or disinfection (kills all vegetative cells but not spores or viruses).

The purpose of sanitation is to control bacterial populations – both

Table 11.1 Advantages and disadvantages of common sanitisers

	Heat	Chlorine	Iodine	Quats	Acid/anionic
Advantages					
Gram-positive and Gram-negative bacteria	x	x	x	—	x
Spores + viruses	x	x	—	—	—
Mould	x	x	—	x	x
Rapid	—	x	x	—	x
Long shelf-life	x	—	x	x	x
Easy to test activity	—	x	x	—	—
Prevents mineral deposits	—	—	—	—	x
No colour/odour	x	—	—	x	x
Disadvantages					
Affected by organics	x	x	x	—	—
Affected by pH	—	x	—	x	x
Affected by hard water	—	x	—	x	—
Corrosive/irritating	—	x	—	—	x
Affected by heat	—	x	x	—	—

pathogens (those causing disease) and non-pathogens (those causing food spoilage). It is important to remember that a thorough cleaning is essential prior to sanitising; effectiveness is greatly reduced if soils are present. Soil deposits reduce sanitiser effectiveness through inability to penetrate and kill bacteria, the dilution effect and adverse reactions of organic material with most sanitisers. Table 11.1 lists some advantages and disadvantages of common sanitisers.

11.1.1.2.1 Heat.   One of the most common forms of sanitising is moist heat – either hot water or steam. In order to be effective, the surface temperature must be brought to at least 70°C. However, this temperature will denature protein so it is essential that soils be thoroughly cleaned prior to application.

Cleaned utensils and machine parts can be placed in a trough containing hot water at >70°C for several minutes. Steam is sometimes used on canning lines and hard to reach areas and has the advantage of promoting subsequent drying. However, high-pressure steam can strip paints and lubricants from equipment and it is quite dangerous in untrained hands. Other disadvantages include the high energy costs involved and the creation of undesirable condensation.

Heat causes broad spectrum bacterial kill but practical contact times have little effect on most spores and viruses.

11.1.1.2.2 Chlorine.
(a) General: chlorine compounds are the most commonly used sanitisers in the food industry and are available in a variety of forms.

They are particularly suitable for the fish canning industry because chlorine is often used to control bacteria during fish washing and in retort cooling water.

Common chlorine sanitisers:

- Sodium hypochlorites (bleach) – usually sold in liquid form but these have a limited shelf-life (available chlorine is decreased by 1/2 in 90 days). Also, the pH of bleach is approximately 12. It must be diluted to achieve a pH of <7 (this is necessary to kill bacteria).
- Calcium hypochlorites – sold in powdered form, longer shelf-life and higher available chlorine than bleach.
- Granular chlorine – based on the salts of an organic carrier which releases chlorine ions; usually also contain buffering agents to control corrosion and antimicrobial activity, e.g. chlorinated isocyanurate.
- Chlorine dioxide – commonly used to chlorinate water and treat sewage. Has 2.5 times the oxidising power of chlorine at lower concentrations and is less affected by organic material. Must be generated on-site and there may be problems in gaining approval for use in fish canneries.

(b) Antimicrobial activity: the active agent in all chlorine sanitisers is hypochlorous acid; its activity is primarily related to the pH of the surrounding solution. As the pH decreases, the relative % of hypochlorous acid increases, causing an increase in activity. With increasing pH, the hypochlorite ion becomes dominant which is much less effective. At pH 5, 100% of available chlorine is in the form of hypochlorous acid, pH 6–98%, pH 7–80% and pH 8–30%.

The mechanism of action is not fully understood although it is believed to act by disrupting cell walls through protein denaturation and enzyme inactivation.

Antimicrobial activity is broad spectrum – effective against Gram-positive and Gram-negative bacteria, bacterial spores and phage, and some viruses. There is a 90% reduction in cell populations in less than 10 seconds with relatively low concentrations of available chlorine. Spores require 7 seconds to 20 minutes for a 90% reduction.

(c) *Advantages*:
- rapid kill, active against a wide variety of microorganisms
- least expensive of the sanitisers
- less affected by hard water
- easy to test levels (many test kits available; note that the use of orthotolidine is not acceptable in many countries)
- easily available in a variety of forms

(d) *Disadvantages*:
- corrosive to iron, steel, stainless steel, copper, brass, aluminium at concentrations >100 ppm; however, bacterial kill is quick and therefore immediate rinsing would alleviate this problem
- effectiveness is reduced in the presence of organic matter
- has a short shelf-life
- activity is greatly reduced at pH values of >7
- skin irritant at high levels, safety issues

(e) *Incompatibilites*:
- alkaline detergents (because they raise the pH)
- produce a strong flavour when combined with cresols or phenols (e.g. paints, fly sprays, wood sealers, some hand lotions)
- very strong solutions disintegrate gum rubber, fabric and concrete
- chlorine gas is driven off with heat (and therefore very hot water) which not only produces a safety hazard but also reduces the amount of available chlorine

(f) Suggested concentrations for use in fish processing plants:

Wash water	2–10 ppm
Hand rinse water	50–100 ppm
Clean smooth surfaces	50–300 ppm
(washing basins, urinals, glass)	
Clean smooth wood, metal and plastic	300–500 ppm
(new tables, conveyor belts, machines, totes/bins)	
Rough surfaces	1000–5000 ppm
(old tables, concrete floors and walls, cutting boards)	

Note: levels in excess of 500 ppm are required to sanitise some surfaces, however, some countries may have regulations restricting levels from an employee safety point of view.

11.1.1.2.3 Iodine.

(a) General: iodine sanitisers come in the form of alcohol–iodine solutions or iodophors. Iodophors are aqueous solutions of a nonionic surfactant mixed with elemental iodine and an acid (commonly phosphoric) to bring the pH to 2.6–5.0. Although iodophors can be used to sanitise equipment and facilities, they are commonly used in fish canneries as hand dips or foot dips and for sanitising utensils.

(b) Antimicrobial activity: both diatomic iodine and hypoiodous acids are the active antimicrobial agents of iodophor sanitisers. Activity is dependant on pH; optimum pH is <3 although they are still effective up to pH 5.

Active iodine solutions are excellent sanitisers for vegetative cells

(Gram-positive and Gram-negative) but are not that effective against spores or viruses.

(c) *Advantages*:
- non-corrosive and non-irritating to skin
- give visual indication of effectiveness (lose brown colour when iodine has dropped to ineffective levels)
- long shelf-life, very stable
- unaffected by hard water
- rapid kill, broad spectrum activity
- good penetration

(d) *Disadvantages*:
- not very effective against spores and viruses
- stains some surfaces
- activity greatly reduced at pH >5
- high concentrations may be corrosive to some surfaces
- may combine with food substances to produce taint

(e) *Incompatibilities*:
- at temperatures $>45°C$, iodine gas is produced
- alkaline detergents (because increases pH)

(f) Suggested concentrations for fish processing plants:

Hand dip	8–50 ppm
Smooth surfaces	8–50 ppm
Rough surfaces	125–200 ppm
Equipment and utensils	12–75 ppm

11.1.1.2.4 Quaternary ammonium compounds (quats).

(a) General: quats are natural wetting agents and therefore have both detergent and sanitising ability. They come in a wide variety of forms and in literally hundreds of commercial products. They are the only sanitisers which form a bacteriostatic film on hard surfaces which has residual activity. Quats are often applied after cleaning and left on equipment surfaces during down time for protection. They are then rinsed just prior to processing. Some countries may allow concentrations of up to 200 ppm to remain on food contact surfaces without rinsing.

(b) Antimicrobial activity: quats are thought to act against micro-organisms by enzyme deactivation, protein denaturation and disruption of cell membranes. They are effective primarily against Gram-positive bacteria and moulds; they have limited ability against most coliforms and other Gram-negative bacteria, and are not effective against spores and viruses.

(c) *Advantages*:
- good penetrants
- long shelf-life

- colourless and odourless
- non-corrosive and non-irritating
- reasonably stable in the presence of organic matter
- accommodates wide temperature ranges and pH values
- test strips available for determining concentrations

(d) *Disadvantages*:
- germicidal ability varied and selective
- expensive
- affected by hard water (must be <200 ppm Ca)

(e) *Incompatibilities*:
- inactivated by acidic solutions
- lose effectiveness when combined with chlorine or soaps

(f) Suggested concentrations for fish processing plants:

Equipment	200 ppm
Hand dips	50 ppm
Cooler walls/ceilings	500–800 ppm

11.1.1.2.5 Anionic-acid sanitisers.

(a) General: these are mixtures of anionic surfactants and an acid, generally phosphoric. This type of sanitiser is particularly useful in automated cleaning systems in conjunction with an alkaline cleaner. Use of the anionic-acid sanitisers eliminates the post-cleaning rinse; the acid neutralises the excess alkalinity left behind by the cleaning procedure, prevents alkaline deposits and sanitises.

(b) Antimicrobial activity: good general bactericidal ability against both Gram-positive and Gram-negative bacteria; ability is limited towards spores and viruses.

The mechanism of action is unclear but thought to be by disruption of cell membranes and alteration of cell permeability.

(c) *Advantages*:
- particularly suited to stainless steel
- broad spectrum bacterial kill
- prevents mineral deposits
- reduces cleaning protocol by one step
- resistant to organic matter and hard water salts
- rapid activity

(d) *Disadvantages*:
- activity decreases with pH >2.3
- corrosive to many surfaces

(e) *Incompatibilities*:
- alkaline water because pH is increased

11.1.1.2.6 Alcohol (post-process area).
- Use 70% methanol or 70% isopropanol on post retort equipment touching cans.
- Dries quickly and produces a broad spectrum kill.

11.1.2 Methods and equipment

11.1.2.1 Dry clean-up.   Refers to vacuuming or squeegeeing to collect gross soils without the use of water. This method is becoming more popular due to increasingly stringent environmental requirements and the increasing cost of water. A dry pick-up system will reduce levels of BOD, TSS and O/ G in liquid effluent by minimising contact time with sump water and will reduce water costs by lowering consumption. Vacuum systems are not used much in the canning industry due to the nature of wet processing area. Much more common is the use of scrapers and squeegees. These should be made of metal or plastic rather than wood and must be cleaned and sanitised to prevent cross-contamination of clean surfaces. Brooms are seldom used because they are so difficult to clean.

11.1.2.2 Manual scrubbing/brushing.   Manual cleaning may be necessary for some heavily soiled utensils, equipment and/or parts. This is a very labour-intensive method and little should be required with a regular cleaning programme in place. Again, the use of wood is undesirable; brushes should be constructed of durable materials resistant to heat, chemicals and moisture. Bristles should be nylon with good water holding action. Brushes, scrapers and scouring pads must be cleaned and sanitised after use to prevent cross-contamination.

11.1.2.3 High-pressure water systems.   These systems use high-pressure, low-volume water to remove gross soils and/or for rinsing off cleaners and sanitisers (Figure 11.1). This reduces both labour and water costs. High-pressure systems include portable or centralised equipment. The high-pressure water provides very effective cutting and penetration action for all types of soils and is good for removing soils from hard to reach areas.

Care should be taken to protect electrical parts and bearings; and to ensure that more delicate items (such as thin pipes) are not broken or ripped apart by the high pressure involved. Painted surfaces may also be a problem, with paint partially removed resulting in flakes which may contaminate product. The temperature of the water is also important; if hot water is used it may bake on protein making it extremely hard to remove (cool water is desirable to remove gross soils).

Figure 11.1 Rinsing off cleaners and sanitisers with high pressure water.

11.1.2.4 Foam cleaning systems. This application style is popular because it can be gently applied to almost any area or equipment; it is very efficient for inaccessible places and vertical surfaces. Foam is generated by special equipment which mixes a metered detergent solution with air; alkaline cleaners are suitable for foaming. A contact time of 10–15 min is common – this longer contact time allows tougher soils to be loosened and then removed. It is important that the foam not be allowed to dry. Foam equipment is available in portable or centralised form (Figure 11.2).

11.1.2.5 Cleaning-in-place (CIP). This system requires that equipment be specially designed; suitable pumps, water flow rate and spray heads must be installed to ensure all internal parts are reached. CIP is commonly used in the dairy industry because it is best employed to clean and sanitise tanks, heat exchangers, pipelines and homogenisers. CIP systems are not widely applicable for fish canneries; there may some specialised equipment where it could be used but generally this is not an appropriate technology for the fish and meat canning industry.

A slight twist to this concept is an automatic conveyor-belt scrubber which has recently come on the market.

Figure 11.2 Cleaning equipment with a foam of detergent solution.

11.1.2.6 Sanitiser application equipment. Sanitisers are generally sprayed on surfaces, although 'foggers' have recently become available on the market. Their advantage is that they lower labour costs and penetrate all surfaces in a facility. Equipment is available in both portable and centralised systems.

11.1.3 Applying HACCP principles to cleaning

Applying the HACCP approach to the development of a comprehensive cleaning and sanitation programme requires a thorough and practical understanding of the entire operation. In order to successfully implement the programme a cross-functional team including management and front line employees from unloading, processing, quality and technical/scientific departments and a representative from a chemical supplier should be set up. This team will be responsible for developing the programme and consulting/training all employees who will be associated with cleaning procedures or with monitoring the results. Without the cooperation and commitment of all employees, cleaning efforts will largely be wasted.

The principles behind the HACCP system of operational control are well documented elsewhere and besides are quite familiar to all canners of low-acid foods. However, there is some confusion regarding the common understanding that the HACCP system applies to 'process' CCP rather than to 'cleaning' CCP. There is no reason that this approach cannot be used to document and implement a comprehensive cleaning programme. It can be incorporated into an existing process style HACCP programme or be delivered as a separate programme presented by specific area or by frequency of procedures.

The purpose of this section is to discuss fundamental HACCP principles as they apply to the development of a cleaning programme for fish canneries. These will be separated into cleaning procedures and monitoring procedures.

11.1.3.1 Cleaning procedures.

(1) Hazards (or risks): for each of the (critical) control points (or surfaces to be cleaned), determine the risk if the cleaning procedure were not carried out. The hazard will be greater if the surface is a food contact surface (such as utensils, conveyor-belts, patching tables). Non-food contact surfaces (such as floors and ceilings) would have a lower risk. It is important to define the various hazards; many use the terms: Critical, Serious, Major and Minor.

The primary hazard or risk involved in canning fish is that of *Clostridium botulinum* toxin. Thermal process times and temperatures for low-acid canned foods have been determined with a wide safety margin to ensure that any potential spores are destroyed. Nevertheless, good manufacturing practices dictate minimising the risk that spores are present. This means a thorough cleaning programme must be in place for both pre- and post-retort processing.

A microorganism of lesser concern is *Staphylococcus aureus* which is capable of producing a toxin which is not destroyed during the retorting process. It is unlikely that *S. aureus* will grow in sufficient quantities to produce toxin during the fish canning operation, especially if temperatures are below 10°C. Again, an effective cleaning programme will reduce the risk.

Spoilage organisms are not a safety risk but a quality risk. If psychrotrophs reach levels of greater than 1 million/g, there is the potential for off-odours and flavours in the canned product and may result in swollen cans. This is undesirable.

(2) (Critical) Control Points: this will include all items/areas which need to be cleaned – equipment, utensils, floors, walls, ceilings, light fixtures, totes, tubs, buggies, baskets, conveyor-belts, tables, cleaning tools, stairs, railings, floor mats and stands, tote tippers, dip stands, washing stations, coolers, racks, freezers and any other surfaces.

(3) Cleaning procedures: there are many things which can be done during processing to make cleaning procedures easier: prompt rinsing to prevent drying of soils, maintenance of gaskets and seals to reduce leakage and splatter, care in handling product and offal, and by keeping work areas orderly and tidy at all times.

The quality of the water used during cleaning is of critical importance. In addition to microbiological tolerances (as per the appropriate regulatory agency), the hardness will influence the choice of an appropriate cleaner and sanitiser.

All cleaning procedures invariably have four to five basic steps:

(i)   Removal of gross soils by flushing with water or a 'dry' method.
(ii)   Removal of remaining soil with a cleaning agent.
(iii)   Rinse with water to remove cleaning agent.
(iv)   Application of a sanitiser.
(v)   Rinse with water to remove sanitiser (optional depending on the situation).

Note: There are a variety of 2-in-1 products which combine a cleaner and sanitiser and reduce the above steps by 2. However, these products are not that effective in achieving good cleaning and sanitation. They may be useful in 'setting the stage' when introducing a new comprehensive cleaning programme, or they may serve a purpose during times when the cannery is in operation around the clock and there is limited time for cleaning.

Choosing a cleaner: choosing a cleaner(s) for a fish canning operation is relatively simple. For routine cleaning, a mild to moderate alkaline cleaning compound is most appropriate because soils are primarily organic (fat and protein). The specific formulation of the cleaner should be discussed with a chemical supplier and will depend on the application method chosen, the temperature of the water to be used, the choice of sanitiser and the degree of soil encrustation. It may be necessary to occasionally use a high-strength alkaline cleaner for areas/equipment that are not cleaned daily or that accumulate tough organic soils. Regular use of an alkaline cleaner may result in inorganic soil deposits and therefore an acid cleaner must be employed to bring these under control. The frequency will depend on the particular situation; if hard water is used in conjunction with an alkaline cleaner then use of an acid cleaner will need to be more often. Solvent-based cleaners are generally used during the end of season clean-up where equipment is dismantled for repairs and maintenance.

Choosing a sanitiser: the choice of an appropriate sanitiser is a more difficult decision. Unfortunately, there is no perfect sanitiser for a fish cannery. All sanitisers have advantages and disadvantages which must be carefully weighed. One solution is to use a combination of sanitisers at different times in the overall cleaning programme. This will address any potential for the development of bacterial resistance to one sanitiser. Note that the sanitiser of choice in the post process area is 70% alcohol during processing.

Choosing an application method: there are many factors which must be considered in choosing the method of application for both cleaners and sanitisers. There are certain utensils and equipment or parts where manual scrubbing is unavoidable. However, because this is so labour intensive it should be kept to a minimum. Many older canneries are equipped with high-volume/low-pressure water; the benefits of switching to a high-pressure/low-volume system are substantial. Savings include the cost of water, the cost of energy associated with heating the higher volume of water and in reducing the amount of time necessary to remove soils. Foaming of the cleaner or the cleaner/sanitiser is a good choice for canners. The longer contact time helps remove soils and is especially useful because of the variety of equipment and facilities associated with fish canneries. Also, the foam is visible and therefore it is easy to spot areas which have been missed.

Procedures: this is the meat of the programme – based on the information presented in the preceding sections, procedures must be designed for all surfaces or control points. As a general rule, all of the basic steps will be performed for each procedure. The following should be spelled out for each surface:

- type and concentration of cleaner
- type and concentration of sanitiser
- application method for cleaner and for sanitiser
- temperature of water at each step
- special requirements: e.g. have conveyor-belts running while cleaning, do not put mats or foot stands on cleaned surfaces

(4) Frequency: depending on the hazard involved and the time available for clean-up, a frequency must be determined for all surfaces. This may be continuous, at every break, end of shift/daily, end of season or a special procedure. Many fish canneries are dependent on natural resources that occur during a limited time period; this will require additional procedures for occasions when the cannery is operating around the clock.

(5) Tolerance: these may be microbiological tolerances based on environmental swabs taken prior to start-up or a description of deficiencies from visual inspections. It is important to spell out exactly what is acceptable and what is unacceptable. The unacceptable category may be further defined as containing critical, serious or major deficiencies. Regardless of how the deficiencies are described, the purpose of determining a tolerance is so that out-of-tolerance situations can be dealt with immediately rather than after a crisis develops.

11.1.3.2 Monitoring procedures.
  (1) *Inspection protocol*: The effectiveness of the cleaning programme
       must be assessed to ensure compliance with tolerances set. The
       procedure should be spelled out and inspectors must be fully trained
       and have the authority (or report to someone with authority) to
       have deficiencies corrected. Many fish plants use a 'checklist'-type
       system where visual inspections of items/areas are rated. Environ-
       mental swabs are an additional check.
  (2) *Frequency*: Inspections may be continuous, daily or random checks.
       A pre-start-up inspection is usual to assess the clean-up prior to
       processing (both visual and environmental swabs). Continuous
       inspections are normally geared to housekeeping issues and to
       ensure no hazards develop during processing.
  (3) *Corrective action*: What will be done if a deficiency is noted? It is
       important to document necessary corrective actions for each type of
       deficiency so that the potential problem can be resolved in an
       appropriate manner. A critical deficiency may require that process-
       ing be delayed until corrective action is performed, whereas a major
       deficiency may be dealt with later.
  (4) *Records*: Documentation of inspections and corrective actions
       performed is essential to the HACCP approach. Design records in
       consultation with those who have to use or interpret them.

Table 11.2 is an example of a general HACCP-based cleaning programme
for a fish cannery. More detailed information and extensive training are
necessary to implement the programme.

11.2 Introduction to cleaning in the meat industry

A wide variety of processes are carried out in the meat industry and the
equipment used is often complex and difficult to clean by traditional
methods. The range of soiling matter includes proteins, fats, blood and
hair, as well as denatured proteins from cooking, and tar residues from
smoking processes. The type of surface to be cleaned also varies and ranges
from concrete (floors) and ceramics (tiles) to plastics and metals, such as
aluminium (smoke chambers) and mild, galvanised, or stainless steel.
   Although factories for the processing of beef, mutton and pork differ,
two distinct areas can be considered:

  • slaughterhouse, and
  • meat processing.

The slaughterhouse covers all stages from arrival of the live animal to the

Table 11.2 Example: general HACCP-based cleaning programme for a fish cannery

Hazard	Control point	Cleaning procedures	Frequency	Tolerance	Inspection procedures	Frequency	Corrective action	Record
Serious	Food contact surfaces	Remove all fish, offal and garbage: remove or protect cans and lids, salt and other ingredients. (1) Hose down everything using high-pressure/low-volume cool water starting from the top and working down. OR Use scrapers or squeegees to collect all fish scraps and bits: dispose of. Hose down as above. (2) Apply a mildly alkaline cleaner as a foam. Leave on 10 min. (3) Rinse off using high-pressure/low-volume warm water starting at the top and working down. (4) Apply a QUAT sanitiser as a spray at 200 ppm. Leave on. ALTERNATE WITH A chlorine sanitiser as a spray at 100–200 ppm. (5) Rinse QUAT sanitiser with warm water prior to processing. Rinse chlorine sanitiser with warm water immediately.	End of every work shift. May be necessary to perform a modified clean-up at breaks on some food contact surfaces.	(1) Micro swabs: <500 CFU/4 in^2 (food contact surfaces only) (2) Visual: No evidence of soil. No pools of water on food contact surfaces. No off-odours. Cans/lids and ingredients protected.	(1) Evaluate effectiveness by rating each surface as acceptable or unacceptable. If unacceptable, define as: Critical. Serious. Major or minor deficiency. (2) Aseptically take environmental swabs of various food contact surfaces. (3) Audit clean-up procedures to ensure chemicals are being used properly, safety requirements are being met and that procedures are followed.	Prior to start-up. Randomly or if a problem is identified.	(1) Ensure that any Critical or Serious deficiencies are corrected prior to processing. Major or minor to be dealt with at next clean-up. (2) If environmental swabs are above tolerance, audit cleaning procedures and ensure improvements are made. (3) Explain importance to employees.	Pre-start-up Daily Cannery Sanitation Report. Laboratory Report. Clean-up Audit Report.

Table 11.2 *Continued*

Hazard	Control point	Cleaning procedures	Frequency	Tolerance	Inspection procedures	Frequency	Corrective action	Record
Major	Non-food-contact surfaces	NOTE: Run conveyor-belts when cleaning and sanitising. Never place floor mats/stands on cleaned items. SPECIAL PROCEDURES: For hard water, alkaline or heavy deposits, substitute an acid cleaner in step (2) above.	1 month or when necessary.		(4) Audit during processing to ensure areas are neat and tidy and that no hazards exsist.	Continuous		
Serious	Hand/foot dips	(1) Clean and sanitise troughs or stands during daily clean-up. (2) Prepare a 50 ppm iodophor solution. Replace as necessary during processing based on colour of solution (i.e. the lighter the brown colour, the less effective).	End of shift and at breaks if necessary.	Must be no less than 25 ppm (pale brown colour).	Check that dips are cleaned and changed as necessary	Continuous	Explain importance to employees.	By Exception.
Serious	Utensils	Wash in warm soapy water, rinse and place in a 50 ppm iodophor solution: rinse in clean warm water just prior to use.	Every break and if falls on floor.	Must be no less than 25 ppm.	Monitor compliance of employees.	Continuous	Explain importance to employees.	By Exception.
Critical	Post-process area	(1) Follow all cleaning procedures listed above. (2) Sanitise equipment touching cans with 70% alcohol.	End of shift. Every break.	As above for surfaces.	As above for surfaces.	Prior to start-up and random	Ensure deficiencies are corrected prior to processing.	As above for surfaces.

departure of meat to either market, or the processor. The processor converts this into a variety of canned meat products.

Common to both of these areas are: general factory cleaning (walls, floors, etc) and personal hygiene (hands, clothing, etc.).

For many applications in the meat industry power cleaning using detergent followed by a high-pressure water rinse is much more cost-effective than manual cleaning.

The main power cleaning techniques are foam, gel and mist cleaning. Manual cleaning, however, may be the only option in certain circumstances and therefore this technique is included in recommendations.

11.2.1 Slaughterhouse

11.2.1.1 Transport and lairage. The lairage is the reception point for animals which are to be slaughtered. The quality of the final meat product will partly be reflected in the quality of these animals, and therefore lairages and transport vehicles bringing them to the slaughterhouse should be cleaned, preferably with foam or gel, each day after production to reduce the risk of cross-contamination, particularly from coliform and salmonellae bacteria. For maximum hygiene security, surfaces should be sprayed with a disinfecting solution after cleaning.

11.2.1.2 Killing area. Animals should be stunned before being killed to make the process painless. This involves either applying an electric shock across the head, or firing a metal bolt into the animals forehead. This latter method is mainly applied with cattle and sheep. After stunning, the animal is hung up by its back legs and its jugular vein pierced by inserting a 'sticking' knife. The blood is pumped out of the animal by its still beating heart and is collected in a trough. The stunning area must be cleaned and preferably disinfected at each change of animal type and at the end of the day. Foam, gel or high-pressure mist cleaning is recommended (altern-atively manual scrubbing), followed by a final disinfectant spray. Clean, sterile knives must be used for 'sticking' the animals. After use, knives must be cleaned in a disinfectant solution and kept available for use in a receptacle containing hot water (at least 82°C). Bleeding troughs should be fitted with fine water sprays to flush them out continuously to prevent clotting. Ideally, cleaning should be carried out at each break in production. Foam cleaning, gel cleaning or high-pressure sprays are most suitable for this purpose.

11.2.1.3 Pre-treatment department. In this area the animal's body is divided into two halves. Before this can be done the skin must be treated. In the case of cattle and sheep, this involves removing the hide. With pigs the skin is not removed, but dehaired and cleaned. This involves special processes and cleaning problems which are described below.

11.2.1.3.1 Scalding tanks. Scalding tanks are tanks which are filled with hot water (60°C). The carcass is immersed in the tank to soften the skin and make it easier to remove the hairs in the dehairing machine. These tanks must be cleaned at least daily to remove grease and particulate matter. Acid descaling may occasionally be necessary to remove water hardness, salts and protein scale which is most easily broken down by an acid detergent.

11.2.1.3.2 Dehairer, back scraper and singers. Dehairing machines must be cleaned daily. After being hosed down with warm water to remove gross soiling, they should be foam, gel or pressure spray cleaned and finally rinsed. Since the dehairing process is not 100% effective, a further treatment is needed to give a completely hair-free body. This is achieved by passing it through a gas-fired oven to singe the hairs and then through a so called back scraper which removes them. Within the back scraper, the carcass is beaten by rapidly rotating rubber strips. The singeing oven and scraper blades should be cleaned daily at the end of production. Owing to the complexity of the machines, foam or gel is considered to be the most suitable cleaning system in this area.

11.2.1.4 Evisceration department. Here the carcass is cut open with knives and the edible internal organs such as heart, lungs and liver, and inedible parts such as intestines (offal) are removed. It is then cut with a mechanical saw into two halves down the backbone and transferred to a cool room to bring its temperature down to 7°C or below. From here, the carcasses pass either to the market or to the meat processing area. The offal is removed from the pre-treatment area to the offal rooms by conveyors, chutes or trays (plastic or stainless steel). Some offal is subsequently used in meat processing (e.g. for sausage skins). The items to be cleaned are as follows.

11.2.1.5 Conveyors, chutes, trays, knives and work surfaces. Most conveyors are made of stainless steel or plastic. Some are equipped to allow continuous cleaning during processing. This is achieved by fixed spray jets, or a facility to allow the belt to pass through a water bath (normally fitted at the end of the return run). Regardless of the presence of such facilities, the belt should be cleaned, preferably by foam or gel, and disinfected at the end of production. Chutes and work surfaces must be cleaned, preferably by foam or gel, or alternatively, by high pressure spray at the end of production. After being rinsed off with hot water, they should be disinfected. Trays are often cleaned by being passed through a tunnel washer. However, trays that are suspended from an overhead rail can also be automatically foam cleaned by installing a fixed foam spray installation. For opening the carcass and cutting out the internal organs, clean sterile knives must be used and replacements kept available. During processing, knives should be stored in a receptacle containing continuously refreshed hot water (82°C). After use they must be thoroughly cleaned using a sanitiser solution.

11.2.1.6 Mechanical saws. The mechanical saws must be dismantled for cleaning after each batch of animals, and whenever they have severed an infected lesion. For optimum hygiene standards disinfection should be carried out after reassembly (where this is possible).

11.2.1.7 Cool rooms (2–10°C). These rooms become soiled with drained blood and walked-in soil and need to be cleaned daily, preferably after production. Cleaning is best done with a scrubbing machine fitted with a hood to prevent splashing since meat will normally be hanging there during the cleaning process. Cleaning solutions should be cold to avoid condensation problems.

11.2.1.8 Transport hooks. These are used to transport the carcasses and some of the internal organs from one area to the next. Systems are often designed so that the hooks pass through a bath for cleaning. Where present, this is the preferred cleaning method. If such facilities are not available the hooks should be foam or gel cleaned. For a small factory, manual cleaning with an alkaline detergent may be preferred.

11.2.2 Raw meat department

11.2.2.1 Cutting boards and trays. Two main types of cutting boards are found in practice, namely plastic (polyethylene or PTFE) or synthetic rubber. The boards have a tendency to distort if heated too strongly and so high temperatures (above 70°C) must not be used for cleaning. Also, high temperatures denature protein causing it to set. Ingrained soil from deep cuts is difficult to remove, and hence spray cleaning in a tunnel washer with a heavy-duty alkaline detergent is the most effective cleaning technique for these boards. However, if a tunnel washer is not available, power cleaning is a good alternative. Once a week the boards should be soaked in a detergent sanitiser solution, and then cleaned in an oxidising solution (chlorine, oxygen bleach, or peracetic acid) to prevent the formation of brown stains. Cuts in plastics can be partially self-healing. This increases the danger of debris being trapped and makes hygiene problems more likely. Thorough cleaning will minimise this danger. Trays are made of stainless steel or plastic and cleaning is often done in a tunnel washer using the same detergent as for the cutting boards.

11.2.2.2 Derinders, mincers, slicers, filling machines. Although these machines are quite different from each other in terms of appearance and function, they have two things in common and these have an influence on cleaning procedures.

- They have electrical parts, including safety switches, which must *not* be wetted.
- They have safety guards which make effective cleaning impossible unless they are removed. Often this means the machines cannot be set in motion during cleaning. Because of this, they can only be cleaned properly if first dismantled which may involve members of the engineering staff.

Once dismantled, the machine parts will normally be manually cleaned. This will involve soaking them in detergent solution in a large sink or bath for 15 min. Where it can be used, power cleaning is the preferred cleaning method for the outside of the equipment, any exposed electrical switchgear first being covered up. For optimum hygiene standards, the equipment should be disinfected after reassembly.

11.2.2.3 Dressing knives, scabbards, sharpening steels, choppers. It is important that these are cleaned frequently, especially:

- after contact with meat known, or suspected, to be diseased;
- after a break;
- at the end of the working day.

During production, knives must be kept in constantly refreshed water at a temperature of at least 82°C. At the end of production, they should be manually cleaned.

11.2.2.4 Meat depositor. This consists of a hopper with an air-operated dosing piston at its outlet. It is used to 'dose' measured quantities of meat paste, e.g. for hamburger preparation. It is necessary to partly dismantle the machine to facilitate cleaning. The dismantled parts should be soak cleaned, while the rest of the equipment should be power cleaned. A final disinfection stage is necessary. This should be done after reassembly if possible.

11.2.2.5 Offal room, chutes, tables. These areas and equipment become heavily soiled during the working day and equipment such as chutes are often difficult to clean by traditional methods. All offal debris should be cleaned away at the end of production (not hosed into drains) and surfaces cleaned by power or manual cleaning, and disinfected.

11.2.3 General factory cleaning

11.2.3.1 Floors and drains. In meat factories, floors rapidly become soiled with fat and grease and so it is important that they are cleaned regularly, not only for hygiene reasons but also for safety. Where sufficient drainage is provided, power cleaning is most efficient, both in terms of time and efficiency. If available on site, specialised floor cleaning equipment, e.g. floor-scrubbing machines, should be used in unobstructed areas. It is recommended that the drains be deodorised and disinfected by pouring a disinfectant solution down the head of each drain channel on completion of the cleaning programme. Pine disinfectants should not be used because of the risk of taint. In difficult areas, e.g. heavy soiling compacted by stacker trucks, an alkaline detergent powder should be sprinkled onto the wetted floor and left for about 1 h before starting the normal cleaning procedure. Some areas are designated as dry areas, e.g. flavour room, packaging, pastry preparation, etc. and wet cleaning methods are not advisable. Vacuum cleaning is then recommended.

11.2.3.2 Walls and ceilings. Walls should be cleaned regularly to prevent the build-up of greasy soil and provide better working conditions. The most suitable general method of cleaning is foam or gel cleaning (solid walls rendered/painted). Ceilings are not normally cleaned as frequently as other surfaces. This is partly because they are less critical and less soiled, and partly due to the difficulties in getting to them to do the cleaning. It is not possible to give a preferred way of cleaning ceilings because they are so variable. In modern buildings, plastic ceilings are often found and these can be power cleaned. In older buildings, the height of the ceilings and the presence of girders and roof supports make this impractical. In this case manual cleaning must be employed.

11.2.3.3 Cold storage rooms (−15 to −20°C). These rooms are used for storing the final food products. Although there is little danger of microbial growth at these temperatures, cleaning is still necessary. Loose soil and material should be swept out daily. On the occasions when the cold storage room has been thawed it can be cleaned, preferably by foam or gel.

11.2.4 Personal hygiene

Regardless of how well the factory is cleaned and disinfected, if the process operators do not practise good personal hygiene the end-product will suffer. This means that regular handwashing and the wearing of suitable, clean protective clothing is essential.

11.2.4.1 Handwashing. Regular washing of the hands is essential, particularly:

- on entering a food area;
- before starting, and on finishing, work
- after all break periods;
- after every visit to the toilet.

A liquid bactericidal hand cleanser is recommended for this purpose. It is also important that this be obtained from a suitable hygienic dispenser. Hands should be dried with a disposable paper towel. For high risk areas, use of an alcohol-based hand disinfectant, applied after cleaning and drying hands, is recommended. To prevent recontamination, wash hand basins should be kept in a clean condition.

11.2.4.2 Protective clothing. All protective clothing such as boots, plastic aprons and gloves should be regularly washed with a detergent sanitiser, preferably after each break, but in any case, at the end of the day. Operators should be supplied with a freshly laundered overall every day, or even earlier if necessary. Before entering high-risk areas boots should be washed in a disinfectant footbath.

Bibliography

Acher, D.L. (1990) The need for flexibility in HACCP. *Food Technol.*, 174–178.
Ahmed, F.E. (ed.) (1991) *Seafood Safety: Committee on Evaluation of the Safety of Fishery Products.* Food and Nutrition Board, Institute of Medicine, National Academy Press, Washington, DC, USA.
Dillon, P. (1990) Sanitation cleans up its image. *Food Engng.*
FAO/WHO (1983) Recommended international code of practice for low-acid and acidified low-acid canned foods. *Codex Alimentarius*, **G CAC/RCP**, 23.
FAO/WHO (1984) Recommended international code of practice for canned fish. *Codex Alimentarius*, **B CAC/RCP**, 10.
FAO/WHO (1985) Recommended international code of practice, general principles of food hygiene. *Codex Alimentarius*, **A**.
Garrett, E.S. and Hudak-Roos, M. (1990) Use of HACCP for seafood surveillance and certification. *Food Technol.*, 159–165.
Giese, J.H. (ed.) (1991) Sanitation: the key to food safety and public health. *Food Technol.*
Guthrie, R.K. (ed.) (1972) *Food Sanitation.* AVI Publishing Co. Inc., Westport, CT., USA.
Hick, G., Kassen, C.L., Huang, F., Ward, R., Thompson, M. and Fletcher, C. (eds) *Sanitation Notebook for the Seafood Industry.* National Marine Fisheries Institute. Sea Grant Extension Division. Dept. of Food Science, Virginia Polytechnic Institute and State University, Blacksburg, VA, USA, VP1-SG-78-05.
Lane, P. (1974) *Sanitation Recommendations for Fresh and Frozen Fish Plants* (Fisher Facts 8). US Department of Commerce, Seattle, WA, USA.
National Canners Association (1962) *The Cannery Sanitation Programme* (bulletin 33-L). Berkeley, CA, USA.
Stevens, B. (1990). Honing in on HACCP. *Meat Proc.*, 44–48.
Tatherson, I.N. and Windsor, M.L. *Cleaning in the Fish Industry* (Torry Advisory Note #45). Torry Research Station.
WHO (1976) *Microbiological Aspects of Food Hygiene* (Report of a WHO Expert Committee with the Participation of FAO; Technical Report Series #598). WHO, Geneva, Switzerland.

Appendix 1

Application area: Slaughterhouse
Reception area: Premises – general
Hygiene standard: Visually clean – disinfection stage optional

Cleaning procedure Remove loose debris

| | Cleaning systems | | |
Manual	High pressure	Foam	Gel
Scrub surface with warm ±55°C) detergent solution.	Spray (mist) detergent solution under low pressure onto surface. Leave for 10 min.	Apply foam onto surface. Leave for 15–20 min.	Apply gel onto surface. Leave for 20–45 min.
Hose down with fresh cold water.	Rinse with fresh warm (±55°C) water at high pressure.	Rinse with fresh warm water (±55°C) water at high pressure.	Rinse with cold water or warm water at high pressure.

Spray disinfectant solution onto cleaned surface. Leave for 10 min (minimum).

Product type
Light/medium-duty liquid manual cleaner.	Medium-duty liquid high-pressure cleaner.	Heavy-duty liquid foam cleaner.	Heavy-duty liquid gel cleaner.
Liquid disinfectant.	Liquid disinfectant.	Liquid disinfectant.	Liquid disinfectant.

Frequency
Daily.	Daily.	Daily.	Daily.

Recommended safety precautions
Gloves.	Gloves plus eye protection.	Gloves plus eye protection.	Gloves plus eye protection.

Appendix 2

Application area: Slaughterhouse
Reception area: Conveyors, chutes, trays, knives, work surfaces
Hygiene standard: Microbiologically clean – disinfection stage required

Cleaning procedure Remove loose debris

| | Cleaning systems | | |
Manual	High pressure	Foam	Gel
Scrub surface with warm (±55°C) detergent solution.	Spray (mist) detergent solution under low pressure onto surface. Leave for 10 min.	Apply foam onto surface.	Apply gel onto surface.
Hose down with fresh cold water.		Leave for 15–20 min.	Leave for 20–45 min.
	Rinse with fresh warm (±55°C) water at high pressure.	Rinse with fresh warm (±55°C) water at high pressure.	Rinse with cold water or warm water at high pressure.
	NB: not suitable for cleaning knives.	NB: not suitable for cleaning knives.	
Product type			
Light/medium- duty liquid manual cleaner.	Medium/duty liquid high- pressure cleaner.	Heavy-duty liquid foam cleaner.	Heavy-duty liquid gel cleaner.
Liquid disinfectant.	Liquid disinfectant.	Liquid disinfectant.	Liquid disinfectant.
Frequency			
Daily.	Daily.	Daily.	Daily.
Recommended safety precautions			
Gloves.	Gloves plus eye protection.	Gloves plus eye protection.	Gloves plus eye protection.

Appendix 3

Application area: Slaughterhouse
Reception area: Mechanical saws
Hygiene standard: Visually clean – disinfection stage required

Cleaning procedure Remove loose debris. Dismantle saw and soak the parts in warm (±55°C) detergent solution for about 15 min. Scrub the parts and rinse with fresh cold water. Alternatively, wash parts in a tunnel washer using hot (±75°C) detergent solution.

| | Cleaning systems | | |
Manual	High pressure	Foam	Gel
Scrub machine body with warm (±55°C) detergent solution.	Spray (mist) machine body with detergent solution. Leave for 10 min.	Apply foam onto machine surface Leave for 15–20 min.	Apply gel onto machine surface. Leave for 20 min.
Rinse with fresh cold water.	Rinse with fresh warm (±55°C) water at high pressure.	Rinse with fresh warm (±55°C) water at high pressure.	Rinse with fresh cold or warm water at high pressure.

Reassemble equipment. Spray disinfectant solution onto cleaned machine surfaces. Rinse with fresh cold water

Product type			
Light/medium-duty liquid manual cleaner.	Medium/duty liquid high-pressure cleaner	Heavy-duty liquid foam cleaner.	Heavy-duty liquid gel cleaner.
Liquid disinfectant.	Liquid disinfectant.	Liquid disinfectant.	Liquid disinfectant.

Frequency			
After each batch of animals.	After each batch of animals.	After each batch of animals.	After each batch of animals.

Recommended safety precautions			
Gloves.	Gloves and eye protection.	Gloves and eye protection.	Gloves and eye protection.

Appendix 4

Application area: Slaughterhouse
Reception area: Cool room (2–10°C)
Hygiene standard: Visually clean – disinfection stage optional

Cleaning procedure Remove loose debris

| | Cleaning systems | | |
Manual	High pressure	Foam	Gel
Wet the surfaces with a *cold* light/ medium-duty detergent solution. Leave for 10 min.	Spray (mist) surfaces with a *cold* medium duty detergent solution under low pressure.	Apply foam onto surface. Leave for 15–20 min. Rinse with fresh *cold* water at high pressure	Apply gel onto surface. Leave for 20–45 min. Rinse with fresh *cold* water at high pressure.
Scrub the surface. Rinse with fresh *cold* water at high pressure.	Rinse with fresh *cold* water at high pressure.		

Spray disinfectant solution onto cleaned surface. Leave for 10 min minimum.

Product type			
Light/medium- duty liquid manual cleaner.	Medium-duty liquid high- pressure cleaner.	Heavy-duty liquid foam cleaner.	Heavy-duty liquid gel cleaner.
Liquid disinfectant.	Liquid disinfectant.	Liquid disinfectant.	Liquid disinfectant.

Frequency			
Daily.	Daily.	Daily.	Daily.

Recommended safety precautions			
Gloves.	Gloves plus eye protection.	Gloves plus eye protection.	Gloves plus eye protection.

Recommended:
(a) Cold cleaning solutions should be used due to condensation problems!
(b) Ceilings to be cleaned twice a year.
(c) High-pressure and foam cleaning are only applicable if the meat is removed from the room.

Appendix 5

Application area: Meat process – General factory cleaning
Reception area: Floors and Drains
Hygiene standard: Visually clean – disinfection stage optional

Cleaning procedure Remove loose debris (not into drains)

| | Cleaning systems | | |
Manual	High pressure	Foam	Gel
Wet floor with warm (±55°C) medium-duty detergent solution. Leave for 10 min. Scrub with hand brush or scrubbing machine. Rinse with fresh cold water.	Wet the floor by applying a medium-duty alkaline detergent solution as a low-pressure spray. Leave for 10 min. Rinse with warm (±55°C) water.	Apply heavy-duty foam onto floor. (Usually done at same time as work surfaces are cleaned.) Leave for 15–20 min. Rinse with fresh warm (±55°C) water.	Apply heavy duty gel onto floor. (Usually done at same time as work surfaces are cleaned.) Leave for 20–40 min. Rinse with fresh cold or warm water.

Dry floor with a squeegee or wet vacuum cleaner. Pour 10% solution of chlorine-based disinfectant into heads of drains to prevent formation of foul odours.

Product type			
Medium-duty powder form detergent.	Medium-duty liquid high-pressure cleaner.	Heavy-duty liquid-foam cleaner.	Heavy-duty liquid gel cleaner.

Frequency			
Daily.	Daily.	Daily.	Daily.

Recommended safety precautions			
Gloves and boots.	Gloves and boots.	Gloves, eye protection and boots.	Gloves, eye protection and boots.

Notes on the manual cleaning technique:
(a) For tenacious soil, wet the floor with water and then sprinkle the powdered detergent over it. This will give better results than wetting with solution.
(b) If the soil is such that it is not possible to achieve a non-slippery surface when cleaning with medium alkaline detergent, a caustic-based powder is recommended.

Application area: Meat process – General factory cleaning
Reception area: Walls and ceilings
Hygiene standard: Visually clean – disinfection stage optional

Cleaning procedure Remove loose debris.

| | Cleaning systems | | |
Manual	High pressure	Foam	Gel
Scrub surface with warm (±55°C) detergent solution.	Spray (mist) detergent solution under low-pressure onto surface. Leave for 10 min.	Apply foam onto surface. Leave for 15–20 min.	Apply gel onto surface. Leave for 20–45 min.
Hose down with fresh cold water.			Rinse with cold water or warm water at high pressure.
	Rinse with fresh warm (±55°C) water at high pressure.	Rinse with fresh warm (±55°C) water at high pressure.	

Spray disinfectant solution onto cleaned surface. Leave for 10 min (minimum).

Product type			
Light/medium-duty liquid manual cleaner.	Medium/duty liquid high-pressure cleaner	Heavy-duty liquid foam cleaner.	Heavy-duty liquid gel cleaner.
Liquid disinfectant.	Liquid disinfectant.	Liquid disinfectant.	Liquid disinfectant.
Frequency			
Daily.	Daily.	Daily.	Daily.
Recommended safety precautions			
Gloves.	Gloves plus eye protection.	Gloves plus eye protection.	Gloves plus eye protection.

Appendix 7

Application area: Meat processing
Reception area: Trays, cutting boards, dismantled machine parts
Hygiene standard: Visually clean – disinfection stage optional

Cleaning procedure The items are washed with a hot ($\pm 75°C$) heavy-duty alkaline detergent solution. After washing, they are rinsed with fresh hot ($\pm 85°C$) water, optionally containing a rinse aid to speed-up drying. If necessary due to staining, cutting boards should be soaked in a hot ($\pm 70°C$) oxidising solution.

Cleaning systems

Tunnel washing machine

Product type

Heavy-duty liquid detergent for machine spray washing.

Aluminium safe liquid detergent for spray washing.

Frequency

Trays   : after every batch.
Other items : daily.

Recommended safety precautions

Gloves and face shield when changing containers.

Appendix 8

Application area: Meat processing
Reception area: Derinders, mincers, slicers and filling machines
Hygiene standard: Microbiologically clean – disinfection stage required

Cleaning procedure Remove loose debris. Dismantle machine and soak parts in warm (±55°C) detergent solution for 15 min. Scrub and finally rinse with fresh cold water. Alternatively, wash parts in a tunnel washer using hot (±75°C) detergent solution.

| | Cleaning systems | | |
Manual	High pressure	Foam	Gel
Scrub machine body with warm (±55°C) detergent solution.	Spray (mist) machine body with detergent solution. Leave for 10 min.	Apply foam to machine. Leave for 10 min.	Apply gel to machine. Leave for 20–40 min.
Rinse with fresh cold water.	Rinse with fresh warm (±55°C) water at high pressure.	Rinse with fresh warm (±55°C) water at high pressure.	Rinse with fresh cold or warm water at high pressure.

Reassemble equipment. Spray disinfectant solution onto cleaned machine surfaces. Leave for 10 min (minimum).

Product type

Light/medium-duty liquid manual cleaner.	Medium/duty liquid high-pressure cleaner.	Heavy-duty liquid foam cleaner.	Heavy-duty liquid gel cleaner.
Liquid disinfectant.	Liquid disinfectant.	Liquid disinfectant.	Liquid disinfectant.

Frequency

Daily.	Daily.	Daily.	Daily.

Recommended safety precautions

Gloves	Gloves plus eye protection.	Gloves plus eye protection.	Gloves plus eye protection.

Appendix 9

Application area: Meat processing
Reception area: Dressing knives*, scabbards, sharpening steels, choppers
Hygiene standard: Microbiologically clean – disinfection stage required*

Cleaning procedure Pre-rinse the articles in warm ($\pm55°C$) water. Soak them in warm ($\pm55°C$) detergent sanitiser solution. Leave for 10–15 min and then scrub. Rinse with fresh warm ($\pm55°C$) water.
*Leave knives in constantly refreshed, hot water, ($\pm82°C$) during production.

Cleaning systems: Manual.

Product type. Medium-duty liquid manual detergent sanitiser.

Frequency   Daily.

Recommended safety precautions: Gloves.

Appendix 10

Application area: Personal hygiene
Reception area: Handwashing
Hygiene standard: Visually clean – disinfection stage optional

Cleaning procedure Regular handwashing should be carried out with a bactericidal hand cleanser obtained from a hygienic dispenser. Disposable paper towels should be used for drying. This should be done:

● before starting work
● on entering a food area
● after visiting the toilet
● after any breaks
● on finishing work

For optimum hygiene use of an alcohol-based post-handwash hand disinfectant is advised.

Cleaning systems: Manual.

Product type: Bactericidal hand cleanser from a suitable dispenser.

Frequency: See above.

Recommended safety precautions: None.

Appendix 11

Application area: Personal hygiene
Reception area: Protective clothing
Hygiene standard: Visually clean – disinfection stage optional

Cleaning procedure All protective clothing such as boots, gloves, face shields and aprons should be thoroughly cleaned with a warm (±55°C) detergent sanitiser solution.

Cleaning systems: Manual.

Product type: Medium-duty powder detergent sanitiser.

Frequency: Daily, more frequently if necessary.

Recommended safety precautions: Gloves.

Index

A seam 100
aluminium *see* can manufacture
amino acids 51
analytical methods 243–269
  available free chlorine 269
  carbohydrates 251, 252, 253
  ethanol 245, 246
  fat analysis 249
  free fatty acids in oils 264, 265
  histamine 253, 256
  hydroxyproline 259, 262
  iodine number 266, 268
  k value 244, 245
  moisture analysis 248
  nitrite 256, 259
  peroxide value 266
  phosphate 262, 264
  salt analysis 250, 251
  starch 253
  Torry meter 246
  total ash 248
  total crude protein 246, 247
  total volatile bases 243, 244
analytical testing 225
antibiotics 24
AOAC official methods of analysis 225

Bacillus stearothermophilus 205
ball datatrace unit 207
base plate load *see* double seamers-target
  setting
batch retorts 172, 188
  full immersion water retorts 186, 187
  showered water retorts 188
  steam/air retorts 184, 186
  steam retorts 182, 184
birds 60–62
Boar taint 48
brailer 6
brightstacking 215
brine fillers 147–150
brining machines 36
brisket beef 137
by-catch 11

can manufacture 88–135
  aluminium 92, 93, 98, 103, 106, 107,
    109, 123, 133
  beading 96, 110–112

can ends 104–107, 109, 110
  coatings *see* lacquers
  easy open 104–107
  flanging 112
  necking 112
  non easy open 104–106
  steel/tinplate 88–91, 94, 95, 98, 109,
    123, 130–132, 134
  tin free steel (TPS) 91, 98, 100, 104,
    107, 109, 121–123, 131, 132
cans
  corrosion *see* corrosion of cans
  double seams/seaming 96, 104–106,
    111
  manufacture *see* can manufacture
  mechanical properties 109–112
  axial strength 110
  panelling resistance 110, 111
  peaking resistance 111
  recycling 133, 134
carotenoids 24
catching fish 4, 5
  line and hook 9, 10
  static nets 8, 9
  surrounding nets 5, 6, 7
  towed nets 7, 8
chilling and freezing of meat 54–56
  rigor mortis 54
chlorinated rubber paints 70
chopped ham and pork 191
chuck lip *see* double seamers-target
  setting
chuck spindle to lifter assembly alignment
  see double seamers-target setting
classification of fish
  demersal 1
  pelagic 1
cleaning materials 271
  acid based 272, 273
  alkaline based 272
  composition 274
  function 273
cleaning methods 283–286, 289–294
  fish 287, 288
  general meat factory 293, 299, 300
  personal hygiene 293, 294, 303, 304
  raw meat department 291, 292,
    301, 303
  slaughterhouse 289–291, 296–298

Clostridium botulinum 200, 237, 238
Clostridium sporogenes 205
Codex 270
cold toughening (shortening) 54
coliforms 226
collagen 47
commercial sterility 178, 192, 199
comminuted meat products 140
composite panel wall
  construction 67, 68
  fire risk 68
computerised warehouse management
  213, 217, 218, 220
conduction packs 180, 193
continuous sterilisers 188–191
  fundamental considerations 188, 190
  hydrostatic cookers 191
  reel and spiral cooker/coolers 191
convection packs 182
conveyor belts 84, 85
corned beef 140, 141
corrosion of cans 125–133
  corrosion promoters 127
  de-tinning 131, 132
  external 125, 126
  hydrogen swells 132
  internal 126–133
  pH implications 128
  pitting corrosion 130, 131
  sulphide staining 128, 132
  theory of corrosion 130
cover curl 162
critical seam parameters 164
curing 50, 51
curing salts 203

decimal reduction time (D value) 200
defrosting frozen fish 26–31
  air blast thawing 28, 29
  air thawing 27, 28
  other methods 31
  vaccum thawing 30, 31
  water thawing 29, 30
DFD (dark, firm, dry) meat 52–54
distribution and shipping of canned goods
  221, 222
  road haulage 221, 222
  shipping containers 222
double seam acceptability *see* seaming
  standards
double seam appraisal 164, 165
  seam sectioning 164, 165
  seam teardown 164, 165
  trend analysis 169
double seam formation 159
  actual overlap 159, 163, 164
  body hook butting 159, 164
  drawn cans 163

end gauge thickness 163
first operation 159, 162
plunge seaming 163
primary seal 159
seaming roll profiles 159
seaming rolls 159, 162
second operation 159
secondary seal 159
tightness rating 159, 164
visual defects 164
double seam/seaming 96, 104–106, 111
double seamers 161
  irregular can seamers 161–163
  round can seamers 161–163
  seamer maintenance procedures-
    cleaning 171
  seamer maintenance procedures-
    lubrication 171
  seamer tooling life-effect of TFS (tin free
    steel) ends 166
  seamer tooling technology 166
  setting and control 166
  setting and control-chuck to end fit 166
  target setting 166–170
double seaming
  technology developments 171, 172
  technology developments – mini seam
    technology 172
  technology developments – two piece
    cans 171
drawn cans *see* double seam formation
drift net 8, 9
due dilligence 195

effluent disposal 60, 79
electrophoresis 47
emulsion paints 69
ends 104–107, 109, 110
enthalpy 180
enzyme linked immunosorbant assay
  (ELISA) 47
enzymes 17, 18, 178
epoxy materials 69–71, 74

factory effluent 79
factory environment 60
  location 60
  potential sources of contamination 60
  surroundings 60
factory layout
  separation of personnel 76
  separation of processes 75, 76
factory lighting 74, 75
factory production area 66–75
  ceilings 74
  floor materials 74
  floors 72–74
  wall finishes 69–72

factory sanitary accommodation 82
factory services 77–79
factory staff amenities 82
factory steam supply
  general 78
  potable 78, 79
factory structure
  access ways 61, 62
  external walls 61, 62
  internal walls 66, 67
  pest proofing 62–66
factory ventilation 75
factory water supply 77–79
  container cooling 78
  general 77
Faraday's Law 130
fat content of fish 25
fillers
  comminuted meats 140, 141
  depositors 150
  liquids 147–150
  mackerel 146
  meat/fish in sauces 150
  operational safety 150
  salmon 144–146
  tuna 142–144
  volumetric 140, 141, 149, 150
filling
  dosing principles 138, 139
  fish products by hand 137, 138
  fish products by hand – sardines 138
  meat products by hand 137
  mechanical – general considerations
    138, 139
  mechanical – fish products 142–147
  mechanical – meat products 140–142
finding fish 2, 3
fish farming 15, 24
fish handling 12, 13
  evisceration 12, 13
  rigor mortis 12, 18
fish nets
  length 8, 9
  mesh size 8, 9
  wall of death 9
fish preparation 31–40
  filleting 33, 34
  heading 32
  pre-cooking 30–40
  skinning 34, 35
  smoking 35–38
fish pump 6
fish quality indicators 242–246
fish storage 25–26
  chilled water 26
  freezing 26
  prepared fish 40
fish supply 1, 11

depletion 1, 2
  total allowable catch 2
flange contamination 137
floor tiles 74
Fo value 200, 202
food poisoning 235, 238
  botulism 237, 238
  staphylococcal 238
Food Safety Act (1991) 178, 195
foods–metal pickup 120, 121, 129
Frankfurters 50
free fatty acid content (FFA) 49
freezer burn 56
Fs value 206
fungicidal and mould resistant paints 70,
  71

glycogen 52–54
GMP 270

HACCP 270, 282–286
ham and shoulder 45, 50, 58, 141, 142
  thermal processes 204
hand filling, fish products see filling
hand filling, meat products see filling
headspace 136
heat penetration tests 206
heat treatment 178
heavy metals 41
hermetic seal 159, 162
high acid foods 199, 200
histamine 13, 41
hydrostatic sterilisers see continuous
  sterilisers
hygienic design of factory equipment
  82–86

immunological test 47
importation of canned goods 220, 221
incubation tests see microbiological
  testing
infestation of warehouses 215
insects 60–62
installation of factory equipment 86
ISO 9000 241, 242
isoelectric point (or pI) 51, 52

laboratory facilities 223
  in-house quality assurance and
    accreditation 239–242
  laboratory design 223, 224
  location 223
  sampling plans 224, 225
  technicians and procedures 224
laboratory simulators 206
lacquers/lacquering 99, 100, 107, 113–125
  acrylic 119
  application 123–125

lacquers/lacquering (*cont'd*)
  as a lubricant   121, 122
  as a protective barrier   120, 121
  coil coating   124
  electrocoating   125
  epoxy based   114–116
  functions and properties   119, 120
  oleoresin materials   114
  phenolic   118
  sheet coating   123, 124
  spray coating   124, 125
  synthetic materials   114
  vinyl based   116–118
Lampara net   7
lead   41
leaker spoilage   184
lethal rate   200, 201
lifter spring pressure   *see* double
  seamers-target setting
low acid foods   199, 200
lower lifter table   161
luncheon meat   50
  thermal processes   204

master temperature sensors   *see*
  Sterilising systems
mean and range charts   153–155
meat storage – freezing   55, 56
mechanical filling   *see* filling
mechanically separated (recovered) meat
  49
mercury   41
mercury in glass thermometers   *see*
  sterilising systems
microbiological testing   225, 226
  incubation testing   228, 229
  sterility tests   229, 234
  swab testing   227, 228
microbiology of meat raw materials   57,
  58
  food poisoning bacteria   58
  spoilage bacteria   57, 58
Miraseam   100
myosin   50

nesting of cans   207
nobbing   32
non round can seaming   *see* double
  seamers

oil filters   147–150
otterboards   7
ox tongues   137

panelling   198
peaking   198
peroxide value (PV)   49
personal hygiene   79–82

personnel health control   81
personnel protective clothing   81, 82
pest control programme   62
picking area   217
pin height   *see* double seamers-target
  setting
platinum thermometers   *see* sterilising
  systems
pleats   162, 163
plunge seaming   *see* double seam
  formation
poly aromatic hydrocarbons   35, 36
pressure gauge   *see* sterilising systems
pressure tranducer   198
pressure/vacuum (P/V) pump   6
PSE (pale, soft exudative) meat   52–54
Pullman cans   203
purse seine   5, 6

quality
  catching practices for fish   12
  chemical indicators for fish   41
  chemical indicators for meat   48, 49
  factors in meat product manufacture –
    curing brine   50, 51
  factors in meat product manufacture –
    meat ph   51, 52
  factors in meat product manufacture –
    pH after slaughter   52–54
  factors in meat product manufacture –
    slaughter   54
  factors in meat product manufacture –
    meat proteins   49–54
  fish   1, 11, 21, 31
  meat   44, 45, 57
  metabolic rate and fish deterioration
    12
  retention – fish   13–15
  size of fish   11, 12
  spoilage factors for fish   17–19

rancidity   18, 26, 49
raw material specification
  fish   21–25
  meat   44, 45, 49
raw material testing
  age and sex of meat source   47, 48
  fish   21
  meat   57
  other factors   48
  sampling procedures for meat   46
  species of meat   47
recycling   133, 134
redox potential   204
reel and spiral cooker/cooler   *see*
  continuous sterilisers
retort drain   *see* sterilising systems

retort instrument pocket   *see* sterilising
  systems
retort log   210
retorting operation   178
  operation of retorts   208, 209
  procedures and records   208
  process audit reconciliation   209, 210
  requirements
    can location   179
    control system   180
    heat tranfer medium   179, 180
    overpressure   191
    pressure vessel   179
    rotation   180, 194
    venting and condensate removal   180
rigor   54
ring netting   6, 7
rodents   60–62
rotation   *see* retorting operations,
  sterilising systems
rusting-testing cans for potential   268

salmon   144–146
sanitisers   271, 274, 275
  alcohol   280
  anionic-acid   279
  chlorine   275–277
  heat   275
  iodine   277, 278
  quaternary ammonium compounds
    278, 279
sardine canning   192
saturated steam   181
sauce fillers   *see* fillers
sausage thermal process   204
sawdust for smoking   38
Scombroid fish   13, 41
sea water for cooling   182
sealing compound   162
seamer corrosion   171
seamer output speeds   162
seaming can   *see* double seamers-target
  setting
seaming chamber   162
seaming chuck   162
seaming chuck to end fit   *see* double
  seamers-target setting
seaming panel   159
seaming panel-waisted   163
seaming standards   163, 164
sexual maturity of salmon   24
showered water retorts   *see* batch retorts
skatole   48
slipsheet   212, 218
smoking kilns   37, 38
spurs   162, 163
stainless steel   84
Staphylococcus   238

steam   180
steam/air retorts   *see* batch retorts
steam bleed   184
steam retorts   *see* batch retorts
sterilising systems   180–199
  classification and selection
    available factory space   181
    factory location   182
    manufacturing output   181
    overpressure   181, 182
    requirement for rotation   181
  instrumentation and control   191–199
    continuous steriliser speeds   194
    control systems   199
    master temperature indicator   184,
      195, 196
    pressure   193, 194
    pressure measurement   198
    rotation speed (batch)   194
    temperature   193
    temperature recorder/controller
      196–198
    time   193
    water flow rate   194
    water level   194
sterility tests   *see* microbiological testing
storage of canned fish and meat   214
stress susceptibility of pigs   53
superheated water   186
swab testing   *see* microbiological testing
Swedish dimple style ends   161

temperature distribution tests   183
TFS   *see* can manufacture
thermal process
  calculation methods   207, 208
  establishment   199–202
  evaluation   205–207
  special considerations for canned cured
    meats   203, 204
  temperature distribution tests   204, 205
  the scheduled process   202, 203
  verification   204
thermophilic organisms   179
thiobarbituric acid value (TBA)   49
three piece cans   96–109
  cement/adhesive side seam   100
  laser welding   98
  side striping   99, 100
  welded side seam   96
tin   41
tinplate   *see* can manufacture
titanium   84
tolerable negative error   154, 155
total volatile basic nitrogen (TVB-N)   41
Toyo seam   100
traceability   208

transportation of fish   13–15, 17–21, 25
  boxing in ice   14
  chilled sea water   14, 19
  cooling with dry ice   20, 21
  cooling with ice   14, 19, 25, 26
  freezing   15, 18, 19, 21
  refrigerated sea water (RSW)   15
transportation of meat   56
  temperature   56
trawling   7
trend anlaysis   *see* double seam appraisal
trimethylamine-nitrogen (TMA-N)   41
trolling   10
tuna   142–144
turret truck   217
two piece cans
  DRD (draw-redraw)   95, 100–104, 108,
    109
  DWI/D&I (draw-wall iron)   95,
    100–104, 108, 109
  PWI (partial wall iron)   109
types of spoilage   235

V cut   32
vacuum
  by hot filling   162
  by steam flow closure   162
vacuum transfer valves   162

vent manifold sizing   183
venting   182, 183, 190
visual seam assessment   164
volumetric fillers   *see* fillers

wall tiles   72
warehouse automation and
  computerisation   212
warehouse operation   212
  third party contract warehouses   219
  block stowed products   212, 215, 216
  electronic data interchange   218, 219
  performance measurement   220
  radio data transfer   217
  semi-automated warehouse systems
    216–218
  stock control   212, 216, 219
water analysis   226, 227
  sampling   226
  standards   226, 227
weight control   152–155
weight control charts   152–155
weight control charts – individual and
  median   153
WHO   127

Z value   200